THE DROWNING OF MONEY ISLAND

THE
DROWNING
OF
MONEY
ISLAND

**A FORGOTTEN COMMUNITY'S FIGHT AGAINST
THE RISING SEAS THREATENING COASTAL AMERICA**

ANDREW S. LEWIS

BEACON PRESS, BOSTON

BEACON PRESS
Boston, Massachusetts
www.beacon.org

Beacon Press books
are published under the auspices of
the Unitarian Universalist Association of Congregations.

Printed in the United States of America
22 21 20 19   8 7 6 5 4 3 2 1

This book is printed on acid-free paper that meets the uncoated paper
ANSI/NISO specifications for permanence as revised in 1992.

Text design and composition by Kim Arney

Map by Paul J. Pugliese. Cover image courtesy of the author

Library of Congress Cataloging-in-Publication Data

Names: Lewis, Andrew S., author.
Title: The drowning of money island : a forgotten community's fight
   against the rising seas threatening coastal America / Andrew Lewis.
Description: Boston : Beacon Press, 2019. | Includes bibliographical
   references and index.
Identifiers: LCCN 2019020188 (print) | LCCN 2019981583 (ebook) |
   ISBN 9780807083581 (hardcover) | ISBN 9780807083727 (ebook)
Subjects: LCSH: Climatic changes—Economic aspects—United States. |
   Sea level—Climatic factors—United States. | Coast changes—Climatic
   factor—United States—Forecasting.
Classification: LCC HD75.6 .L49 2019 (print) | LCC HD75.6 (ebook) |
   DDC 974.9/94—dc23
LC record available at https://lccn.loc.gov/2019020188
LC ebook record available at https://lccn.loc.gov/2019981583

To my parents, for letting me fly

CONTENTS

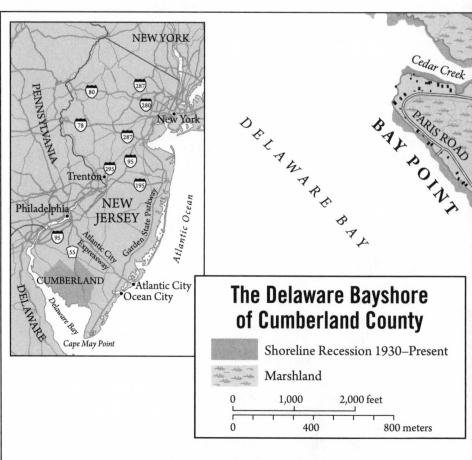

The Delaware Bayshore
of Cumberland County

Shoreline Recession 1930–Present

Marshland

| 0 | 1,000 | 2,000 feet |
| 0 | 400 | 800 meters |

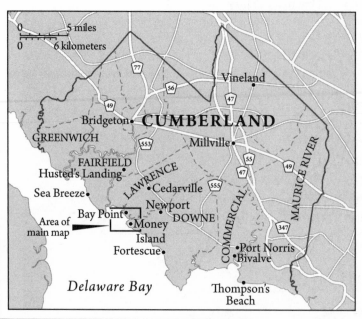

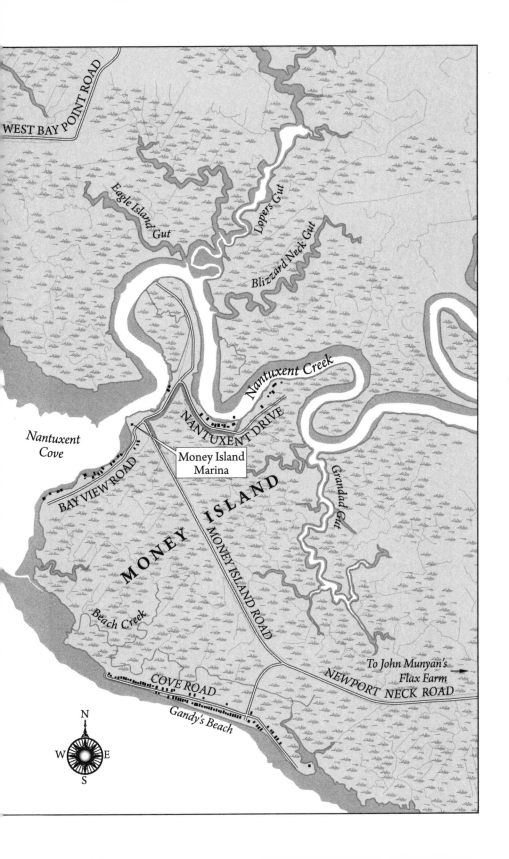

DEMO DAY

NOVEMBER 21, 2017

The foxhounds' wails rolled like a wave across the marshland. They joined the roar of the Komatsu excavator, owned by Site Enterprises, the company contracted by the state for $1.2 million to demolish all but three of the remaining twenty-three homes in Bay Point. The engine revved, and the excavator's thirty-five-foot boom stretched out and in as its huge, rusted claw opened and closed. Its metal treads rattled as they rolled over the unpaved road's potholes. At the little bridge that led over Cedar Ditch and into Bay Point, the machine swiveled around slowly, then stopped to face the one-story home once owned by an old man named Bones Batten. The grasses that had grown up around Bones's place shifted in the wind, a blush of summer green still visible in their stalks.

In recent years Bones's driveway had become more muck than dirt. Back when Bay Point consisted of more residents than just Mike and Kate Nelson, Bones had served as the Bay Point Rod & Gun Club's custodian. His was the first house you passed driving into the hamlet. It was a typical South Jersey Bayshore home—boxy, weather-beaten, its front yard cluttered with a small fishing boat, trailer, outboard motor, crab pots, and coolers. Around here, it was less about what you did with your home and more about what you did with the land surrounding it. Just outside Bones's house was the place where the club had installed its first security camera, which had long since been turned off.

The excavator stopped, turned, and contemplated the back corner of the house, where a small porch was half slumped into a stand of foxtails. The boom reached out, sunk its claw into the structure as if it were nothing but paper. Wood framing split. Drywall crunched. Window glass exploded. Shreds of pink insulation floated like feathers in the breeze. And then a different sound rose, impossibly, above all the others—a sound that I recognized well. It was Parker, Mike and Kate's five-year-old Chesapeake Bay retriever, desperately barking from inside their nearby bungalow. Parker only barked like that when he was alone and frightened. Mike and Kate had left for the day—they weren't interested in watching Bay Point get torn to the ground.

All afternoon, I had been standing beside Cedar Creek, where Bay Point Marina once stood, watching the excavator transform Bones's house into a neat, unremarkable pile of building material. I tried to imagine what the creek had looked like with the marina's many docks floating on its surface. All the noise of one of Mike and Kate's famous summer fishing tournaments. The laughter, the cracking of beers, the whine of boats heading out to, and coming in from, the bay. The smell of grilled fish and hamburgers and hot dogs, sunblock. The odor of the marshland, sulfurous but somehow also sweet. I'd seen some of the pictures by now— the glossy red faces of Mike and Kate twenty years younger; their two children, Katie and Mikie, hoisting up fish nearly as big as themselves. Forever-unknown fishermen who showed up from out of town for the tournament and stayed for the party.

The foxhounds must have moved on—or they'd gone quiet, having finished their job. I had been hiding long enough, so I started walking toward the demolition. I stopped on the little bridge spanning Cedar Ditch. The bent and twisted metal sign at its entrance read "Anthony Zadlo Memorial Bridge: 1995." A young man held a hose that cast a limp stream of water, pumped from the ditch, onto the debris that was once Bones's house. He offered a friendly wave and then went back to watering the pile. The other workers looked at me with puzzlement, wondering why anyone cared to come all the way out here to watch an old house get torn down.

While it was true that I had come far to get here, it was also true that I had come home. I had grown up eight miles to the northwest, across a stretch of nearly unbroken marshland, but I'd only recently returned to South New Jersey after being gone for fifteen years. I needed to see this piece of my past before it was erased and returned to nature. In the years I had been gone, the Delaware Bay had been rising ever faster, consuming the worn, tired communities that dotted the Bayshore, as it is called. The wild vastness of the open spaces that surrounded me was woven into my DNA— no amount of distance could untangle me from it. I had never expected that, one day, there would have to be a choice like the one made in Bay Point— one that pitted the Bayshore's people against nature rather than in harmony with it, as I and my ancestors had always understood the relationship.

After standing on the bridge for a while, a man approached me. He was tall, and a pair of wire-rimmed glasses were perched low on his long nose. He wore a red hardhat and an orange reflective vest. His khaki carpenter pants were clean.

"Are you with the state?" I asked.

"Blue Acres," the man yelled over the roar of the excavator, which was just a few feet away. He introduced himself as Gary Parent. He was the on-site representative for the Blue Acres Superstorm Sandy Program, an open-space acquisition initiative under the DEP, New Jersey's Department of Environmental Protection. After the October 2012 hurricane, Blue Acres had been infused with $300 million in federal funding to purchase, at pre-storm value, the homes of willing sellers living in repetitively flood-prone areas of the state, then demolish those homes so that the land could return to open space. The Bay Point acquisition would mark a milestone in the program's five-year history—its five hundredth demolition. In 2015, the Federal Emergency Management Agency, better known as FEMA, had recognized Blue Acres as a "Best Practice" in flood mitigation and a blueprint for other states with low-lying, flood-prone areas, highlighting Blues Acres' cluster approach to buying properties: by targeting whole sections of neighborhoods, New Jersey has been able to both reduce its amount of repetitive-loss properties—of which the state has the third most in the nation—and create buffer zones to better protect adjacent upland communities from future flooding. Climate resilience and adaptation experts from around the country—as well as the deeply in-debted National Flood Insurance Program—had lauded Blue Acres for its

effective cost-benefit approach, especially given that the program was being implemented in the most densely populated state in the United States.

Parent and I talked for a moment about the twenty homes scheduled
for demolition. "Sometimes, if you have an owner that's a little reluctant,"
Parent said, "they see the houses starting to come down and they're like,
'Oh, okay!'" He nodded toward the excavator. "It's kind of amazing how
long it takes to build a home with a hammer and nails and then . . ." He
trailed off before making a long, low sound through his teeth, mimicking
the sound of paper shredding.

It was 1:30 p.m., and since Site Enterprises could not work past five, it
looked as if Bones's house would be the last, and only, demolition for the
day. The sun was tilting toward the bay, still obscured behind a gray film
of cloud. Long shadows, the silhouettes of marsh grasses, stretched across
the gut that meandered beside the road. Across Cedar Creek, the skeleton
of an old wooden-hulled barge protruded from the muddy bank.

"What are you working on?" Another man stood above me, his face
wind-burned and square. He was gruff and his leather work boots were
well broken in. He introduced himself as Jimmy DiNatale, the owner of
Site Enterprises.

I explained I was working on a story about the Bayshore. "About here,"
I said, "and Money Island," referring to another forlorn bayside community a mile across the marshland.

"How they ain't going to exist anymore?" DiNatale said. "Shame.
They're taking them down all over the state."

"It's been going on for a long time."

"But nobody belongs here, anyway. Can't even get your car in here at
high tide."

"Well, it didn't flood like it does now."

"I think it did, but it's just . . ." he trailed off. I got the sense he was
about to bring it up—climate change, sea level rise, the phrases that were
so loaded around here—but thought better of dredging up "politics" with
a perfect stranger. Anyway, DiNatale redirected his thoughts. "What are
you going to do?" he said. "That's life."

There wasn't much left to see, so I walked back over Anthony Zadlo's
little memorial bridge and to my car, at what was once the Bay Point

Marina parking lot. It was still warm and the sky was starting to clear; it would be a fiery sunset over the bay that evening. Driving back onto high ground, I passed between a series of empty vegetable fields—the last crops before winter were pretty much picked clean. After watching the demolition of Bay Point begin, it was comforting to think about the repetition of the planting and harvesting of the fields—a familiar aspect of my childhood that, at least for now, was not threatened by state buyouts or the rising bay. Three miles inland from Bay Point was the village of Cedarville, where pumpkins sat on the porches of the old homes along Main Street, left over from Halloween. Work on a nearby Dollar General store continued at a rapid pace—the parking lot was finished and all that was left to add to the building were the windows. Just outside of town, right before the turn-off to Money Island, a sign in the yard of Mark's Shedder Shack, which sold blue crabs and oysters, read "CLOSED FOR THE SEASON."

PART ONE

THE STORM

ONE

"OUR AMERICAN DREAM"

AFTER THE HARD RIGHT BEND, where Jones Island Road turns into Bay Point Road, the pavement shook out into a straight black line. On both sides, cabbage, asparagus, and romaine fields stretched like patchwork, their seams a series of low earthen dikes bristling with marsh grasses. Beyond the fields were a few homes—small modulars at the end of driveways crowded with pickups, tractors, and boats. After the last dike, the land slipped back into its natural state. A thin stand of cedar and oak and briar thicket gave way to the bone-white trunks of trees long since inundated and killed by salt water: the ghost forests. The road then meandered for another mile, globs of dead grass, leaves, and bits of Styrofoam gathered along its yellow dividing lines, deposited there by the morning's high tide. At last it reached Bay Point, where Mike and Kate Nelson's one-bedroom bungalow stood at the edge of Cedar Creek. It would be another year before the excavator showed up to demolish their neighbors' homes.

I had made the hour drive from Ocean City, a Jersey Shore community jammed onto a narrow barrier island, just south of the casino town of Atlantic City. I had only recently moved there after living in Manhattan for two years, and California for thirteen years before that. It seemed that Ocean City, with its touch of the cosmopolitan, was as close as I could bring myself to returning home to the intensely rural Bayshore. I had talked to Mike on the phone before driving to Bay Point to meet him and Kate, and in that first conversation, he'd answered many of my questions with "Yes sir," as I would come to realize he often did with people who weren't from the Bayshore, and who, he understood by now, perceived themselves as more intelligent than him. He wasn't sure if he wanted to talk to me about the nearly four years that had passed since Hurricane Sandy decimated the Bayshore. Or about how dealing with the government—all of it, from federal to state to local—had given him and Kate nervous breakdowns, and, as Kate believed, post-traumatic stress disorder. It was a story that they had once wanted to tell as many journalists as they could—journalists from as far away as New York City—when it seemed nobody else cared to listen. But with the state's Blue Acres Program succeeding in buying out most of the rest of Bay Point, Mike felt that, now, maybe all the government officials and "nature folks" would stop harassing him and Kate about "managed retreat," "resilience," "mitigation," "living shorelines"—terms that, to Mike and Kate, were at best abstract and at worst unfair. "We just want them to forget about us," he had told me, "so we can live in peace."

In Mike and Kate's driveway was an aged but neatly kept fishing boat, the *Katie Ann*, parked on a trailer. A grimy, tattered American flag was tied onto the wooden railings of a wide front deck. As I approached the house, I could see Mike's big, six-foot-four, nearly three-hundred-pound frame behind the glass of the front door. Behind Mike, Parker barked incessantly, most interested, I would quickly find out, in being scratched behind the ears. Mike was smiling as he opened the door. This time, he didn't say "Yes sir," because I had told him, in another phone call a few days before my visit, that I had grown up just across the marsh.

Even though I had mud on my boots from the walk up the driveway, Mike told me not to worry. "Are you kidding?" he said. "Keep them suckers on." Just beyond their small kitchen, Kate sat at a long high-top table that she and Mike called "the bar." Its top was a massive slab of resin-coated wood, in which various fishing lures and coins were permanently encased. It was early afternoon, thus late enough to have a beer, Kate said. She pulled one for herself and one for me from a whirring, commercial-grade ice machine sitting next to the head of the bar.

Mike no longer drank, so he poured himself a glass of fruit juice. The other side of the table was almost all windows. They looked out over a placid and gray Cedar Creek and the marshland beyond. The trees of Cedarville, where the bottom edge of South Jersey slipped from solid ground to floodplain, appeared as a line on the horizon. I noticed that the wood-paneled walls were, like the table, coated in resin. "I learned my lesson after the storm," Mike said. "This whole damn house is sealed tight." Just past the end of the bar was the living room. It was a small space stuffed with two puffy reclining chairs, a flat-screen television, and, below that, another screen displaying three different video feeds from security cameras stationed outside the house—one of the front porch, another of the driveway, and another of Bay Point Road. I asked Mike what they were for. "We're out here by ourselves now," he said.

BAD WEATHER, along with isolation, was part of the deal in Bay Point, but for Mike and Kate, and everyone who lived on the Bayshore, Sandy was not a storm; it was an act of a wrathful God. Like Mike, Kate sometimes couldn't say the name—when recalling her and Mike's struggle to rebuild and remain in Bay Point over the last four years, she simply called Sandy "the storm," or "the tragedy." When she did finally say the name, it induced in her a physical revulsion—the word came out quiet and through clenched teeth.

Talking about Sandy caused her to nervously make a little pile with her keys, cell phone, and can of Miller Lite, which was stuffed in a Bay Point Marina koozie. She pushed the keys and phone left and right, then spun the beer around in her hands, over and over, before taking a gulp. Her eyes darted to some distant place out the window, over the creek, over the marshland, toward the trees. Initially, Mike had more success hiding his pain—until he didn't. I'd asked him to talk about the days when they owned and ran the marina. His eyes pooled. "The marina was our American Dream, you know?" he said. "There's been some big tears."

Although I hadn't yet fully realized it, I knew enough to understand that getting emotional was not something Mike and Kate did freely. Everyone around the Bayshore seemed to have a tragic story—many having to do with fishing or hunting accidents on the bay or in the marshland, or the hurricanes, nor'easters, and nameless storms that came with each season, year in and year out. Or, if the tragedy wasn't natural, it was societal.

People didn't stick around Cumberland County, where the majority of the Bayshore's communities lived, to get rich or rise up America's social ladder. You stuck around because you were from here, and—for some reason many of us could never quite figure out—you loved it here. There was plenty to complain about—lack of jobs, rising crime rates in the nearby towns, the dismal state of the county's public health services, the viciousness of the summer gnats, mosquitoes, strawberry flies, and greenheads. But there was the breathtaking natural landscape—somewhere along the line, a visiting researcher had dubbed the Bayshore the "Serengeti of the West." If your ancestors had lived here, it was as if you had an obligation to live here, too, if only to keep the place from going extinct.

There was something to be said about seeing a family name in the earliest records of the place where you grew up. The name (or names) put words to roots, made tangible the abstractness of heritage. In the places I had lived in Manhattan and California, everyone seemed to be a transplant, as if they'd arrived yesterday. For a long time, when I was asked by people in those places what my European roots were, I didn't have a real answer, because I had never taken the time to trace my roots far enough back to get beyond South Jersey. When asked the question, I often used an old family joke: we didn't come from Europe; we came from the marsh mud. In Mike and Kate, I had instantly seen two people with the same mud in their veins.

Mike was fifty-nine, with graying, curly black hair that was almost as full as it was in his and Kate's wedding photo, which sat on the windowsill. Mike was a true waterman, as the crabbers, fishermen, and oystermen are called on the Bayshore. He'd spent most of his life in Bay Point. Though he was born about forty-five minutes inland, his father had purchased a home here not long after returning from World War II, as a way, Mike believed, to seek refuge from the PTSD he'd developed from the war. Back then, Bay Point was in its infancy—the dirt road that ran from Cedarville and through the marshland to the mouth of Cedar Creek had been fortified with car parts, cedar poles, and any other refuse that might prevent cars from sinking into the mud. At first, the land along the bay where the first collection of shanties were built was called Eagle Island. It was named after a nearby patch of high ground that was elevated just enough to sustain a stand of trees where eagles often perched. By the time Mike was born in 1957, his parents were spending the summers in Bay Point. They rarely left, besides the occasional trip to pick up groceries in town.

Kate, who was two months younger than Mike, was no less suited to the bay and its culture. She had cropped, slightly graying brown hair and stood a full foot shorter than Mike, and she could out-cuss and out-drink most of the tough watermen who were always stopping by the house. She loved nothing more than a hot day on the water, drinking beer and filling up the cooler with fish. She was not, however, a Bayshore native—she'd been introduced to Bay Point later in life, in 1985, when she was working for the energy company PSE&G. One day a coworker named Ray Sileo asked her if she might want to sacrifice a weekend helping him drill and set steel plates onto the piling foundation of a house he was building on the bayfront section of Bay Point. That weekend, while she was working on Sileo's house, she met Mike, who was helping with the carpentry. They were both twenty-seven.

To thank everyone for working on the house, Sileo threw a party that Saturday night. Mike worked up the courage to ask Kate to dance. Afterward, he asked her if she'd like to go fishing with him in the morning. They'd gotten a late start, since everyone was nursing hangovers, but by noon they were out on the bay, drinking beer again and catching weakfish and blue crabs. Up to that point, Mike hadn't found the right woman. "I took some girls out fishing and all, but they were prudish," he told me as we sat at the bar. Kate chuckled, rolled her eyes. Mike went on, "One girl didn't pee all day, 'cause she was too vain to pee in a bucket." He had invited his brother and a few other guys on the boat that afternoon—Kate was the only woman onboard. But when she had to go, Mike said, "she just turned her head and went in the bucket." Mike raised both hands, palms up, and shrugged his broad shoulders, as if to say, *Sometimes you just get lucky.* By the next summer, they were married. "She's been my partner ever since," he said.

"I'LL TELL YOU WHAT," Mike was saying. "It was a real special place." He was describing his and Kate's previous home that had been on Paris Road, the gravel-and-clamshell drive that horseshoed off Bay Point Road as the land followed Cedar Creek's mouth. The properties along Paris had been the most coveted real estate in Bay Point because they fronted the bay. Along with Sileo's, Mike and Kate's had been one of the nicer homes. It was a two-bedroom, one-thousand-square-foot rancher raised on timber pilings, with a spacious deck that looked out across the bay. "We got sunsets over the water," Mike told me. "You can't get that on the other side." He was talking about the Jersey Shore, on the Atlantic coast, where I now lived.

On the evening of October 27, 2012, Mike and Kate had been at home. The house was a cluttered mess. Katie, their twenty-five-year-old daughter, had been living there with her five-year-old son, Eugene, with whom she shared a bedroom. In the other bedroom was Mikie, who was two years younger than Katie. He'd recently gotten a good job with a marine construction company over on the Delaware River, near Philadelphia. He'd tried to move closer to work, but he'd decided the drive was worth it if it meant being able to live in Bay Point. The only place left for Mike and Kate to sleep was a small shed that Mike had built alongside the house, years before, with the intention of making it his man cave. "It became the honeymoon suite," Kate said, laughing. Neither one of them cared about the tight quarters. Eugene's toys were everywhere, muddy footprints tracked across the kitchen floor, and the dogs, Parker and Paris, who were just puppies, constantly yelped from inside their crate. But, Kate said, those years just before Sandy, with everyone living together in Bay Point, were "the best times of our life out here."

A cool west wind had been blowing that October night. Below the rancher, the bay moved listlessly. Freighters, en route to Philadelphia, fifty miles up bay, slipped along quietly, retreating from the ocean, their lights like rogue stars rising from the watery horizon. It was like any other day. The summer before, in 2011, as Hurricane Irene bore down on the Northeast, Mike and Kate had decided to evacuate, which they'd never done before. "In the past," Mike said, "we'd just go into town and pick up some food and alcohol and have a hurricane party." For Bay Point, at least, Irene's damage wasn't much worse than the countless other storms they had dealt with in the past. They figured Sandy would be the same.

But on the big-screen television in the rancher's living room, the news reported that New Jersey governor Chris Christie had declared a state of emergency in anticipation of Sandy's landfall. Journalists and commentators were preemptively drawing parallels to Katrina, the hurricane that devastated New Orleans in 2005 and exposed the fragility of the Federal Emergency Management Agency under President George W. Bush and sent the National Flood Insurance Program into spiraling debt.

Twenty-four hours before, most of the forecast models had showed Sandy, a mere Category 2 hurricane, tracking northwest toward the Outer Banks of North Carolina, before swinging east out to sea with the Gulf Stream, as most Atlantic hurricanes did, especially this late in the year. Then, Sandy's track changed drastically. The models now showed the storm turning not east, but west, directly into the Jersey Shore. The meteorologist on the nightly news became excited, worked into a froth. Standing before a glowing map that showed Sandy's various, potentially devastating landfall scenarios, he called the hurricane the "Frankenstorm," since it was ballooning into an unprecedented one thousand miles in width and would be making landfall just before Halloween.

Four years later, as we sat at the bar, Mike remembered seeing the one track that had the storm running directly into the Delaware Bay. "I'd never seen a storm do that before," he told me. Once they saw that, they decided to evacuate. "Why not?" Kate recalled thinking. No one was too worried. "We figured we'd be back home in a few days' time."

THAT WASN'T HOW THINGS TURNED OUT, of course. Since October 29, 2012, through the entirety of Barack Obama and Chris Christie's respective second terms, Mike and Kate had simply been trying to rebuild. It was now 2016, and they still weren't finished. For instance, they wanted to box in the piping that snaked beneath the bungalow, to insulate it from freezing in the winter. But the insurance money they'd gotten for the Paris Road rancher had to be spent on building the bungalow. Other than a fifty-dollar gift card from Catholic Charities, there had been little other aid money. Mike had been digging into his pension for years now and was desperately waiting for his early Social Security. Really, it felt like they'd never be finished rebuilding. A new president would be coming into office soon; a new governor not long after that. What would these political shifts at both levels of government mean for Mike and Kate and the rest of the Bayshore? Looking around, it was easy to think that they wouldn't mean much at all. Many of the homes that had been abandoned and sold to Blue Acres still showed their prominent scars from Sandy, as if they were forced into a catatonic state by the confluence of an indifferent climate, government, and country—a world that had no need for such a place anymore.

After leaving Mike and Kate, I took a walk around. At the bend where Bay Point Road turned into Paris Road, on a utility pole, there was a rusted sign that read "SLOW: CHILDREN AT PLAY." On top of the pole was a bald eagle, watching me as I walked. At one of the homes now owned by the state, I entered a side door that was unlocked. A black spiral staircase ran up to an empty second floor, where a lone piece of furniture, a red plastic chair, sat in a bolt of sunlight coming through a sliding glass door. The sun was just beginning its drop into the bay. It was a warm, lucid afternoon—the kind that made you wonder why everyone had given up on such a dazzling place.

I sat down in the red chair and looked out over the water. Didn't people often refer to views like this as priceless? I'd recently had a conversation with Jeff Tittel, the senior chapter director for the New Jersey Sierra Club, about the Blue Acres buyout in Bay Point and the program's growing interest in neighboring Money Island. Since Sandy, Tittel had been a vocal advocate for retreat along New Jersey's coastlines, especially on the Bayshore. He had no qualms about saying that the best course of action for the people who lived along the bay was to move to higher ground. Tittel didn't blame people like Mike and Kate for being in the predicament they were in; he blamed the politicians. They'd forgotten about the Bayshore, he said—its rich history and environmental vulnerabilities that had culminated with Sandy and led to the slow-moving crisis that continued to torment its residents. Personally, Tittel thought ecotourism was the answer. But then again, he worried it was too late. "You walk in those little shops down there and you get looked at sideways," he told me. "It's just a time-forgotten place."

TWO

"WHERE POOR PEOPLE CAME TO GET AWAY"

THE GEOGRAPHY OF THE DELAWARE BAY offered a hint at what Sandy would bring to the Bayshore. Between the Cape May Peninsula and the narrow spit of sand that makes up Delaware's Cape Henlopen State Park, the bay's mouth stretches just over eleven miles, nearly identical to that of the Chesapeake, 130 miles to the south. Unlike the Chesapeake's mouth, however, the Delaware's tips due southeast, with the shorelines of both Delaware and New Jersey curling inward toward its mouth, like the wide ends of a great funnel. For a storm like Sandy, which spun northwest, directly into the Jersey Shore, the mouth of the Delaware was the perfect siphon for the enormous seven feet of storm surge that arrived on top of an already higher-than-usual full moon high tide that October night.

Once Sandy's surge entered the bay, there was little to absorb its inevitable collision with land. The bay—which resembles the outline of South America tipped on its side—is nearly eight hundred square miles and can plunge more than one hundred feet deep in areas around its shipping channel, but along the Bayshore coast, its depth averages only about ten feet. The shoreline here is barely above sea level, presenting no barriers for floodwaters. From its mouth at the Atlantic Ocean to the beginning of the Delaware River, forty miles to the northwest, the bay is ribbed with shoals that have challenged mariners for centuries—during Sandy, they served to refract and break apart swell, which fomented tall, wild surf, as if the bay were a shallow bathtub being whipped up by a child's hands.

A shallow area of the bay just offshore from far South Jersey's Cape May peninsula is referred to as "The Rips," for its tempestuousness and danger. On the morning of August 28, 1609, Henry Hudson came upon the bay for the first time in the eighty-five-foot *Half Moon* and was quickly deluged by breaking waves and side-slipping current near where The Rips are located today. Catching sight of "Breaches and drie Sand," Hudson ordered a retreat. While anchored safely offshore that evening, Hudson's first officer, Robert Juet, recounted in his journal the morning's drama: "And hee that will throughly Discover this great Bay, must have a small Pinnasse [boat], that must draw but foure or five foote water."

A later account of Hudson's failed attempt to enter the bay that August morning in 1609 noted that as the *Half Moon* tacked north the next day, toward the river that would soon bear Hudson's name, the coastline appeared to be "a white sandy beach and drowned land within, beyond which there appeared a grove of wood." The account, recorded by Joannes de Laet in his *History of the New World*, was referring to the barrier islands that make up New Jersey's Atlantic coast, from the Cape May Peninsula 130 miles north to Sandy Hook, which today resemble de Laet's description only in his mention of white sandy beaches.

By 2019, those barrier islands had been engineered and fortified with hundreds of jetties, bulkheads, piers, miles of asphalt, and nearly two hundred million cubic yards of sand fill—all to slow the ocean and back bays' natural erosive currents and, now, their accelerated, climate change–induced rise. From this grotesque profusion of infrastructure has sprung boardwalks and roller coasters and T-shirt shops and mini-golf courses, hotels and casinos, and the second homes of the wealthy. And all of it for a summer season of just fifteen weeks, between the end of May and the beginning of September, when tens of millions of souls pack onto these mutated sandbars. Of New Jersey's twenty-one counties, only four encompass the Jersey Shore, and yet these four make up half of the state's $43 billion tourism economy.

If Hudson had been able to squeeze the *Half Moon* into the Delaware Bay, however, he would have seen more than just white sandy beaches and drowned land within. He would have entered one of the largest estuaries in North America. Beginning far to the northwest, in the Great Appalachian Valley, the six-thousand-square-mile Delaware Estuary—as it is called today—descends southeastward toward the Atlantic, following the lead of a valley carved out by the last glacial retreat. Along the north shore of the bay are some eighty-five thousand acres of salt marshes, which are dominated by long cordgrass (*Spartina alterniflora*) and low, dense salt hay (*Spartina patens*). To Hudson and his crew, the marshland would have appeared as a green and yellow sea, unfurling to the horizon in rolling swells beneath the hot, southwest wind blowing that August day.

If it seemed implausible to Hudson that something as architecturally monolithic as the modern Jersey Shore could be built on such unstable earth, he would have found it hard to imagine anything human at all inhabiting the northern shore of the future Delaware Bay. Rivers, creeks, ditches, and tidal guts laced their way through the bogged and often impassable estuary like dark brown arteries winding toward a golden, grassy heart. Mosquitoes, gnats, and other insects swarmed so thick they could be mistaken for puffs of black smoke. If Hudson had explored this infirm land, he would have observed only traces of human habitation, in the form of temporary fishing and hunting camps made by the local Lenni Lenape Native Americans. In the absence of permanent inhabitants, however, Hudson would have been overwhelmed by the animal life—eagles, osprey, red knots, sandpipers, ruddy turnstones, dunlins, dowitchers, yellowlegs, and some three hundred other bird species roamed the sky above, perched in the marshlands' hardwood trees, or scuttled along its beaches. Sturgeon, whales, horseshoe crabs, otters, and reams of other marine wildlife crowded the brown, nutrient rich water below. Because, in the 403 years that passed between his last look at "South River," as he called the Delaware Bay, and that October night when Mike and Kate saw the television image of Sandy's strange track leading directly to their doorstep, little had changed on the Bayshore.

Mike knew this. It was precisely why he and Kate loved Bay Point so much—why, in the decades before Sandy, they'd endured countless storms that had caused severe flooding across the Bayshore. In more recent years, the trouble had extended beyond foul weather, to "sunny day" flood tides.

Mike liked to say that Bay Point—and the Bayshore in general—was "the place where poor people came to get away." The Jersey Shore could have all the glitz and attention. Folks on the Bayshore just wanted to be able to fish and hunt and live quietly, untouched by the crush and clamor and fierce modernity of what is the biggest megalopolis in the Western Hemisphere—the sprawl of urbanity, industry, and suburbia stretching from Washington, DC, in the south to Boston in the north.

The Bayshore sits squarely in the center of this corridor, and yet, few people in the region—even many South Jerseyans—know it exists. New Jersey's entire Delaware Bay shore cuts a ragged, seventy-mile path through three counties, but its epicenter—what is generally considered the capital *B* Bayshore—is a forty-mile stretch of coast in Cumberland County where a handful of fishing villages, covering just four miles in length and having a total population of around fifteen hundred, dot the otherwise barren landscape. At Cumberland's southeast corner, beside the county's largest tributary, the Maurice River, sits the town of Port Norris and its Bivalve and Shell Pile communities, which were the heart of an oyster industry once so flush with money that, in the 1920s, the town of around a thousand residents had more millionaires per square mile than any other town in New Jersey. At the other end of the county, there is the now-disappeared hamlet of Bayside, where a railroad once ran to the water's edge, to service one of America's most prosperous ports for sturgeon, whose roe was distributed to caviar importers around the world.

With the turn of the twentieth century, however, all that would soon be gone. The bay's sturgeon had been fished nearly out of existence—in 1890, when the fishery was booming at Bayside, an average of sixty sturgeon were caught per gill net; by 1899, the average had dropped to just eight. Although the bay's sturgeon population could not withstand the pressures of overfishing, its oysters, and the industry built around them, seemed to only thrive. In Port Norris in the early 1900s, there were some twenty-nine processing houses standing along the docks in Bivalve and Shell Pile. A passenger train ran regular trips to Bridgeton, the county seat. By the 1920s, a freight rail was shipping sixty-seven carloads of oysters to Philadelphia, Baltimore, and New York every day. Port Norris's oystermen, made rich by the hundreds of thousands of oysters being dredged daily from the bay's seafloor, built hulking Victorians along the town's Main Street. Oysters became so important that the state started monitoring the bay's population through a permanent shellfish laboratory it opened in a space among the processing houses.

The industry managed to survive the Depression and remained strong in the 1940s after power dredging replaced the manual method on the schooners. But in 1957 the shellfish laboratory's scientists noticed that a disease was beginning to infect the bay's oysters. Dr. Thurlow C. Nelson, who was internationally recognized for his research on the physiology of the *Crassostrea virginica*—the species of oyster that inhabited the bay—noted that his samples weren't growing and that their meat were "puffed and white." On a cold, windy November morning in 1958, Nelson reached into his tank of samples and pulled out another oyster to examine. It was, Nelson wrote in his "Oyster Pathology" notebook, "the thinnest oyster I have ever seen." Nelson had discovered MSX, a parasitic disease that had never been seen before. By 1960, about 95 percent of the bay's oyster stock had died, and the industry collapsed.

By then, the great vision to connect the cities of the Northeast Megalopolis had mostly succeeded, spawning an endless network of highways and cities and suburbs. In northern New Jersey, the smokestacks of factories and refineries bristled everywhere, billowing the kind of mysterious, foul-smelling smoke that has made New Jersey synonymous with decay—the "armpit of New York," as those who know the state only from Newark and its ilk are wont to say. But that's a fallacy. One hundred thirty miles south of Manhattan, less than forty miles from Philadelphia, Cumberland County is by and large deeply rural—it makes up the natural end of the splash of wilderness that begins with the Pine Barrens to the north—despite being surrounded by a landscape glazed over with concrete and asphalt and crosshatched by development.

Since its founding in 1748, Cumberland has been dominated by agriculture; today, a quarter of the county's nearly five hundred square miles is farmland, divided into some six hundred farms. The Northeast Corridor's major highways steer clear of the county's huge tracts of fields and forest and wetlands, despite decades' worth of pleas from various county stakeholders for a southward extension of the nearest highway, State Route 55.

The Megalopolis's greatest legacy—its sprawling suburbs—have mostly avoided Cumberland. Local officials, who constantly fret over the state's disinterest in the county's many plights, often say that if only we still traded and traveled by boat, the county would have remained a shining example of American progress. "The south [of South Jersey] seems to illustrate a principle of economic development," the *New York Times* wrote in 2000. "To be unspoiled is to be left behind."

In the realm of health, poverty, and political demographics, much of Cumberland County today is far more emblematic of Appalachia than it is of the region of the country in which it is so oddly trapped. New Jersey has one of the highest per capita income rates in America, while Cumberland's rate of just over $22,000 is well below the national average. Cumberland's overall population is also in decline and aging, as young residents leave permanently for opportunities elsewhere. On the Bayshore, it's stagnated. In the 1870s, when the Bayshore's oyster and agricultural industries were growing at a rapid pace, the population of Downe Township—where the Bayshore's three largest hamlets, including Money Island, are located—was just over three thousand. Today, it is around fifteen hundred—about the same as it was in 1798, the year Downe was created. Countywide, the poverty rate hovers at 18.5 percent. And in Port Norris, once home to so many millionaires, the per capita income is just $17,000.

Cumberland's decline is a typical rural American tragedy. Before globalization and industrial consolidation decimated small shipping ports like Bridgeton, Greenwich, and Port Norris, quaint, family-owned farms blanketed the county's rich, sandy soil. The glass giant Owens-Illinois, located in Bridgeton, used that soil to become one of the largest glass factories in America by the 1960s. Companies like P. J. Ritter, Hunt-Wesson, and H. J. Heinz Company operated processing plants near the Cohansey River, which bisected Bridgeton, to be closer to the many Cumberland farms that supplied their tomatoes. South Jersey's sandy soil, along with the fruits and vegetables that grew so well from it, was one of the primary reasons New Jersey was nicknamed "The Garden State."

As late as the early 1990s, downtown Bridgeton's main thoroughfare, Laurel Street, had hardware stores and shoe shops, florists and cafes, art supply stores and a J. C. Penney. In the mid-nineteenth century, in Cumberland's largest city, Vineland, John Landis Mason invented his screw-top glass jar, Joseph Fourestier Simpson created the arcade game Skee-Ball, and Thomas Bramwell Welch figured out that if he pasteurized grape juice, he could market it to churches as an alternative to Holy Communion wine. Thomas Edison's forgotten rival, Oberlin Smith, lived his entire life in Bridgeton, where he found that sound could be recorded on magnetic tape.

Mine was the last generation to experience a thriving downtown Bridgeton, before its sharp decline in the late 1980s and '90s. By the time I graduated high school, in 2000, there were few career opportunities for Cumberland County kids who did not want to move away from home. The only somewhat abundant, decent-paying jobs available were those at one of the four huge state and federal correctional facilities that had sprouted up on the Bayshore in the 1990s.

Like so many of the kids who decided to leave, I gravitated toward a prosperous corner of the country. I went farther than most, to San Diego, where I sought to replace my rural American identity with a new, modern one. For thirteen years, I achieved just that. I traveled the world, scrapping by as a freelance journalist, writing about the sport of surfing, which I had become obsessed with as a teenager. I returned home for the holidays, weddings, funerals, but rarely stayed long enough to revisit, much less think about, the places that defined my childhood. Even if I had wanted to make a fishing trip out on the bay, I couldn't, because the weakfish, flounder, and striped bass had all but disappeared, forcing the state's Division of Fish and Wildlife to impose strict catch limits that virtually ended recreational fishing on the Jersey side of the bay. Sadly, everyone now abbreviated the name "Gandy's Beach"—one of Downe Township's bayside hamlets—to "Gandy's," since its beach had long been swallowed by the water.

In the years prior to Sandy, I'd come to disrespect my home for what I saw as its failure to evolve, without fully understanding the undercurrents that kept it down. So I attempted to graft the identities of the places I saw in my travels onto my own, as if I could permanently cover over my backwater self. The kid who had spent his summer days slogging along the muddy banks of the Cohansey, fishing for carp and catfish, was rarely recalled. The kid who walked countless miles of salt hay meadow, muddy ditches, and dense woods to hunt ducks, deer, and turkeys became a secret that the adult did not share. In doing so, that life became fogged and fractured beneath the crush of newer, shinier, more cosmopolitan memories. I secretly looked down on my peers who chose to never leave home—but I also admired them for making lives out of so little, and thought of myself as traitorous.

MIKE AND KATE had never entertained such conflicted thoughts. Bay Point, living in the Paris Road rancher together, running the marina to make some extra money after Mike retired—that was the script they had written for the story of the rest of their life together. "I think this is what heaven looks like," Mike told me one afternoon as we sat at the bar, looking out the windows at Cedar Creek and the landscape beyond. "At least, I sure hope so." The rancher, which Mike built in the '80s, had been their dream home. But year by year, the sandy beach below it had been gnawed away by the high tides, exposing a muddy, Swiss cheese–like base. In 2011, when Mike retired from the Delaware River Port Authority, he made $40,000 in improvements to the rancher—new vinyl siding, windows, heater, insulation, and a steel roof—that he thought would last forever.

In 2004, along with two partners, Mike and Kate purchased Bay Point Marina, which had fallen into disrepair. They built an office and tackle shop and installed floating docks for 120 slips. Mike and Kate were the kind of people whose door was open at all times—they could make anyone who walked inside comfortable and, shortly thereafter, drunk and stuffed with food. The refrigerator or cooler was always filled with beer, and you were always welcome to one. The marina became a hub for local, as well as visiting, fishermen. The annual Cumberland County weakfish-flounder fishing tournament was a big draw, and many years, Kate checked in the winning fish. The tournament had a first-place pot that went into the thousands. Other local marinas—including the one my mother's cousin owned on a nearby creek—donated prizes that included fishing rods, reels, tackle, even outboard engines. "There was always something happening then," Mike told me.

The marina's end-of-summer pig roast might have been the biggest party in Lawrence Township, the municipality where Bay Point was located. Local mayors stopped by, as did county legislators—called "freeholders" in New Jersey—and other small-town big fish. Kate ran the marina's bait and tackle shop next to the boat ramp, and all the regulars called her "Mama Kate." Once, when she suspected a guy named Eddie of cheating in the tournament, she dumped a beer over his head. "He kept winning every year," Kate said. "He had a real fast boat—I think he was going out to the ocean or something, where the fish are bigger." About once a week, a writer for the local newspaper would call Kate for a fishing report.

Kate relished what she called the "social aspect" of the marina. It wasn't that the surrounding beauty of the bay, the creek, and the marshland was lost on her or Mike or anyone who chose to live in Bay Point; it was just that the tight-knit community was an intrinsic part of the pleasure of living there. In the years since Sandy, this was what she missed most.

Although I'd left the Bayshore in 2000, before I had a chance to see the marina in its halcyon days, I'd grown up hearing about it, before it was owned by Mike and Kate. As a kid, all I wanted to do was fish, and Bay Point Marina, along with the other little marinas dotting Cumberland's portion of the Bayshore, existed in my mind as a kind of tantalizing sportsman's utopia. I knew I'd get there someday. I just didn't know that, when I did finally get there, it all would be gone.

When they evacuated for Irene in 2011, Mike, Kate, and the kids had packed up their guns, meat slicer, sewing machine, family photos, the brand-new forty-inch flat-screen television, the two boats, and, most importantly, Mike's La-Z-Boy recliner. But since nothing much happened in Irene, they packed very little when they finally decided to evacuate on October 28, a day before Sandy's landfall.

Plus, with all the improvements Mike had just made to the rancher, he felt confident it would survive the storm. Once the floodwater receded, they would come back and start cleaning up the mess, just like always. After packing a few changes of clothes, the family—which included Katie, Eugene, and Mikie—took off for a nearby hunting club, where Mikie was a member. On the evening of October 29, as the skies turned heavy and dark and Sandy's landfall on the Atlantic coast was imminent, Mike,

Kate, and Katie had driven in to Bay Point to check on the house. The tide was rising and the water was already creeping up over the road, but otherwise the weather and the bay's conditions didn't appear any more severe than they had in the hours before past hurricanes. "It was dark and we couldn't really see much, but everything seemed fine," Katie told me. Kate remembered her daughter say, "We could've stayed home. It's not going to be that bad."

They turned around and went back to the hunting club, thinking everything was fine. But in Downe Township, a fire captain named Cliff Higbee discussed the situation with a local newspaper reporter. He was worried. "With the amount of water we are facing coming in from the bay—it has nowhere to drain," Higbee said. "If this storm hits the way some weather experts are predicting, it could be one of the worst disasters this area has ever seen." Higbee and other firefighters had been holding over in the firehouse, staying on call. Multiple reports of serious flooding were beginning to come in, and Sandy's landfall was still hours away. Higbee then offered the reporter a prediction. "This is a little area," he said. "Bigger places are going to be prioritized."

THREE

"THUS FAR, AND NO FARTHER SHALT THOU GO"

BAY POINT MAY have only existed as local legend in my mind, but Money Island I had touched, seen with my own eyes. And like most poignant memories of the Bayshore, mine also is anchored by a storm.

It was 1991, in the middle of a hot, rainy summer. I was nine years old and wanted nothing else but to go fishing on the bay. My uncle owned a small boat that wasn't much different from Mike and Kate's *Katie Ann*. Same yellowed fiberglass, same bloodstained decks. On most Saturday or Sunday mornings that summer, my father, older brother, and I would arrive at the wharf where my uncle kept his boat. The wharf was located a few miles back from the bay, on the crook of a shallow, serpentine tributary called Back Creek. It wasn't much to look at—just a horseshoe-shaped parking lot paved in crushed clamshells, tucked behind a wall of foxtails and connected to the main road by a perpetually rutted dirt lane. There were about a hundred slips framed out with warped cedar poles and splintering, fish-gut-coated docks.

The wharf, called Husted's Landing, and the land surrounding it had been owned by various relatives in both my mother's and father's families for the better part of the last century. Both families were farmers and fishermen and, during Prohibition, enablers of bootleggers who paid off many Bayshore landowners in return for access to the bay. My grandfather often talked about being woken as a child in the middle of the night by the headlights and gurgling engines of the bootleggers' trucks driving past his home near the Cohansey River, pulling trailers loaded with liquor and concealed by bales of salt hay. In summer, the insects—mosquitoes, gnats, strawberry flies, blackflies, and greenheads—can be intolerable. But for the beer-numb old men and women who would sit on the reeking bench next to the fish-cleaning table, they were no problem. Only outsiders, they'd say, had that sweet blood the bugs like so much. They would plant themselves on the bench for hours, offering *humpfs* and dismissive waves for bad catches, and long, low whistles for good ones.

My father, uncle, brother, and I got a lot of whistles. Fishing was in our DNA. Both of my parents could trace their Bayshore roots nearly back to the American Revolution, and our collective family's history was full of watermen—boat captains, muskrat trappers, salt hay farmers, oystermen, and, my father regularly and proudly reminded us, the painter Warren W. Sheppard, whose evocative depictions of life at sea made him one of the most iconic American naval painters of the nineteenth century. After almost every fishing trip on the bay in those days, we'd have a cooler full of weakfish, bluefish, and flounder to take home for dinner. My father and uncle had taught my brother and me how to fillet, and I can re- member how good it felt when I finally figured out how to cut close and evenly along the spine and ribs so as to leave little meat on the carcass. My mother, who'd grown up among brothers who hunted and fished, would wrap the fillets in tinfoil and cook them on a rusted-out charcoal grill that was perched on our back step.

As the crow flies, we lived four miles away from the wharf—by land, it was eleven, since the road had to trace the circuitous path of the Cohansey. In the mid-1970s, my uncle, who was a carpenter, had been working on a stately nineteenth-century farmhouse on a patch of land that abutted the marshland along the river. When the owner said he wanted to refur- bish and rent out an old hay barn on the other side of the property, my uncle told my parents, who were then living in a tiny apartment closer to Bridgeton. When my parents first saw the barn, goats were living inside, jumping in and out of the low, open windows. They fell in love with it immediately, and gradually began converting it into a home. In 1976, they had my sister; three years later, my brother was born. I arrived in 1982. With the woods and fields and endless miles of *Spartina* marshland surrounding us, we spent little time indoors. Our finger- and toenails were permanently crammed with dirt and our knees and elbows skinned from climbing trees and traipsing through briar thickets. No one seemed to care when our television broke and our parents didn't get a new one until months later.

That morning, as we glided along the inky skin of Back Creek, mallards and mergansers, teal and black ducks, sprang from the narrow ditches hidden throughout the marshland. I liked the way my uncle gripped the base of the throttle, rather than the handle, so that he could make subtle adjustments to the boat's speed. The way he and my father—they were brothers—simultaneously leaned forward from their ankles into the bow as it rose up on the water. The way the boat's green and red running lights glowed like Jolly Ranchers in the predawn.

Back then, before the bay began to rise and eat away the marshland, it took exactly ten minutes to reach the mouth of Back Creek. My father and uncle grew up fishing and crabbing and duck hunting in the creek (they, like most everyone who grew up on the Bayshore, pronounce it "crick"). They'd done this trip hundreds of times. I was still working on my first few dozen. But I'd been studying. The first bend was called Bridge of Sticks, named for the tiny cedar-pole bridge, built a half century before by salt hay farmers, spanning a nearby ditch. The next bend, called Drum Bed, was the most exciting. Here, Back Creek opened wide and redirected ninety degrees to the southeast. The width was deceiving: there were two shallow, cigar-shaped sandbars that came to inches below the surface at high tide and were dry at low. Before the black drum were overfished and nearly vanquished from the bay, they would venture up to these shallows every spring to spawn. Outsiders were often running aground here, but it never posed a challenge for my uncle. He opened up to full-throttle, toying with the shallows in the darkness.

The first sign of the last bend was "Deany's Cabin," a salt- and sunbleached clapboard shanty where, as teenagers, my father, uncle, and their friends spent many cold nights during duck hunting season. My mother had also grown up exploring Back Creek and hanging out in Deany's

Cabin, though she was never a hunter. Just past Deany's was where swell from the bay would start trickling in. If the water's surface went from smooth to agitated, we knew the bay would be rough. If it was choppy *and* rolling underneath with swell, we knew the bay would be angry. Here, Back Creek whipsawed directly into what was, to my young eyes, a wondrous and terrifying continent of open water—the Delaware Bay.

The conditions seemed fine that morning. A few miles out we dropped anchor at a known flounder spot. My uncle tuned the VHF radio to channel thirteen. The staticky voice of the NOAA marine forecaster—still a human back then, rather than the automated voice used today—filled the silence between the sloshing of the waves. The forecaster's voice was as familiar to me as my own—on the tank of our toilet at home was a battery-powered radio; there wasn't a single morning that my mother or father didn't turn it on the moment they woke up.

On this morning, the forecast seemed benign enough: *The marine forecast for lower Delaware Bay—East Point Lighthouse, New Jersey, to Slaughter Beach, Delaware: This morning, east winds fifteen to twenty knots. This afternoon, conditions easing. East winds ten knots. Clear skies. Seas one to two feet.*

While we trusted the weatherman, we were also aware that, around these parts, he could be deceived. Every season had its own brand of foul weather—autumn hurricanes, winter nor'easters, dense spring fog, summer squalls. The ability to adapt to bad weather was essential to living on the Bayshore.

We kept fishing. But soon, boats were streaking along the bay's western horizon, like white paint drips sliding laterally across a gray canvas. The wind began to swirl. A single drop of rain fell on the boat's deck, then a deluge, like thousands of buttons being unsnapped all at once. One of the heavier clouds in the distance sparked, and a ragged bolt of lightning drilled into the bay. Gusts whipped and twisted in every direction. Then came the splitting, gut-wrenching boom. "She's close," my uncle said.

There were three miles of open water between us and the safety of Back Creek. The wind became more confused, the rain heavier. The boat bucked wildly. My father began pulling the anchor. I stood close to my brother, the fear surging within me, watching our father balance himself on the bow, thighs braced on the rail, arms pinwheeling one over the other as fast as he could make them go, his tanned forearms bulging against the weight of the anchor and the pull of the current.

Once the anchor was in and stowed, my uncle jammed the throttle. The boat danced left and right before finding her line. A column of lightning dropped from the sky directly in front of us and plowed into the water. My uncle instinctively turned hard to the right, out of the bolt's way. The sky flickered between darkness and luminous clarity. The air surged with electricity. "I can feel it," my brother said.

There was no making it to Back Creek—too rough, too much lightning. Maybe if it had been just him and my father, my uncle would have given it a shot, but not with us boys onboard. He yelled that we had two options for taking refuge: Bay Point or Money Island. Bay Point was a little over a mile away; Money Island a bit less. They agreed Money Island was the better choice. "Let's ride it out there," my uncle said.

I had never been to Money Island before, but I'd heard about it. This was where the watermen lived, along with a smattering of second-homers, mostly from inland Cumberland County and the Philadelphia suburbs. During the late nineteenth century, when the Bayshore was just acquiring its "Oyster Capital of the World" status, the oyster beds near the mouth of Nantuxent Creek, where Money Island would later be situated, were some of the bay's most fertile. Early maps demarcate the beds, as well as the areas within Nantuxent Cove and Creek for the safe mooring of the multimasted, spoon-bowed oyster schooners that filled the bay during summer. No town yet existed, but there were plenty of recorded accounts that proved the mouth of Nantuxent Creek was a popular place. Before European settlers showed up in the early seventeenth century, the Lenni Lenape Native Americans, who had inhabited the Bayshore region for millennia prior, established summer camps there for stocking up on fish and oysters. By the time I came around in the 1980s, the boom that came with the oyster and sturgeon fisheries had gone bust, but a raucous, antiestablishment attitude—compounded and calcified from centuries of isolation and living by the whims of water and wind—remained in full force.

We tied off the boat to Money Island Marina's main dock. There was a small clubhouse nearby, and it was full with a rowdy crowd of patrons drinking beer, smoking cigarettes, and yelling over one another about fish, the weather, and women. The air was hot and damp and the din was almost loud enough to drown out the thunder rumbling outside. Someone handed my brother and me sodas, on the house. The pouring rain blurred our view out of a large picture window. To that point I hadn't known any other marina but Husted's Landing, which only had a leaky, screened-in shack nicknamed "the Gnat's Nest." Compared to that, Money Island's clubhouse was luxury. I could see pastel-colored homes stretching from both sides of the marina—little shanties and trailers set upon piling and cinderblock foundations, the bay sloshing over a sandy beach below them. Beyond the neat row of homes was an expanse of verdant foxtail stands and *Spartina* meadows undulating in the wind. I thought in that moment that there was no better, or sturdier, place in the world.

I WAS OF COURSE VERY WRONG. At the time, the Bayshore marshland was just beginning to lose the length of one football field a year due to a confluence of sinking land, called subsidence, and sea level rise—a disastrous phenomenon that climate scientists refer to as "relative sea level rise."

While sea level rise, driven by human-caused climate change, began accelerating only in recent decades, subsidence has been occurring for thousands of years. Southern New Jersey rests on the Outer Atlantic Coastal Plain, a flat, porous bed of sandstone, shale, limestone, clay, and other sedimentary formations created by the retreat of the Late Pleistocene glaciation—the last ice age—which began around eighteen thousand years ago. Because of an ongoing seesaw-like process called "glacial isostatic adjustment," in which land released upward by the weight of a retreating glacier continues to gradually settle, the Coastal Plain is sinking.

In 1855, New Jersey's first state geologist, George Hammell Cook, documented the subsidence of the Bayshore. "Several rods in width of the marsh," he wrote, "are sometimes worn away during a single storm." In his research, Cook consulted the manuscripts of a prominent Cape May County legislator named Aaron Leaming, who had written that, in 1734, his grandfather's grave in Town Bank—an area of present-day Cape May, where the first Dutch settlers established a whaling colony—was "fifty rods" (nearly three football fields) "from the Bay, and the sand was blown upon them." Leaming then noted that Town Bank "was formerly between [the graves] and the water." In other locations where graveyards had been set near the water's edge, the skulls of residents' buried relatives and neighbors were often sighted after heavy storms, unearthed, lying in the marshland or a pasture, or what was left of a beach. At a pond mill near the Maurice River, Cook talked to the mill's owner, Nicholas Godfrey. Fifty-two years before, the mill's "wheel-pit floor was carefully set, so that it might be as low as possible, and not be affected by the tide which flows up to it." Cook went on: "When first built it was only an extremely high storm-tide that would stop it; now, a common perigee tide will stop it; and it is stopped in this way perhaps twenty times a year."

An 1868 article, titled "Subsidence of the Coast of New Jersey—Facts which Prove the Encroachment of the Sea" and appearing in the *New York Times*, summarized Cook's findings. "If this subsidence shall proceed in the future as in the past, great calamities are in store for portions of the State," the article concluded. "We can only surrender the future into the hands of Him who laid the foundations of the earth, whose is the sea and its fullness, and who in his time will say, 'Thus far, and no farther shalt thou go.'"

Today, thanks to humanity's imprint on the natural world, subsidence is just one of three forces transforming whole swaths of the Bayshore into water. The Kirkwood-Cohansey aquifer, a seventeen-trillion-gallon expanse of freshwater that sits beneath the entirety of southern New Jersey, is being drained faster than it can be replenished, causing the land above it to slowly cave. And then there is the sheer weight of human lives—our highways, vehicles, office buildings, homes—that adds further pressure on the weak earth beneath our feet.

Natural subsidence and the draining of the Kirkwood-Cohansey aquifer is, of course, just the landward part of this troubling equation. In the sea, there are more dire realities, especially in the mid-Atlantic region of the United States. Since 1880, global mean sea level has increased by about eight to nine inches—with about three inches occurring in just the last twenty-six years. In his paper "History of New Jersey Coastline," written in 1950, U.S. Army Corps of Engineers chief C. F. Wicker pointed out "the rising elevations that have been noticed in recent years." Whether this confounding phenomenon was "due to a subsidence of the land mass or a gain in the volume of water present in the ocean," Wicker wasn't sure. Whatever the cause, Wicker noted that "this change in sea level has moved both the mean high water and the mean low water lines landward about 20 ft. on a 1 on 40 [2.5 percent] sloping beach without the assistance of any accompanying erosion."

This uptick in the rate of global mean sea level rise since 1880 has been faster than that of any other comparable period in at least 2,800 years. Relative sea level rise is more complex, because it takes into account both natural and anthropogenic forces. The US mid-Atlantic coast just happens to be suffering from several of these afflictions—climate scientists have called it a sea level rise "hot spot." The Gulf Stream, which flows just off the coast, is slowing, causing the current's warmer water to stall out and stack on top of the colder, denser subsurface waters. Like any liquid that is heated, the warming ocean is expanding. And Greenland's 680,000 cubic miles of land ice is rapidly melting and pouring into the ocean—this alone has accounted for 15 percent of global mean sea level rise since the 1990s. Couple all of this with the sinking of a coastline that is already barely above the water, and you get 3 to 5 millimeters (0.12–0.20 inches) of relative sea level rise a year—one of the fastest rates in the world. This accelerated rate of relative sea level rise means that by 2050, the bay will rise around a foot above its current level, and, around four feet by 2100. Such inundation will erase some 10 percent of Cumberland County's land, beginning with the Bayshore lowlands and its waterfront hamlets.

MIKE NELSON KNEW BETTER than most the challenge of keeping Bayshore property above the water. Nearly every year since his childhood, he'd helped pour gravel and crushed shell fill around the piling foundations of his home and those of his neighbors. As an adult, he'd begged the township and county to raise Bay Point and Paris roads, or at least grade them flat so that corrosive saltwater from flood tides wouldn't sit in potholes where it would be splashed onto vehicles' undercarriages. He watched as the patch of beach and marshland that used to extend beyond the point where Bay Point Road turned into Paris Road was overcome by the bay.

In Money Island, problems with flooding and erosion had been menacing residents for just as long, and were becoming equally severe.

Mike didn't deny that something was happening—Cook's research had long since proved that—or even that the climate was changing. He just wasn't sure the extent that humans had to do with it. For him, the reason was simple: if Bayshore towns like Bay Point and Money Island had been given the same kind of infrastructure that the Jersey Shore towns had been given over the years, then they would be thriving and growing too. "The world's climate's been changing for hundreds of thousands of years," he told me. "We've been seeing it for a long time."

FOUR

"THE NEXT LEAST LIKED"

"SOME OF THE LOCAL YAHOOS RIPPED MY FIRST SIGN DOWN," Tony Novak said, shaking his head. "I don't get what it is with these guys." He threw both hands in the air and lifted his feet slightly off the floor. Tony had thought that the upscale La Colombe coffee would be a welcomed addition to the menu at Money Island Marina—a source of attraction, even— but apparently he had been wrong when he put up the sign promoting it. The vandalism hadn't stopped him, however, and he had quickly replaced the sign with a newer one on the telephone pole at the entrance to the marina's parking lot. He'd even doubled down and put a second sign a mile up the road, at the spur where Money Island Road branched off toward Gandy's Beach.

It was the beginning of November, around the time I'd first visited Mike and Kate. Tony and I were sitting at a round table in a utility shed, the kind you buy prefabricated at Home Depot, that Tony had converted into the marina's office-cum-tackle shop and called the "bait shack." The table was cluttered with a bulky construction-site radio, a few old boater directories, and a lamp with a crooked shade. Outside, Money Island's small, sodden homes and trailers lined the narrow beach along the bay, then continued along the mouth of Nantuxent Creek, past the marina, and on around a quarter-mile thumb of marshland. Tucked just inside the first bend of the creek, protected from the lashing wind and waves of the bay, was Money Island's tiny commercial oyster fleet. Just past the oyster docks, on a strip of high ground between Nantuxent Drive and the creek, were sixteen homes half concealed by Money Island's last trees. To the northwest was the outline of Bay Point.

Technically, Money Island was not an island, though it was a sliver of high ground in an otherwise empty landscape regularly flooded and made inaccessible by high tides. One thing, however, was for sure, and that was there was no money. The rusted oyster boats, several of them approaching their hundredth year at sea, were barely visible behind a dense fog—the kind that lingers in fall, when the air has grown colder than the water. With the foul weather and ramshackle homes and slumping docks and piers that stretched out into the water in front of them, Money Island was a desperate sight.

Sitting next to Tony and me, sunken into a tall swivel chair with the name "Bruce" embroidered in its backrest, was Tony's marina manager, a frail, leathered man in his sixties named Bruce Muenker. Muenker wore wire-framed glasses and a bushy, graying blond mustache. He spoke little and propped his forearms on the desk in front of him, which held a computer, printer, a pile of Tony's mail, a bottle of outboard engine fuel additive, and Muenker's ashtray. In between rolling his cigarettes, Muenker pressed a thumb into his mustache and concentrated on a small flat-screen television propped on a table on the other side of the room, beneath a No Smoking sign. A daytime soap opera played on mute. To the left of Muenker was another screen, this one displaying, as with Mike and Kate's surveillance monitor, three different angles of the property.

Muenker had recently been diagnosed with cancer, and Tony was driving him back and forth from the hospital, which was a forty-minute drive away. "Bruce is our main priority," Tony had recently told me. "He *is* Money Island Marina." When he wasn't feeling completely exhausted, Muenker drank and could be cranky. He also had a reputation for being mischievous—when out-of-town fishermen called the marina on stormy, rough mornings to get a bay report, Muenker liked to tell them, "Looks great." It was a habit that didn't exactly serve the credibility of Tony as the marina's latest owner. Muenker had a freshly rolled cigarette to smoke, so he excused himself without saying a word and walked back to his place, a camper trailer that was parked next to the bait shack, on the other side of the boat ramp.

The camper sat on the edge of the bay, at the southern mouth of Nantuxent Creek, on a small wedge of land. In the 1970s, when Money Island's population was at its peak, the area where Muenker's camper now sat was the back corner of a wide, grassy beach lot that extended another hundred yards beyond where the shoreline was now. Where a half-dozen shanties and several boats had once sat was now nothing but open water. It had been an ill-advised decision to build on such earth, which was not meant to be static but to expand and contract with the constant friction of the tides and weather, just like the barrier islands on the Jersey Shore.

Downe Township had never had the funds to construct any kind of jetty or bulkhead that could stop the erosion, leaving the work up to individual property owners. The resulting piecemeal construction of shoreline protection did nothing but exacerbate the problem. Beginning in the 1990s, as global sea levels began to accelerate, the point was rapidly carved back to a slice just big enough to hold Muenker's camper, a few boats, and the bait shack. The Money Island tax maps still listed whole lots that now sat entirely underwater. In their fight to stay above water, previous marina owners had taken erosion control measures into their own hands, building flimsy seawalls and dumping gravel, quarry rock, and slabs of concrete to beat back the water—activities that, as years passed and environmental regulation became more stringent, fell in violation of the state's Wetlands, Waterfront Development, and Tidelands regulations. None of the previous owners had addressed these issues, so Tony had inherited them all.

Tony had been on a quest to revive Money Island Marina since November of 2012, when he bought the property in bankruptcy court for $12,000, just a couple of weeks after Sandy. Outsiders like him had come and gone in the recent past with big plans for turning around Money Island, and the Bayshore in general, but none had been successful. Tony would break the curse, he told me, by transforming Money Island into an oyster and blue crab aquaculture hub. This he was sure of.

As late as 1999, when he was thirty-eight, he had been one of the nation's top Greco-Roman wrestlers—he was short, sturdy, and could hold a long stare; he had been a real challenge to pin down or push out of the ring. Although he'd grown up just outside of Philadelphia, among the idyllic, historic Appalachian foothills near Valley Forge, on what his brother later described to me as a "gentleman's farm," Tony seemed used to the grit of Money Island, if exasperated by the local yahoos' constant tampering with his La Colombe coffee sign. Sitting in the bait shack, he had his hands jammed into the pockets of his Carhartt jacket and his left leg bounced constantly.

He was waiting for two men from Atlantic Capes Fisheries, a seafood conglomerate based in the nearby Jersey Shore town of Cape May. The men were from the company's latest venture—a sub-brand called Cape May Salt Oyster Company, which sold oysters raised on a stretch of Bayshore tidal flats about an hour's drive away, in the county of Cape May. Tony had recently learned that Cape May Salt had purchased a barge retrofitted with a floating upweller system known as a "FLUPSY," employed for raising baby, or "seed," oysters that could then be transplanted to mesh bags on the flats, or in cages offshore. Tony had pitched Atlantic Capes on the idea that Money Island was the best place on the Bayshore for this new aquaculture system, and they'd bitten.

When the Cape May Salt men arrived a few minutes later, Tony and I stepped outside the bait shack to meet them. Although it was late in the morning, there was little light. The cold fog remained heavy over the mouth of Nantuxent Creek and the bay beyond. Small beads of condensation gathered on Tony's jacket as he made small talk with the men about the terrible fishing season that summer and fall and his concerns about winter ice wrecking his docks. Tony acknowledged the foul weather, but didn't apologize for it. "Let's do this from north to south," he said to the men and me with a level of excitement that defied, or simply didn't notice, the lousy conditions. "We'll get a little bit of a leg stretch."

Tony had stumbled upon Money Island in the late 1980s, when he was in his late twenties and recently divorced, after a friend and fellow recent divorcé saw an ad in the paper for a "cabin" on the South Jersey

Bayshore—a place neither Tony nor his friend knew existed. In truth, the cabin, which was located at the entrance to Money Island, just across the street from the marina, was a 1960s-era vinyl trailer that had been set permanently on a raised foundation.

At first, the Bayshore's forgotten-by-time culture hadn't appealed to Tony. Although he had grown up on that gentleman's farm, and had originally majored in animal husbandry with the hope of owning his own farm after college, Tony had moved on to a successful career as a health care benefits consultant and, later, a Certified Public Accountant. He remarried, had a son and daughter, and bought a nice home in the upper-class Philly suburb of Bala Cynwyd. But as he continued to visit his friend's trailer throughout the early '90s, Money Island's rough charm began to grow on him. The locals' reliance on the land and water for income, sustenance, and recreation reminded him of both his childhood and his undergrad studies, when he'd spent a lot of time thinking about the decline of rural America in the face of technologization and globalization. "Rural people are at least as much concerned about conservation as the rest of the population," Tony once wrote in an article for his college newspaper. "They only need a little help, in the form of professional advice and financial assistance, to put these concerns into action for the benefit of us all."

With its gruff watermen and -women, whose livelihoods remained dependent on the land and water, Money Island offered something that Tony's life growing up on the gentleman's farm had not. The Bayshore seemed to possess an unabashed self-awareness. Born and raised Bayshore people understood perfectly that their region existed as a strange Neverland floating in the middle of the urbane epicenter of the West. They knew that that other world had left them behind long ago, along with the prosperity it offered, and by now had forgotten them completely. But if being left behind and forgotten meant not having to deal with the noise and complexities of modernity, that was fine with them. They had a stubborn, if risky, pride for a parallel America—one that had never lost sight of where it came from, even if they weren't sure what that "from" was. In a strange way, it was an enviable perspective, because it freed one from certain societal expectations, like the accumulation of wealth and influence. And maybe a part of Tony, whose life up to that point was perfectly emblematic of that outside world, wanted to achieve such a perspective, to feel it.

In 1996, Tony bought the cabin next to the marina, hoping it could be a sort of country retreat from his new life in Bala Cynwyd. In the twenty years that had passed since he had bought the cabin, Tony had gone on a bit of a real estate spree. Closer to the oyster docks, at 228 Nantuxent Drive, he had purchased another trailer, this one in worse shape than the cabin, since it had never been raised and was now sinking into the mud. Then, after Sandy, he'd gotten the marina, which consisted of thirteen forlorn, flooded lots scattered across Money Island's one-and-a-half-mile bay and creek shoreline. He had no experience running a marina, and he often joked that he could hardly drive a boat. Not long after he'd purchased the property, Bob Campbell, the mayor of Downe Township, where Money Island was located, paid Tony a visit. "Congratulations," Campbell had told him. "You now own a marina that no one uses."

As the two men from Cape May Salt and I followed Tony past the trailer at 228 Nantuxent, he pointed to his and others' dilapidated properties and asked us to envision a great oyster and blue crab aquaculture operation. The marina's empty, rotting docks would be replaced by Cape May Salt FLUPSYs, which would produce tens of millions of seed oysters annually. The seed would be transplanted onto artificial reefs in Nantuxent Cove, built through "living shorelines" collaborations with the Nature Conservancy or the American Littoral Society, on the exact site where the Lenni Lenape had harvested oysters so long ago. A few Cape May Salt employees could live and work out of 228 Nantuxent. Rutgers University, which operated the Haskin Shellfish Research Laboratory in nearby Bivalve, where the remaining packing houses were still located, could open up a satellite lab on the site where the bait shack now stood and assist Cape May Salt with the cultivation of superior oysters. With the introduction of aquaculture, the traditional Bayshore oyster industry, which already landed around $10 million in wild-caught oysters annually in Money Island, would be made twice as strong and many times as rich. (However, after applying to the catch the government's standard sixfold multiplier, which is based on the exponential rise in the value of seafood as it moves from the fishery to the consumer, Money Island's annual oyster intake was worth closer to

$60 million.) There would be seafood cookouts in summer. Live bands. Boating excursions. Jersey Shore tourists would finally get off the Garden State Parkway's southern exits and, instead of turning east toward Ocean City or Cape May, would turn inland, to the Bayshore.

Just past the trailer, where the road hooked ninety degrees to the southeast as it traced the bend of the creek, there was a patch of land overgrown with tall foxtails and small trees, which suggested the land was just high enough to avoid being fully inundated at high tide. The property's location beside the creek, where the water was deep and the current flowed strongly, would be perfect for the FLUPSY, one of the Cape May Salt men said. Tony shuffled uneasily. "That property's off-limits," he said. "It's owned by one of the watermen, and unfortunately we don't see eye to eye on this aquaculture thing." He then told us a story about another outsider who had bought a place in Money Island and had apparently gotten on the bad side of the watermen. The cabin, he said, had "accidentally" burned down one night. "He was the least liked," Tony said. "I'm the next least liked."

There was also the issue with one of the marina's previous owners, Roger Mauro, who had tried to run Tony down with his pickup on a Saturday in 2006, two days after Thanksgiving. At the time, a portion of Bayview Road in front of Tony's cabin had washed away. In order to reach Money Island's west side, people had to partially drive across Tony's lawn. To stop them, he had planted some small shrubs and flowerbeds to keep everyone on what was left of the crumbling road. On higher tides, his blockade prevented Bayview Road residents from reaching their homes. Mauro, who also lived in Money Island, was angrier than anyone about Tony's tactics—he was also a drunk. When Tony stepped out into his yard, Mauro had gotten in his pickup, hit the gas, and barreled directly toward Tony.

Just seven years removed from his national Greco-Roman wrestling championship in the master's division, Tony turned toward Mauro's truck as if it were an opponent in the ring. In that split second, he decided he could leap forward and cleanly roll off the hood. He almost pulled it off. While he avoided being run over, Tony was still launched in the air, then slammed to the ground. Laying in the muddy, saltwater-saturated soil of his yard, he checked himself for any broken bones or bad cuts. Everything seemed fine, save for a creeping headache from hitting either Mauro's truck or the ground—he couldn't recall which. The headache eventually led to periodic bouts of memory loss. Back home in Bala Cynwyd, he'd leave his favorite coffee shop and forget where he'd parked his car. When it came time to take his CPA recertification test, he couldn't remember any of the correct answers, and his license lapsed.

Tony was able to regain his CPA license, but he claimed that for the next several years, the bouts of memory loss still occurred. Nevertheless, he seemed unbothered today by the prospect of being run over by another neighbor, or having his cabin be the most probable candidate for the next accidental fire in Money Island. Instead, he spoke about his vision for Money Island as an aquaculture hub so emphatically and incessantly that I could almost see it as clearly as he saw it in his head. It was hard not to hope that such a thing would come true, but I didn't want to look away, get caught in the quick pauses between his grandiose dreams for Money Island. Because when I did, the impossibility of it all screamed from every collapsing home and dock and stretch of shoreline that was no longer there. "Hope" was not the word that came to mind. In fact, long before I had met Tony, I had told myself that the Bayshore would never be prosperous again, and nothing I saw that morning convinced me otherwise.

When we returned to the marina parking lot, the Cape May Salt men seemed eager to leave. Later, one of the men, Brian Harman, who was the company's general manager, told me that Tony's tour hadn't given him much hope for Money Island or Tony's grand plan, either. He'd done some asking around among his contacts within the DEP and the Shellfisheries Council and was told that Money Island was "basically going to be gone." With all the problems with flooding and decay and lack of infrastructure and regulatory violations, Tony was "in over his head," Harmon said. "I'm not sure he realized what he was trying to get into."

FIVE

"WE KNOW NOT WHAT A DAY MAY BRING FORTH."

THE SNOW HURRICANE OF 1804 was the first tropical cyclone to produce snowfall since the first appearance of detailed records in the fifteenth century—Hurricane Ginny, in 1963, was the second, and Sandy the third. The Great Coastal Hurricane of 1806 sank the *Rose-in-Bloom* off South Jersey's Atlantic coast, killing twenty-one. In September of 1821, the Norfolk–Long Island Hurricane slammed into Cape May, bringing a five-foot storm surge and 110 mile-per-hour winds. Atlantic City's Category 2 "Vagabond Hurricane," in 1903, had a track that closely resembled Sandy's and was the first-ever tropical cyclone in recorded history to make landfall in New Jersey. September 1944's Great Atlantic Hurricane was "the worst hurricane ever to hit New Jersey in the twentieth century," according to one state climatologist. A 1950 winter storm hit the Bayshore dead-on, causing a tidal-wave-like storm surge that killed fourteen, left another 2,500 homeless, and resulted in over $3 million in damages, which prompted President Truman to set up a $5 million disaster fund. Connie and Diane were the back-to-back hurricanes of August 1955 that killed twenty-six. The previous summer, Hazel and Carol. Category 4 Donna, in 1960. More storms in 1962, 1972, 1985. Then Bertha, Floyd, and Irene.

But until Sandy, nothing was as devastating for Bay Point and Money Island as the nameless storm that arrived on the morning of Saturday,

October 25, 1980—almost exactly thirty years before Sandy. "That was the writing on the wall," Mike told me. "We should've known then."

In Money Island, Joseph Pollino, then the owner of the marina, described to a local newspaper reporter being trapped in his home and feeling the waves tear the structure apart. Realizing that the place was about to be swept away, Pollino had forced a door open to find his boat just outside, held there by his garden hose, which had somehow gotten caught around the boat's cleat. "God saved us," Pollino told the reporter. "He pushed that boat there so we could find it and be saved." Asked if he'd rebuild, Pollino said he wasn't sure. "How much can you take?" he said.

In Bay Point, boats and pieces of docks, porches, and homes were strewn across the marshland. Fifteen structures had been washed off their foundations, including Mike's parents' home on Paris Road. The bay's storm surge had been so strong that it had dislodged the entire road-side section of the house. Mike, then just twenty-three, was living at home with his parents even though he was making pretty good money at the Delaware River Port Authority. His father had fallen ill, and his mother was struggling to take care of him, so Mike had moved in to help them out. "I redone Mom and Dad's house because I was working and had some ability," Mike said. "And the damn storm took that out." During an emergency meeting in which all five Bayshore municipalities were declared disaster areas, one freeholder told the local newspaper, "This may be the worst bayshore storm this county has seen." A formal request was made for state and federal emergency funding after it was determined Cumberland County suffered more than $19 million in property damages.

Despite the destruction, Mike and the rest of the Bay Point and Money Island communities simply rolled up their sleeves and started rebuilding. The decision to put back what had been taken wasn't an act of defiance against Mother Nature—it was just instinctual. Storms and the damage they brought were a part of the deal on the Bayshore. It had always been that way, ever since the eighteenth century, when the first English settlers began to carve out communities within the shady eastern red cedar, oak, and elm woods that stood at the edge of the Bayshore's high ground, where the earth gracefully transitioned into miles of marshland before slipping beneath the bay.

IN THE SPRING OF 1766, Philip Vickers Fithian, an eighteen-year-old farm boy and aspiring Presbyterian minister, wrote of a storm that had just pummeled the Bayshore. Fithian lived in a settlement called Greenwich, which sat along the Cohansey River a couple of miles from where I would grow up just over two hundred years later. "There hath been the most shipping wrecked upon our coast the last winter than ever was observed a season before," Fithian wrote. "I expect to hear of more vessels cast away by this storm, as it hath been exceeding violent." In the following months, as the cherry and apple trees began to blossom, and news of the Stamp Act's repeal reached Greenwich, Fithian spent his days harvesting wheat, corn, and salt hay. He also devoted a lot of time to working on the dike that protected his father's farmland and pastureland from flooding. (On the Bayshore, dikes were called "banks," as they continue to be known today.) In July, while Fithian toiled on a sluice built into the bank, another storm raged in off the bay. To Fithian, it was "as if the Bottles of Heaven were opened." Despite more torrential rain the next day, he continued his work on the bank. "Blessed be the name of our God," he wrote of the weather's constant punishing of the land. "We know not what a Day may bring forth."

Nearly a century and a half before, in 1630, the Dutch captain David Pietersz de Vries was sent to the shores of what was then called Cape Mey, named in honor of another Dutch explorer, Cornelius Jacobsen Mey. Lured by stories of the bay's abundance of whales, whose oil "brought sixty guilders a hogshead," de Vries's bosses at the Dutch West India Company had sent him to Cape May to oversee the construction of a whaling colony—more than two decades before the New England colonies, made famous by Herman Melville, were established. The Delaware Bay colony has been forgotten, however, because the Dutch whalers were lousy at their job. "Could have done more with good harpooners," de Vries wrote in 1633. After one report of over a dozen botched landings, de Vries called his Delaware Bay harpooners' incompetence "astonishing," and in little more than a year, the colony was abandoned. While de Vries's vision of the Bayshore as a haven for whaling was ultimately unrealized, his observation that the land was well suited "for cultivation of all sorts of grain" was prescient.

When the Dutch surrendered New Netherland to the British in 1664, and the New Jersey Colony was founded, the English settlers that arrived were less concerned about making quick money from animal pelts and more interested in long-term real estate. Acre by acre, tract by tract, English settlers in what was then West and East Jersey (before it became South and North Jersey) devoured the land through one-sided purchases that the Lenni Lenape could not fully understand, given that to them land was not a commodity but akin to air, sunlight, or water. (The province of New Jersey was originally divided into West and East Jersey, given that the border began near the province's northwest corner and ended in the southeast, near present-day Atlantic City.)

As English settlers drilled east from the banks of the Delaware River, where Philadelphia and Trenton would soon take root, they increasingly manipulated the marshland and its salt hay meadows, cedar islands, rivers, creeks, and ditches for agriculture and pastureland. In 1685, a surveyor named Thomas Budd noted that the "big rich fat marsh land" of the Bayshore could be utilized even better if it were banked and drained. By 1688, Bayshore towns had begun forming "meadow companies"—also called "bank committees"—to more efficiently develop and manage the network of banks keeping the tidewaters from swamping their farmland and pastures.

Between 1697 and 1783, the provincial legislators passed over seventy laws to encourage the construction of bridges, banks, dams, and sluices for, predominantly, salt hay farming. After New Jersey became a state in 1787, its assembly did not slow down on marsh-banking legislation. In the early 1800s, several bills were passed "authorizing the banking and improving of certain marsh, meadow and swamp" throughout Cumberland County, including in Downe Township. Thomas Gordon, in his 1834 *Gazetteer of the State of New Jersey*, wrote, "Adjacent to the Delaware Bay and sea coast, are wide tracts of salt meadow, some of which have been reclaimed by embankment; and the rest afford abundance of coarse hay, free in many places to all who seek it." If one had the luxury of viewing the Bayshore from high above in the mid-nineteenth century, they would have seen hundreds of acres of once naturally incongruous and serrated edges of Bayshore marshland already smoothed, angled, or straightened, like a Rorschach test gradually being covered by a patchwork quilt.

The reengineering of the Bayshore marshland continued in earnest throughout the nineteenth and twentieth centuries, as farmers ceaselessly drained and banked salt hay meadows to protect them from flooding. The marshland was manipulated further to help curb the Bayshore's most vicious and abundant insect—the mosquito. As early as the 1620s, when the Swedish had a settlement called Fort Elfsborg, which they nicknamed "Fort Myggenborg," on the southeastern bank of the Delaware River, they showed begrudging respect for the mosquito and its torturous nature—translated, *myggenborg* means "fort mosquito." By the early 1900s, New Jersey began passing laws to deal with the pests. County Mosquito Extermination Commissions were established and tens of thousands of acres of marshland were drained and etched with some five million feet of shallow-water ditches, which helped to flush out mosquito habitat and introduce fish that fed on the insect's larvae.

The early banking and draining of the Bayshore's marshland encouraged its inhabitants to expand all the way to the edge of the bay, where the small, fitful waves splashed, pushed, and receded day in and day out. Ping-ponging between the *Spartina* meadows, bogs, and ditches are islands of higher, drier ground, where briar thickets and clusters of hardwood, like eastern red cedar and oak, grew. The Lenni Lenape had followed these islands, like stars on a map of constellations, to string together footpaths to their summer camps at the mouths of creeks like Nantuxent and Cedar. European settlers often just followed the scars of these routes, gradually expanding their girth with mules, horses, and, eventually, "corduroy roads"—vehicle paths laid with cedar poles, brush, mud, sand, old tires, engine parts, and pretty much any other refuse that might slow the inevitable encroachment of the wetlands.

Though there is no proof that he followed one of these Lenni Lenape routes, Fithian nevertheless offers an early account of his fellow settlers expanding farther and farther into the marshland. In September of 1773, Fithian and three friends traveled across the Cohansey River to the cabin of a Governor Reily, which sat "open to the Bay." In addition to meeting the governor's daughter and developing a crush on her ("who knows but I might then have made my Fortune?"), Fithian and his friends followed their host through a "long, muddy, trackless Marsh to the Place of Fishing," where they loaded up on more fish than they could eat.

Three years later, just as the US Declaration of Independence was ratified, an English lord named John Fortescue and his wife, Mary, sold a ten-thousand acre expanse of land about ten miles down the bay coast from Governor Reily's cabin for five shillings, the equivalent of about twenty-eight dollars today. Fortescue Island, as it was briefly called, was about a dozen acres of high ground situated beside the bay, bordered by a creek and an elbow of boggy, almost impenetrable marshland called Egg Island. Fortescue's beach was wide and sandy, with a spine of dunes that stretched for nearly the entirety of its two-mile length. Even for the Bayshore, Fortescue was an outpost—Newport, the nearest village, was a three-mile jaunt away along a muddy, perpetually flooded corduroy road. By the 1820s, Fortescue, despite its remoteness and the back-shattering carriage rides one had to endure to get there, became a budding resort town, with a hotel near the beach that grew to three stories and held forty-eight rooms.

Through the end of the nineteenth century and into the start of the twentieth, the town was a sought-after seaside destination, with a seasonal population of four hundred, a pier, boardwalk, large public marina, and a steamer called the *Charlotte* available for daily trips to and from Philadelphia. "Fewer seaside resorts possess greater advantage than this, it being located in a healthful region," read an advertisement for a Fortescue hotel in 1874. "The beach has no superior, and the bathing is superb during the heated season." At some point, Fortescue was given the nickname the "Weakfish Capital of the World." But already, the town was experiencing problems with erosion. In 1898, a local newspaper article described a landowner named William Riley as having to build "a bank along his beach front at Fortescue where the high tides have washed out the beach." To fortify the bank, Riley was "driving piling and filling in with cedar brush, hay and sand."

In the last half of the nineteenth century, a booming oyster industry, and the success of Fortescue, sparked ever-increasing interest in Cumberland

County's forty miles of Bayshore coast. In 1877, not far from Governor Reily's "Place of Fishing," two local men purchased 120 acres of bayfront beach to establish the village of Sea Breeze in the resort-town mold of Fortescue. Like Fortescue, Sea Breeze also offered ferry service to and from Philadelphia, via a 527-ton decommissioned Union Army munitions steamer called the *John A. Warner.* A huge hotel, called the Warner House, was built in the dunes, with a wraparound porch that allowed guests to watch the sun rise above the marshland to the east and set into the bay to the west. By the 1950s, little saltbox cottages, painted in various pastel hues, stretched along Sea Breeze's cedar-lined waterfront thoroughfare, called Beach Avenue. The homes were mostly second homes, owned by Cumberland County residents who lived inland or people from the Philadelphia area. Everyone loved fishing; most loved a stiff drink. No one cared much for the Jersey Shore, where America's infatuation with the beach was surging, from Long Branch in the north to Cape May in the south. The Jersey Shore might have been only forty miles to the east, but if you loved the bay, you stayed on the bay.

In 1872 a Downe Township landowner named John B. Munyan submitted an application to the Cumberland County Court of Common Pleas for a public road that would fork off Fortescue Road and wind for about two and a half miles into the marshland and terminate at his farm. Munyan's 350-acre parcel was known locally as the Flax Farm, and it sat on the farthest edge of a finger of dry land called Newport Neck. A November 1817 advertisement for the Flax Farm's sale described it as being "enclosed by a good bank to keep off the overflow of the tide which sometimes would otherwise intrude." A "new two Story Frame dwelling House, and a kitchen attached to it" was also on the property, along with a new barn, wagon house, cedar fencing, and a young apple orchard. An adjoining 125 acres of salt hay meadow ran to the mouth of Nantuxent Creek. Munyan's proposed road would end at the Flax Farm's bank. For every landowner whose property would be damaged in some way by the road, Munyan requested the county reimburse them ten cents, including himself. Once completed, Munyan's road, then called Nantuxent Neck, offered Downe Township another access point to the bay, where a new "island" resort town like Fortescue and Sea Breeze might one day be built.

Few improvements were made to Munyan's road for the next six decades, until 1935, when President Franklin D. Roosevelt's Works Progress
Administration allocated just over $5 million to New Jersey for the im-
provement of the state's more than ten thousand miles of "farm to market"
dirt roads. Cumberland County's share of the fund was $180,000. Up to
that point, the state had never spent a dollar on the county's nearly four
hundred miles of unpaved roads, and they were in desperate need of repair, especially those on the infirm land of the Bayshore. The county invested in connecting existing roads, like Nantuxent Neck, to its bayfront
beaches. "I can remember when it was only my dad and me and we didn't
even have electricity," Mae Griffith, who owned the Seabreeze Tavern,
told a local newspaper in 1978. "Thank God for Franklin D. Roosevelt."

In December of 1938, the marshland beyond Munyan's bank was surveyed and mapped for the construction of a road that would stretch another 1.8 miles to the mouth of Nantuxent Creek, near where the Lenni
Lenape had made their fishing camps in summer and where John Munyan's
livestock had grazed. There, another untouched sand beach curved from
the mouth of the creek, around a plain of *Spartina* meadow marbled by
salt ponds and tangled with narrow ditches and creeks. The bay's current
swept along the beaches, creating alluvial spits of sand and sea grass, teeming with birds and horseshoe crabs and oysters. The earliest aerial image of
the area, from 1930, shows no evidence of development on the shoreline.
But out on the water, in the creek's wide mouth and on the placid waters
beyond its first, lassoing bend, there are the unmistakable silhouettes of
nearly a dozen evenly spaced oyster schooners.

After the county's roads had been improved, in 1941, Lucy Bateman,
who owned the land surrounding the mouth of Nantuxent Creek, con-
veyed a portion of her property to Downe Township for the construction
of a road called Bayview. Bateman's land was soon subdivided into lots,
and almost immediately, advertisements began popping up in local newspapers. One enterprising businessman bought a summer's worth of postage
stamp–sized advertisements in the local newspaper, promoting "Rowboats
& Bait now available at Money Island." Similar to development in Sea
Breeze, tiny one- and two-bedroom saltbox shanties, raised on pilings,
started growing from the water's edge. Long finger docks stretched from

some of them, motorboats moored to their edges. On June 2, 1942, a man named Tony Zitto reported that he and some pals "went a-fishing off Money Island and caught so many croakers and weakies they had to quit for fear the boat would sink!" In 1946, a thirty-six-foot boat called the *Cruiser Rose* was running daily fishing excursions out of Money Island, no reservations required. For years after, there never seemed to be a single bad fishing report to come out of Downe Township's newest beach town.

Despite the small explosion of development on the Bayshore, few improvements were made to the banks, dams, sluices, and mosquito ditches that had been built by Philip Vickers Fithian and those settlers who followed. By 2010, the condition of South Jersey's inventory of earthen banks was alarming enough that the US Department of Agriculture's Natural Resources Conservation Service, in collaboration with the Army Corps of Engineers, conducted a study to determine the type and extent of residents' vulnerability and the vulnerability of property protected by these centuries-old structures. The study surveyed eighteen miles of banks and found that 40 percent were located in Cumberland County. Nearly every bank analyzed in the county was critically degraded in some way, whether from inadequate grass cover, general erosion, cracking, subsidence, development, burrowing animals, or a combination of some or all those factors.

Like the bank on the Fithian farm in Greenwich, many of Cumberland County's banks had been built and maintained by individual landowners. The study's report referred to a majority of the privately owned banks as "orphans," meaning centuries of transferred deeds and subdivision had left the banks spanning the properties of multiple landowners. No one knew who was obligated to take care of what section of bank, although, generally speaking, few individuals or municipalities were taking care of the banks at all. The state and Army Corps had done little because the banks were on private property. Owing to the "lack of local sponsorship, archaic legal entities for sponsorship, fragmented ownership, lack of funding for ongoing operation and maintenance, permitting costs and timeframes," the report stated, there was no discernible party who could be charged with the upkeep of the banks. The report concluded that the lack of policy coordination and communication between federal, state, and local governments posed serious risks for the communities and agricultural land that the banks (barely) protect. "The failure of these structures," the report's authors concluded, "would have incalculable adverse economic and public health consequences similar to what took place in New Orleans following the Hurricane Katrina event in September 2005."

ON THE NIGHT OF OCTOBER 29, 2012, while the Nelsons watched the latest Sandy update from the hunting club in Cedarville, water began creeping around the oyster-packing houses in Bivalve, at first slowly and then in a rush. Sandy was just a few hours away from making landfall fifty-five miles to the northeast, near Atlantic City. Somewhere beyond the black clouds was a true full moon. The tide was coming in and it was going to be high—5.71 feet, storm or no storm. On top of that would be Sandy's seven-foot surge. When the water did finally come in at full force, somewhere in the middle of the night, most of the Bayshore's ancient banks were broken, breeched, or simply overtaken. Along the bay, where there was no protection of any kind, a twelve-foot wall of water rose from the darkness and met head-on the worn and weary homes of Fortescue, Sea Breeze, Gandy's Beach, Bay Point, and Money Island.

I was living in California at the time. When I woke up on October 30 and saw the first images of the destruction in New Jersey and New York, I booked a flight home—not to check on the Bayshore, but to cover the recovery effort on the Jersey Shore and Long Island, like most every other journalist rushing into the region in those first chaotic hours after the storm. In the days that followed, I walked through one ravaged community to the next, from the northern Jersey Shore to Staten Island to Rockaway Beach. I thought little about Sandy's impact on the Bayshore, until I was finally able to visit home. My parents still lived in the same house. Because four miles of marshland stood between them and the bay, it had been spared any flooding. The bayfront towns, my mother and father told me, had not fared so well.

On November 3, five days after Sandy, I was finished with my assignment on the Atlantic coast and able to survey the Bayshore's damage. I borrowed my mother's car and drove toward the bay. It had been so long that I figured I'd need a map to find my way, but as I got closer, I began recalling the route to the water. I weaved down Newport Neck Road and stopped at the spur—to the left was Gandy's Beach; to the right was Money Island. All around, the marshland spread flat and ghostly gray, its color drained. In the far distance, back on higher ground, the trees, whose leaves should have been an autumnal firestorm of reds, oranges, and yellows, were stripped nearly bare from the wind. The sky remained a low, lardy belly the hue of worn steel, as if hung over from the storm.

A Cumberland County sheriff was blocking the way into Gandy's Beach. Only homeowners were allowed in, and even they only had two hours to salvage what was left of their belongings. Later that afternoon, inspectors from the state's Department of Community Affairs would be arriving to assess the town's roughly seventy homes for structural damages. From the fork, which was about a football field away from the bay, Gandy's Beach's homes looked fine. I told the sheriff as much. "Wait till you see the bay side," he said. While the sheriff and I talked, a township councilman stopped by to give the sheriff some company. The councilman and the sheriff fretted about an impending winter storm that was now in the forecast. Both of them kept looking up at the sky confusedly, wondering out loud how less than a week ago a hurricane had roared up from the tropics, and now a bitter, snowy front was settling in. The sheriff apologized for not being able to let me enter Gandy's. Apparently, there had already been some looting. "You can go to Money Island if you want," the councilman said. "No one'll stop you there."

The last time I had been to Money Island was that day in 1991, when my father, brother, uncle, and I had been chased off the bay by the summer squall. I could never have imagined that the place I recalled in my mind was the one I now saw as I reached the marina, at that point frozen in bankruptcy and still a few weeks away from Tony Novak's purchasing it. In the distance, along the bay, some of the same colorful homes I'd seen as a boy were still there, though they were badly faded and waterlogged, barely hanging on to their pilings, the bay sloshing underneath them. The Bayview Road side of town, or the west side as locals called it, had borne the full brunt of the surge and wind. The small bridge connecting it to the rest of Money Island was cracked, crumbling. Several homes had been completely ripped away and thrown into the water. One shanty had been pushed completely across the road and was now sitting, disembodied, out in the middle of a patch of salt hay meadow. The marina's dock was violently twisted and splintered. I walked out on a flimsy board and watched the dark water beneath me move back and forth. There wasn't a soul stirring, except for a few gulls screaming into the cold wind. An oil tanker en route to Philadelphia slipped soundlessly along the bay's razor-edged horizon, its crew probably oblivious to the fact that life existed on this shore.

Across the marshland in Bay Point, Mike, Kate, and the kids were finally able to access Paris Road to rummage through the wreckage that was, just a few days before, their dream home. Sandy's surge had blown open the rancher's bayside windows and doors and rushed through the house. The force of the water pushing against the back walls had knocked loose the entire structure from its piling foundation, almost exactly like the October 1980 storm had done to Mike's parents' home. If it hadn't been for the $40,000 in improvements that Mike had made to the rancher the year before, he was sure it would have been completely wiped away.

Because the front steps had been devoured by the surge, Katie had to use a ladder to climb inside. "The whole front of the house was gone," she told me. "So you could see out over the whole bay." The forty-inch television—the same one they'd taken with them when they evacuated for Irene—was ruined. A chest that held family photos and other memorabilia had simply vanished. In other places, it was as if nothing had happened at all. The Halloween stickers, of pumpkins and autumn leaves, that the family had put on the front door were still there. In her room, Katie collected two trash bags' worth of clothes that had somehow stayed dry. At some point Kate and Katie noticed a waterline mark on a framed canvas map of the Bayshore that hung on the wall. Then they looked up at the ceiling fan and saw that its cupped light fixture was full of brown-green bay water. That was the moment when Kate thought, *We're ruined.*

PART TWO

NO RETREAT

SIX

"DRAIN THE SWAMP."

THE TREES WERE ABLAZE WITH AUTUMN COLOR, the sky a lucid blue. It was cool and dry. No heat to ratchet up the stench from the shell piles down by the oyster docks in Bivalve, and no bugs to attack you the minute you stepped outside. It was almost too beautiful to keep driving, as if doing so would rush time into a lesser day. For all the foul weather that marched across the Bayshore, from autumn to winter to spring to summer and back, there were also days like this one—November 8, 2016—that reminded me of Mike's constant fretting that, if God should let him into heaven, it might turn out to be not as perfect a place as the Bayshore.

I was driving through Port Norris, on County Route 553, otherwise known as Main Street. The bygone oyster tycoons' Victorians, now mildewed and slumped, along both sides of Main appeared as if they'd regained some of their old sturdiness—they were even a little more regal in such crisp light. The enormous Hoffman Funeral Home, with its wrought-iron gate, carefully landscaped lawn, and white, ornate columns, stood in defiance of time. My great-uncle had operated the funeral home when Port Norris had not yet fallen on hard times. Four miles down Main Street, in another tiny town called Dividing Creek, I passed Zion United Methodist, the Bayshore Mennonite Church, and Dividing Creek Baptist Church, all within a quarter mile of each other. Main Street's old sycamore trees, their trunks the color of worn bone and their leaves radiating yellows, oranges, and crimsons, soared above all. In many front yards, shaggy grass was overtaking kids' toys, broken-down cars, deflating Halloween ornaments, trailered fishing boats, and yard signs that read "Make America Great Again."

In recent decades, Cumberland County had collectively voted Democratic, because close to 75 percent of the county's population of 157,000 is concentrated in the county's perennially blue cities—Bridgeton, Millville, and Vineland. But the Bayshore, encompassing the length of Cumberland's southern half and dwarfing the area of the three cities by an order of magnitude, had long voted bright red Republican. There was clearly no reason to infer that the outcome would be different this time around, but I was certain that, in less than twenty-four hours, America would be waking up to its first female president in Hillary Clinton. It just seemed impossible that the country's sparsely populated rural places, like the Bayshore, could ever eclipse the force of its Democratic urban centers.

In Money Island, I found Tony Novak on the marina dock, fiddling with the shallow tanks he had recently built to hold molting blue crabs. Bayshore watermen called the soon-to-be soft-shell crabs "shedders." They were the most valuable of any blue crab harvest—not only did restaurants pay top dollar for soft-shells, but a crab in its shedding phase was also irresistible bait for the bay's weakfish. The tank system had been inspired by a trip Tony and his family had taken to Tangier Island, Virginia, in 2011, after Tony had founded a nonprofit, called BaySave, to attract private investment in wetlands restoration and conservation projects, including oyster and crab aquaculture, in Money Island. Apparently, Tangier's mayor, James "Ooker" Eskridge, had taken Tony out on his boat and given him a tour of the island's famous crab shanties, where generations of Tangiermen, including Eskridge, had perfected the art of soft-shell crab production. Tony had been impressed by Eskridge and Tangier's small but mighty crabbing industry. "So I based our business model on that," he told me.

Tony had no such relationship with Bob Campbell, Downe Township's mayor. "Bob and I, we have the same goals in mind, but we differ on a few things," he told me. "And some I can't overcome." I asked Tony what those were. "I'm more willing to accept the inevitable," he said. "I don't believe that whatever I do, or Bob Campbell does, is going to keep this place from being underwater."

Compared to recent years, 2016 had been a good season for the oystermen out on the bay. The crabbing hadn't been bad either. All of this buoyed Tony's belief that things would finally start going his way. That the water was rising didn't bother him, because he'd already thought that through. "I think we can have a viable community, particularly an aquaculture community in a space that's underwater," he said. "We can survive. We can deal with that with floating platforms, with barges, with whatever technologies we need to bring in." He was speaking fast, getting more excited. "*If* government will let us."

Nantuxent Creek lay flat beneath the still evening. The foxtails and *Spartina* meadows continued to hold on to their summer green, though they had taken on a slight golden hue. A profoundly battered commercial crab boat slipped past, hanging tight to the marina dock, since that was the only section left in the mouth of the creek that was deep enough to get a boat of any size through. Nantuxent Cove was already shallow, but Sandy had exacerbated the issue with silt, sand, mud, and debris from elsewhere in the bay. It was a cruel irony that, on some high tides, watermen couldn't reach their boats because Money Island Road was too flooded to drive through, and on some low tides they couldn't get their boats out into the bay because Nantuxent Creek's channel was too shallow. Tony waved at the crabbers, but they didn't wave back. No matter where America stood the next morning, those men would be here before sunrise, pulling on their rubber boots and oilskins for another day out on the water.

A FEW WEEKS AFTER THE ELECTION, I met Campbell for breakfast at the Landing, a restaurant that sat in between a small marina called Sundog and a cluster of trailers along a wide bend of Nantuxent Creek that the area's first European settlers called East Landing. Four and a half winding, shallow miles to the southwest was Money Island. The restaurant was full of watermen with muddy boots that made heavy, hollow thumps when they walked through the door. Hanging on one wall was a wooden-framed, shallow glass case with various nautical knots inside. A nearby print depicted three fishing boats, their outriggers stretched outward like a dragonfly's wings, emerging from a gray, featureless background. Next to the painting was a T-shirt for the 2017 Sundog Marina Flounder Tournament. A two-day-old *Press of Atlantic City* sat, disheveled, in the newspaper rack. When a customer asked how one waitress was making out, she simply responded, "I'm here."

Campbell was sitting at the head of a table in the corner of the dining room, next to a picture window with the view of Nantuxent Creek and the marshland beyond. Through a lingering fog, there were the silhouettes of ghost forests in the distance. With Campbell was the township's latest engineer, a burly, red-faced man who seemed a little uneasy to be dining with the mayor—or a journalist, I couldn't figure out which. They were discussing the latest hang-ups surrounding Campbell's most ambitious infrastructure plan since coming to office in January of 2012—a public wastewater system that would eliminate the need for individual septic tanks in Fortescue, Gandy's Beach, and Money Island.

One of the biggest problems these three communities—as well as Bay Point—faced was the fact that they did not have a public sewer. Much of the Bayshore was within the state's designated Environmentally Sensitive Areas, which were prohibited by the state from having public sewer service. As their shorelines receded, many properties' septic tanks had become exposed. Some rose several feet above ground and were within the high tide line, raising serious pollution concerns and alarming the county health department and the DEP, who worried most about the contamination of nearby oyster beds. There simply was not enough suitable earth remaining to fit the thousand-gallon tank now required by New Jersey law. Sandy had made the situation much worse—the surge and subsequent erosion had broken the septic tanks' pipes, dislodged their lids, or washed them away completely. Campbell's plan would cost between $12 and $15 million—most of which would have to come from state and federal grants, since Downe Township could never afford such an ambitious infrastructure project on its own.

After New Jersey finally received its first payout from the $60 billion Hurricane Sandy Disaster Relief Appropriations Act in April 2013—$1.83 billion through HUD's Community Development Block Grant Disaster Recovery Program—it designated nine counties to receive 80 percent of the funds. All nine counties were on the Atlantic coast; Cum-

berland County was not included. This had to do with FEMA fine print—
in order to be included on the emergency-aid priority list, FEMA required
that a county had to have endured a loss of at least 1 percent of its total tax
base as a result of Sandy. Campbell estimated that Downe had lost 10 percent of its tax base, since Fortescue, Gandy's Beach, and Money Island held
the township's most valuable real estate. But because the Bayshore made
up just a sliver of Cumberland, the total damages didn't meet FEMA's
threshold. Now, nearly five years later, the DEP's Superstorm Sandy Blue
Acres Program was interested in buying out Money Island's remaining
homeowners, as it already had done in Bay Point. Unlike the mayor of
neighboring Lawrence Township, where Bay Point was located, Campbell
had been fighting the buyouts at every turn. When Blue Acres case officers
began direct talks with Money Island homeowners in 2014, Campbell said
that the state had crossed a "line in the sand." When some owners indi-
cated they were ready to sell out and retreat, Campbell declared a fiscal
emergency.

In order to pressure the state for the funding that Fortescue, Gandy's Beach, Money Island, Bay Point, and other devastated communities needed to begin rebuilding, Campbell helped spearhead the creation
of a coalition of county stakeholders. The group called themselves the
New Jersey Delaware Bayshore Long Term Recovery Committee, and
tasked themselves with identifying twenty-six projects that could get the
Bayshore back on its feet, without the help of federal disaster emergency
money. The group integrated into the plan projects that would address
sea level rise, like living shorelines, which use nonstructural elements like
sea grasses, oyster- and conch-shell reefs, and thin-spread dredge spoils to
reinforce and elevate existing beaches and marshland. Campbell, however,
wasn't interested in such passive measures. His passion was infrastructure,
starting with wastewater management.

Campbell had long been a tumultuous presence in Downe Township.
Prior to becoming mayor, he had been the township's zoning officer, a position he was fired from in 2009 by Downe's then mayor, who Campbell
had publicly accused of buying up land and illegally mining it for silica
sand. That mayor claimed she had bought the land to avoid yet another
tax-exempt state acquisition in the township, and had fired Campbell to

cut municipal costs; Campbell claimed he'd been dismissed for snooping around the mayor's business, and also because he was a Republican. He'd sued under the state's employee protection act and won. Instead of asking for his job back, he ran for a seat on the township committee, and won that too. Three years later, in January of 2012, he was elected mayor. Because he'd come into office just before Sandy, he liked to call himself the "hurricane mayor."

Campbell was seventy, and what was left of the gray hair on the sides and back of his head was slicked back and brushed into a little wave against his neck. He had long, deep creases running from his nose to the corners of his mouth, which accentuated the smile he always beamed when making a point that pleased him. He had a broad, round belly and wore a plaid shirt tucked into jeans. The pair of leather boots he wore were new and clean. His skin was not the tanned, leathery type that defined the watermen walking through the door of the Landing. Though he'd lived in Downe Township for some thirty years, he wasn't from there—like Tony, he came from the suburbs near Philadelphia.

It was immediately obvious that Campbell was a man armed with a quick response to any question. When one waterman came through the door, dressed head to toe in camouflage, he immediately stopped and shouted to Campbell across the room, over several tables full of retirees eating eggs, pancakes, French toast, and sausage. "Hey mayor," he said. "What's gonna happen with Money Island?" Campbell told him not to worry; he had a plan. "I love to talk to people," Campbell told me. "I'm a people person. I guess that's why I'm a good—or at least I think I'm a good—politician." He needled me about my interest in the Bayshore. I told him I was from here, and that its story was my own. That I'd grown up on the Bayshore seemed to please him, and it also seemed to put the engineer at ease. Campbell said breakfast was on him. He ordered a cup of lima bean soup, a dinner roll, and coffee.

In the first few years after Sandy, before I returned to South Jersey, it had been easy to keep up with Campbell. There were many newspaper articles about the Bayshore's woes following the hurricane, its seemingly endless recovery. Some of the stories addressed the fact that sea level rise was hampering the ability of the Bayshore communities to rebuild, and in each story Campbell was clear about his position on sea level rise—it wasn't happening. In one *Philadelphia Inquirer* article, Campbell was quoted telling the reporter Frank Kummer, "There is no sea-level rise, and it's a bunch of hogwash."

"The tree huggers have always been the enemy," Campbell told me as the Landing's waitress set down our breakfasts. He was still buzzing from the election. In a joking tone, Campbell lumped journalists into this enemy camp, along with environmentalists and "Crooked Hillary." He had all the Trump campaign talking points down pat. His favorite was "drain the swamp," given its unique tie-in with the Bayshore, which Campbell felt could use some literal draining itself.

I was curious about his rift with Tony. It seemed to me that, other than one being a Democrat and the other a Republican, and there being a clear disagreement over the existence of sea level rise and climate change, they both wanted the same thing for Money Island—reconstruction, state and federal investment, a wastewater system. In other words, infrastructure. Wouldn't it be beneficial to work together to make at least some of it happen? "I like Tony, I really do," Campbell told me. "He's a character, a dreamer—he has the best intentions. But I like people who get things done, and Tony doesn't get anything done."

Campbell reminded me that Tony had been a prolific blogger since starting his nonprofit BaySave in 2008—his primary subjects being sea level rise and how, if Bayshore communities like Money Island didn't adapt, they'd soon be gone. Tony had also taken plenty of shots at Downe Township's government, accusing it of making bogus tax assessments of Fortescue, Gandy's Beach, and Money Island. More than anything, Tony's dreams of recasting Money Island into an aquaculture hub, which he wrote about often on his BaySave and Money Island Marina websites, were agitating many of the town's residents who loved the place for its isolation and solitude.

The Bayshore's problems, Campbell told me, were too dire to be approached in the context of something as abstract and long-term as climate change. What his residents should be focusing on, he said, was the township's lack of shore protection. If there had been investment by past local, state, and federal governments, he complained, then adequate coastal-hardening projects, like seawalls, jetties, bulkheads, and beach re-plenishment, would have been built along the Bayshore, and the bayfront towns would not have shorelines so severely eroded that they no longer had space for septic tanks. And relatively new residents like Tony wouldn't be screaming bloody murder every time the tide spilled onto the road. Campbell didn't recognize the irony when he asked, "How can the tree huggers be so naïve to believe that humans have control over nature?"

CAMPBELL'S DENIAL OF SEA LEVEL RISE, and climate change in general, was of course problematic, but it was based on a very real fact, which was that when it came to New Jersey's two coasts, the Jersey Shore got all the at-tention—and all the money. In the same *Inquirer* article in which he had told Frank Kummer that he believed sea level rise was hogwash, Campbell explained: "We seem to get the brunt of all the talk about sea level rise . . . but I don't hear about it in Margate" (the affluent Jersey Shore town just south of Atlantic City). "What's the difference? I'll tell you why: We've had no maintenance along the bay shore." Kummer, who had traveled to the Bayshore to report the story, noted that Downe's slogan was "A Nature Lover's Paradise." But, he concluded, "this paradise is crumbling."

For millennia before humans showed up, the barrier islands on New Jersey's Atlantic coast had gently, naturally drifted in and out, north and south, in chorus with the ocean's currents, its waves, and its storms. The islands accumulated in some places and dipped to sea level in others, at the hands of the wind and the paths of natural drainage basins. In a word, they breathed. They were no more habitable than the marshland of the Bayshore. And yet, at the start of the nineteenth century, Jersey Shore hotels were marketing their services in Philadelphia newspapers—"fish, oysters, crabs and good liquors" and "sea bathing," as Army Corps chief C. F. Wicker noted, in his paper "History of New Jersey Coastline," of one Cape May hotel's advertisement. In "A Winter Day on the Sea-Beach," a short work of prose that Walt Whitman wrote in 1870, the Jersey Shore's beaches and ocean strike in him "emotional, impalpable depths, subtler than all the poems, paintings, music, I have ever read, seen, heard. (Yet let me be fair, perhaps it is because I have read those poems and heard that music.)" As more and more communities sprouted up on the sand, feet away from the Atlantic, individual home owners and hoteliers defied nature by building jetties, groins, and seawalls to save their increasingly valuable properties from being swallowed by the sea. By the early 1900s, a kind of war had broken out between the Jersey Shore's barrier island towns, which began building large "spite groins," located at their borders, in order to capture as much sand as possible before it drifted over to the next town's beach.

While such structures delayed the destruction of properties, the beach was displaced or consumed, leaving a vivid line between armored land and the sea crashing against it. As the coastal geologists Orrin Pilkey and Katharine Dixon pointed out in their 1996 book *The Corps and the Shore*, this sacrifice of beach for property became known as "Newjerseyization." "What became apparent after a century of shoreline armoring," Pilkey and Dixon wrote, "was that those hard stabilization structures worked modestly well to save buildings but, sooner or later, destroyed the beach—the very reason the buildings were there to begin with."

By the 1920s, at the same time the Bayshore oyster industry was booming, so too was America's infatuation with the beach—and the Jersey Shore had become the epicenter of the cultural phenomenon. It was simply too late to retreat, so New Jersey doubled down. In 1922, the state stepped in to assist communities that up to that point had been stabilized by individual shorefront home and business owners. (In Atlantic City, much of the work had been funded by mobsters like Enoch Lewis "Nucky" Johnson, who controlled large portions of the beachfront in the early 1900s.) The state issued its *Report on the Erosion and Protection of the New Jersey Beaches*, which led to New Jersey senator Walter Edge introducing a bill in 1929 that would authorize the Army Corps of Engineers to conduct shoreline erosion studies and work with state governments to protect vulnerable coastal communities. Up until that point, the primary coastal responsibilities of the Corps, which had been formed under George Washington, was channel dredging and structural construction associated with waterway commerce and national defense—certainly not erosion control studies and beach replenishment projects to protect private interests. But the economic force of the Jersey Shore, as well as other increasingly popular coastal communities up and down the East Coast, had become too important for the federal government to ignore.

From the 1930s onward, Congress began passing a series of shore protection acts that provided for a cost-sharing agreement between state and local governments, and the federal government. At first, the federal government was responsible for covering up to a third of the cost of these projects, but after several deadly hurricanes in the 1950s and '60s, it increased its share to as high as 70 percent. After conducting a "National Shoreline Management Study," which began in the 1960s, to develop "general conceptual plans for needed shore protection," the Army Corps concluded in 1971 that, of the nine regions it investigated, "the North Atlantic has the greatest percentage of critical erosion." New Jersey, the report said, had "miles of critical erosion." As part of the study, one of the first places to which the Corps turned its attention for potential projects was not the Jersey Shore, but in fact the Bayshore.

While the Jersey Shore communities had been implementing shoreline protection measures with the help of the state and federal government since the 1920s, residents of the Bayshore in the 1970s were still working alone and piecemeal, building ad hoc structures sturdy enough to get through only the next storm or two. In Sea Breeze, the shoreline was a smattering of seawalls, riprap, and other drastic protection projects, each done and paid for by individual property owners. "My dad said that you never fight Mother Nature," Mae Griffith, who continued to operate the tavern her father had opened during Prohibition, told the *Philadelphia Inquirer* in July of 1973. So, instead of fighting her, Griffith had bought and sunk four wooden river barges just off the beach in front of the tavern to "help nature along." All the other Bayshore communities mirrored Sea Breeze's rudimentary measures, and yet the earth beneath their homes, marinas, and taverns continued to disappear. Stewart Farrell, who is the director of Stockton University's Coastal Research Center, and who began his research of the New Jersey coast in the 1980s, told me of one property owner, in the Bayshore community of Thompson's Beach, who had built a seawall out of old Cadillacs. "I have a picture of six students sitting in this Cadillac," Farrell said. "The thing is half filled with sand." In Money Island, then marina owner Joseph Pollino, who would narrowly survive the 1980 storm, told Corps fieldworkers that he'd recently had to replace the floor of the luncheonette he'd built along the water, as well as raise the marina's walkways. The bay's natural tidal swing of six feet had, in Pollino's observation, somehow risen to nine.

In a 1973 Corps report called *Delaware Bay Shore of New Jersey: Supplemental Information to Accompany Beach Erosion Control and Hurricane Protection Survey Study,* the authors included clippings of newspaper stories chronicling Downe Township's inability to receive help from the county, state, or federal governments to fortify Money Island, Gandy's Beach, and Fortescue from further erosion. In Fortescue, Irvin Meyer, who operated a boat rental business, told the *Atlantic City Press* (as the paper was known then), "What we need is a jetty all the way across the beach. I can't understand why they don't help us. We pay taxes, too." Meyer, one of several Fortescue residents who had been calling their district representatives, also complained about "environmentalists," who he said had forced him to obtain a permit for no clear reason other than "this ecology bit." Another clipping described Downe Township Committee members' opposition to a bill proposed by Thomas Kean, a Republican state assemblyman— and future governor—from the North Jersey county of Essex. Kean's bill would curb any kind of development on land less than ten feet above sea level. If passed, the bill would limit development in Downe Township "to about one square mile," committeeman Talbert Blizzard said. At the time, Downe had a land area of about thirty-two square miles, fourteen of which were already owned by the state. "I think my property is just about the only one in the township that is over ten feet," Blizzard said.

Kean's bill never passed, but it did suggest an ominous future for New Jersey's coasts. It also helped the Army Corps reach a conclusion about the Bayshore's erosion problem. In its 1979 *Survey Study Feasibility Report: Beach Erosion Control and Hurricane Protection, Delaware Bay Shore, New Jersey,* which included the findings of the 1973 supplemental survey study and others, the Corps concluded that the cost-benefit ratio simply did not add up when it came to investing in the kind of shoreline-hardening infrastructure that the Bayshore needed. By then, the oyster industry had collapsed and industry was exiting Cumberland County's cities. At the same time, the Jersey Shore continued to boom. This reality led the Corps to conclude that no federally funded work should be authorized for the Bayshore. The Corps' own history of the Philadelphia District, written in 2012, best summarizes the Bayshore surveys and feasibility study of the 1970s:

> This study highlighted the conundrum that some coastal communities faced. Residents might feel that coastal protection was necessary, but if projects did not meet or exceed the required benefit–cost ratio, the Corps could not implement them, regardless of the needs of communities and individuals. In addition, in the eyes of many, using federal money on coastal protection projects was not an acceptable option, because it benefited only a few (those residing on the shore). "The problem is we built too close to the ocean," one critic said. "Is the solution putting all this sand endlessly in front of these structures at taxpayers' expense?"

Investment in the Jersey Shore has only skyrocketed since. In the last three decades, more than $1 billion, the bulk of it federal, has been spent on beach replenishment projects in New Jersey, making the state, in terms of this funding, second only to Florida, which has ten times more coastline. In 1986, under the Water Resources Development Act, the entirety of New Jersey's developed Atlantic coast came under the management of the Army Corps. In the arrangement with the state, the federal government would contribute 65 percent toward the cost of beach replenishment work in Jersey Shore towns, while the rest of the money was covered by the state and local municipalities. Although beach projects in other coastal states have been gradually eliminated from the federal budget, only New Jersey legislators have successfully persuaded Washington to include money for projects as special earmarks. From 1995 to 2009, those earmarks have brought well over $330 million to New Jersey beach projects, more than any other state. A staggering 177 million cubic yards of sand has been pumped onto Jersey Shore beaches over the past three decades, at a cost of $1.8 billion. Much of it has washed away.

Ocean City, often voted as New Jersey's best beach community and nicknamed "America's Greatest Family Resort," has always been the most vociferous spender—no beach town in America has been replenished more.

In the 1960s and '70s, the city owned its own dredge, allowing it to pump a steady stream of spoils from its lagoons, until federal permitting became too cumbersome. In 1982, the city received a $5 million beach nourishment that lasted just two and a half months before it completely washed away. Under President Obama's budget after the 2008 financial crash, just $55 million was allocated for beach replenishment projects nationwide, and the only New Jersey beach project that survived was a $6.5 million project for Ocean City. The city's seven miles of beachfront has been replenished with nearly twenty million cubic yards of sand, the volume equivalent of five Great Pyramids of Giza.

For those Jersey Shore replenishment projects that came as a result of Sandy, the federal government, via the Army Corps, has covered 100 percent of the cost, through the January 2013 Disaster Relief Appropriations Act. As long as engineered beaches like Ocean City's is considered by FEMA as a part of a city's infrastructure, the cost to replenish it will continue to be the responsibility of American taxpayers. "We seem to be trying to hold every shoreline in place forever by pumping sand onto them, largely at federal expense," Robert S. Young, the director of the Program for the Study of Developed Shorelines at Western Carolina University, wrote in the *New York Times* in 2016. "But this is folly. As sea-level rise continues, and if storms intensify as predicted, the projects will require more sand, and more dollars. We are going to run out of both." Stewart Farrell, who is arguably the most knowledgeable scientist of the New Jersey coast's endless battle to save itself, put it to me more succinctly. "If you're looking with a 150-year point of spectrum," he told me. "Yeah, we're all gone."

TO CAMPBELL, IT WAS CLEAR AS DAY—lack of infrastructure was the reason he was losing Money Island, not sea level rise. Tony could go on with his reeducation campaigns about sea level rise and aquaculture while the rest of the community went on with actually getting something done. His cup of lima bean soup was now empty, and the Landing's breakfast crowd was thinning out. At one table near the restaurant's counter, an older man remained, reading the paper, the regulator for the oxygen tank connected to his nose hissing every few moments. Outside, the fog remained low and heavy and cold over Nantuxent Creek. A white heron stood motionless along the water.

"Have you seen our slogan?" Campbell asked. I said I had, but only recently, when I was in Money Island with Tony. In the weeks after Sandy, Campbell and the Downe Township Committee had come up with a campaign to inspire the community to get behind their commitment to rebuild Fortescue, Gandy's Beach, and Money Island. The state had adopted a slogan too, but only for the Jersey Shore—they called it "STRONGER THAN THE STORM." Downe Township's was more to the point, perhaps less a rallying cry than a demand directed at the state, which they believed had abandoned them. They'd printed up stickers and signs and asked residents to plaster them everywhere—on windows, bumpers, yards, wherever. While there were a handful of stickers in Fortescue and Gandy's Beach, nearly every front door in Money Island had one. "NO RETREAT," they read. "SAVE THE BAYSHORE COMMUNITIES."

SEVEN

"HEY MAN, THAT'S COOL."

ON THE FRIGID MORNINGS of the first weeks of 2017, Mike got into the habit of getting up before dawn to take Parker for walks. At this time of the year on the Bayshore, sunlight came slow. In the hour before the sun cracked through the eastern wall of woods that made up the Nantuxent Wildlife Management Area two miles away, the sky was cast in the deepest blue and strewn with stars. If it wasn't for the glowing deck lights and gurgling diesel engines of Money Island's oyster fleet in the distance, Bay Point would feel as desolate as some remote patch of arctic tundra. The *Spartina* meadow that spanned between Cedar Creek and the mouth of Nantuxent Creek lay flat in its winter dormancy, made heavy by a web of ice. Piercing northwests clawed at the surface of the bay, whose waves smashed into the shore and froze into broad, rumpled sheets as white as snow.

Mike and Parker's puffs of breath caught in the wind, were swallowed in its rushing immensity. Mike's career had been spent in the elements, hanging hundreds of feet above the Delaware River, maintaining the Commodore Barry and Delaware Memorial bridges. He'd seen every condition. He could stare down the cold, but even his weather-beaten, dark brown eyes watered up against these heavy northwests. At the end of the driveway, he and Parker usually turned right, to walk down Bay Point Drive, past the empty homes of his and Kate's departed neighbors.

There were a lot of memories behind all those old screen doors, now emblazoned with white DEP placards that read "RESTRICTED AREA: KEEP OFF." Walking past Anthony and Jenny Zadlo's place, a few doors down from where Mike and Kate now lived on Cedar Creek, was especially bittersweet. Zadlo had been one of the first Bay Point residents to live on the island year-round, along with Mike and his parents. Soon after the road was laid in the early 1940s, made possible with the money that Cumberland County had received from the WPA, Bay Point's first property owners chartered the Bay Point Rod & Gun Club, which essentially made the hamlet a private village. Zadlo had been one of the club's longest-standing treasurers. After he died in 1994, the club named the tiny bridge that spanned twenty-five feet over Cedar Gut and onto the island in his honor. Mike, then the club's vice president, had paid for the sign commemorating Zadlo, which stood at its entrance, out of his own pocket.

The cold didn't slow Parker down any. In the good years, when every one of Bay Point's sixty-some homes were jammed with families in the summer, the club had to enforce a leash law because there were so many dogs running around. Now, Parker was the only dog left in town—he was free to roam as he pleased. At least for him, Mike and Kate often quipped, the Blue Acres buyouts were a good thing. He loved to chase anything that moved in the water and bring it back to show Mike or Kate—dead crabs, live crabs, fish carcasses, driftwood. In summer, he spent the better part of every day playing in the shallows just off the little beach next to the bungalow, snapping at real and illusory critters, fending off the armies of mosquitoes and greenheads and blackflies that could chew the edges of his ears raw and bloody. Even on these cold winter days, with the protection of his matted, rust-colored coat, he was tempted to jump in the water. At the far bend, where Bay Point Road horseshoed into Paris Road and the creek drained into the bay, Parker would dash out onto the narrow, concrete-and-brick-littered shore. "Park, no!" Mike would shout at him. "You'd be dead in a minute, old boy."

Mike and Kate still called this part of the island "the point," even though there wasn't much left of it. When Bay Point and Paris Roads had been put down, the marshland and beach extended nearly a football field's length out from the bend where the two roads met. Now, most of that was gone. In fact, almost immediately after the Bay Point Rod & Gun Club had begun developing Bay Point, it was clear that erosion was a major issue. As early as 1967, some Bay Point lots still being taxed by the township had become fully submerged, as was also the case in Money Island. Club members, several of them well-connected local bankers and business owners, were not shy about raising awareness of Bay Point's problems with erosion. They attended township meetings and communicated with friends who were county freeholders, state senators, and assemblymen, asking for help. There was enough political leverage locally to keep the township busy providing loads of gravel to be dumped along the road and around houses. The problem was that local political sway, and the Band-Aid solutions it brought, was never enough.

New Jersey was one of the first states to regulate the development of its coasts. In 1914, the state legislature enacted the Waterfront Development Act, which restricted the construction of docks, piers, bulkheads, and bridges. But the economic pressures of the Depression and World War II, and the subsequent massive infrastructure efforts of the 1930s and '40s, like the WPA-funded roads to Cumberland's bayfront, cut against New Jersey's efforts to manage shoreline development. As roads were laid to Bay Point, Money Island, and Cumberland's other Bayshore communities, the message ostensibly was to continue building. For years after the Bay Point Rod & Gun Club was established, if a member wanted to add on to their home, or build a second one, they basically needed only to bring it up for a vote during the club's monthly meetings, then get it approved by the township, which was easy.

With the 1960s and the environmental revolution, coastal development became even more regulated. In 1970, the same year that the Environmental Protection Agency was created, New Jersey's Department of Conservation and Economic Development became the Department of Environmental Protection—it was officially established on April 22, America's very first Earth Day. That same year, New Jersey passed the Wetlands Act of 1970, which gave regulatory teeth to the Waterfront Development Act of 1914. With the creation of the DEP, there was now staff and dedicated funding in place to regulate beyond small-scale structures like docks and bulkheads, and expand to cover "a broad range of activities and disturbances in coastal wetlands." In 1973, New Jersey's coastal wetlands were given a defined border under the Coastal Area Facility Review Act (CAFRA), which provided the DEP with additional resources to restrict the location, design, and construction of "major facilities" contained within a 1,376-square-mile area that encompassed the Atlantic and Bayshore coasts.

At the time, as the Army Corps' National Shoreline Study was underway, concern was mounting among Bay Point Rod & Gun Club members that these new rules would hinder Bay Point's ability to construct other erosion controls. For their monthly meeting in September of 1975, the club's president, Ted Hudson, pulled a few strings and was able to get John Higgins, the district coordinator for New Jersey's Environmental and Economic Development Department, to pay Bay Point a visit. After Hudson reported that the much-anticipated basketball hoop had been installed on one of the telephone poles next to the community pump house, Higgins explained to members the Wetlands Act and how it might affect their riparian rights. Hudson then talked about a group of citizens from the nearby Mullica River who had organized an association with the hope of "preserving private ownership of lands within the coastal area wetlands," and suggested club members consider creating something similar.

The club then began a letter-writing campaign to Cumberland's representatives in Trenton and DC, even to President Jimmy Carter, to express their concerns about the lack of state and federal help that the Bayshore was receiving to address erosion, and how the Wetlands Act and CAFRA might affect their land and development rights in Bay Point. For another meeting, Hudson invited a soil conservationist from the USDA who agreed to help the club develop a plan to slow the erosion along the bay shoreline. Nothing much came of it. The following year, the club drafted a letter to send to South Jersey newspapers and television stations, comparing their erosion situation to that of Atlantic City, which by then had received millions of dollars' worth of shoreline protection projects, and was now undergoing another.

The fate of Bay Point, and the Bayshore as a whole, was being pulled ever further into the orbit of the DEP, whose regulatory scope and reach was growing by the year. New Jersey's citizens and lawmakers were growing increasingly concerned about the state's deeply problematic industrial pollution, especially those areas in the EPA's Superfund, which is an inventory of the US' most dangerous toxic waste sites. In 1983, when the EPA finalized its first Superfund "National Priorities List," sixty-five of the sites were located in New Jersey, the most of any state in America. Dan Fagin, who wrote the Pulitzer Prize–winning book *Toms River*, which told the story of a Jersey Shore town ravaged by industrial pollution, called New Jersey "the undisputed capital of hazardous waste dumping in the United States." Meanwhile, in Cumberland County, only two sites were listed in the original Superfund National Priorities List, both of them located in the city of Vineland, twenty-five miles away from the bayfront.

The environmental movement, coupled with advances in technology and globalization, had, in effect, stanched the cancerous spread of industrial pollution to the Bayshore. Therefore, as New Jersey finally began to right its environmental wrongs in the 1970s, there were few large, ecologically diverse areas of the state that remained unsullied. The Pine Barrens, a 1.1 million-acre swath of forest and swamp that spans the center of southern New Jersey, was the state's top conservation priority. "New Jersey was a great place to be involved in these issues," Michael Catania told me. In 1979, as a twenty-seven-year-old supervisor in New Jersey's Office of Legislative Services, Catania drafted the act that led to the preservation of the Pine Barrens. "We were tackling problems that other states didn't have to." The next great, undisturbed region of the state was the Bayshore. By the time Catania became the executive director of the Nature Conservancy of New Jersey in 1991, the Bayshore had long been one of the nonprofit's focal points. "There was still time there," Catania said.

By then, New Jersey had had an open space preservation program that was thirty years old. Established in 1961, the Green Acres program, which fell under the DEP, had already purchased and preserved hundreds of acres of Bayshore land. The state's ever-increasing environmental regulation and pursuit of open space didn't leave much room for development or infrastructure of any kind on the Bayshore, which among residents didn't engender much love of any kind for the state, given that the Bayshore was not in dire need of open space preservation to halt sprawl. In the 1973 Army Corps supplemental survey study of the Bayshore, the authors noted that cooperation with Lawrence Township officials was "practically non-existent." Repeated attempts to arrange meetings "to gather the necessary data . . . were repeatedly thwarted."

Thus, instead of the jetties or bulkheads or piers that the Jersey Shore's towns were receiving—because *their* tourism dollars justified the development, not to mention could cover the huge expenses of the required permitting—Bay Point, with its nonexistent contribution to the state's economy, was left with an old barge that the Bay Point Rod & Gun Club had purchased and grounded on the point in the 1960s, around the same time that Mae Griffith had sunk her barges in Sea Breeze. Like Griffith, the club believed that the structure would help build up the surrounding beaches and slow the erosion and help nature along, as Griffith had put it.

Instead of becoming an eyesore, or simply a passive piece of infrastructure, "the barge," as everyone came to call it, quickly evolved into the centerpiece of the community. The club sometimes held their monthly meetings inside the spacious, wood-slat room encompassing the barge's deck, as well as their annual Labor Day Outing and other picnic parties. There was a pool table and a soda machine that charged a dime for a 7UP or RC Cola. In the 1960s, Mike would spend his summer days on the barge with the other Bay Point kids, playing ring toss with rubber quoits and fishing and crabbing off its deck. The kids would leave the barge just long enough to grab lunch from one of the many mothers who always seemed to have ham sandwiches or homemade crab cakes to eat. The Bay Point kids were such a force that, in 1968, the club voted to allow them to form their own club, whose meetings would—of course—be held on the barge. "It was a kid's paradise," Mike told me. "We spent many hours there, out of our parents' hair."

Also on the point, where Bay Point Road and Paris Road came together, was the pump house. While the barge was the entertainment center of Bay Point, the pump house was its beating heart. Annual club dues mostly went to maintaining the pump and the water it provided from the pristine Cohansey Aquifer, then located just below the earth. Month after month, year after year, club members fretted over the pump house, since maintaining it was a constant, increasingly difficult battle—not only because of the corrosive salt air, but because of the fact that the bay was inching closer and closer. The club spent thousands of dollars on gravel, crushed clamshell, and concrete to shore up the disintegrating earth beneath the pump house. Like their parents and grandparents, new club members like Mike and Kate attended township meetings and wrote letters to, and developed relationships with, county freeholders and state representatives. They invited the legislators to the annual Labor Day Outing and other club parties, to remind them of the community that Bay Point residents had built way out here at the edge of America. They implored them to secure funding to bring in more barges and more fill to rebuild their eroding beach, to raise the road to save their cars from the rust caused by flood tides, to pave the road, to give them just a fraction of the attention the Jersey Shore was receiving.

Help eventually came in the usual form—a few truckloads of fill from the township. There were also bigger victories, like a new bridge. Mike, Anthony Zadlo, Bones Batten, and other members spent much of their time on weekends and after work maintaining the pump, replacing its rusted-out lines, or running a backhoe to spread the latest load of gravel or shell. The first well had been drilled in 1939, at a depth of thirty-five feet. By 1971, salt water had started to seep into the upper aquifer, so another well had to be drilled deeper—this time down about seventy feet. After Sandy, the well had to go deeper still, completely past the upper aquifer, down five hundred feet into its belly, to find water Mike called "wonderful, probably the best you'll get."

All of the extra work required for maintaining the Bay Point residents' existence, however, didn't seem a burden at the time of the second well's drilling. Even after the 1980 storm destroyed Mike's parents' home along with fourteen others, including the pump house and the barge, everyone just licked their wounds and rebuilt. When the warm weather came back around, and the majority of Bay Point's homeowners returned for summer, the club organized cleanup days and held their rowdy monthly meetings. While the damage was too severe to hold the 1981 Fourth of July party at the pump house, everyone decided that they'd have Bay Point back in good enough shape for the Labor Day Outing, which had never been cancelled since it began decades before. If a neighbor's driveway became too muddy from the constant flooding, a few guys from the club would find cedar poles and other lumber to build up the ground. If someone wanted a longer pier or another floating dock, "we'd jump the pilings in and just build it," as Mike put it. They built a 1,400-square-foot picnic pavilion in the summer of 1985, and to fortify it against the next storm, they ordered a ton of sand and a ton of stone for its foundation, then set its pilings in concrete. "Back then," Mike told me, "the building inspector come down and have a few beers and say, 'Hey man, that's cool.'"

For Mike, those were the best years of his life. He'd met Kate in 1985 while helping to build Ray Sileo's house. They'd danced all night, fished all the next day, fallen in love. He joined the club's board of directors and was quickly establishing himself as one of Bay Point's patriarchs. He and Kate hosted pig roasts and many of the club's monthly meetings. They took over the annual fishing tournament—and almost always won. The club published a newsletter, screened in the pavilion to keep the bugs out, and set up a volleyball court nearby for when there was a breeze and the bugs weren't too bad. At the Fourth of July parties, everyone would take turns manning the grill, cooking hot dogs and hamburgers, or making sure the cooler was full of ice and beer and soda. In 1989, to celebrate Bay Point's fiftieth anniversary, the club hired a group called the Hawaiian Revue to throw a traditional Hawaiian luau for the Labor Day Outing. Not long after, the township finally received some funding to repair and resurface Paris Road. In this way, the Sisyphean task of living in a place not meant to be lived in—a place that, by the 1990s, was losing around a foot of shoreline a year and rising—became not only a Bay Point resident's way of life, but a piece of their heritage.

After Katie and Mikie were born, Mike and Kate spent the school months in Salem County, in a nice two-story home that Mike had built, but their hearts were in Bay Point. On the kids' last day of school each June, Kate would pack the family "wally wagon," as she called their Buick station wagon, full of clothes, groceries, the dogs, even the aquarium and its fish. "We left school that day," Kate said, "and never come back till September."

ON THOSE BITTER MORNING WALKS, while Parker ran around, toying with the edge of the bay, Mike climbed the steps up to the pump house to check and make sure nothing had frozen. A seized pump meant he and Kate would have to go and stay at one of the kids' homes until they could get someone out to have it fixed. Because Mike had to prop the pump house on pilings after Sandy, the wind blew underneath the structure, making the pump more difficult to insulate from the cold, since its pipe had to run down through the floor and out into the open air before entering the ground. Mike had sheathed it with a PVC tube, and he'd found that he could dangle a construction light down inside the tube to keep the pipe just warm enough to avoid freezing. The floor of the pump house was dusty with the dried mud of Mike's many footprints. Extension cords lay in a knotted pile, next to burned-out bulbs and other construction lights that no longer worked.

It wasn't easy bending over, plugging in cords and changing bulbs. The pain in Mike's knee had gotten so bad that cortisone shots didn't work much anymore, so his doctor had him on experimental injections—"chicken fat, or something," Mike called them. Nevertheless, the joint pain was a small price to pay for his decision to get sober a couple of years before. He'd long been a drinker—everyone was in Bay Point, what with all the parties and fishing tournaments and club meetings. But back then, it was all done in a social context. After Sandy, that all changed.

Mike could trace it back to a particular moment, a few days after the storm. From the hunting cabin in Cedarville, where he, Kate, and the kids were staying until they could get back into Bay Point, Mike watched on television as President Obama and New Jersey governor Chris Christie gave a press briefing from the Jersey Shore town of Brigantine, fifty miles east of Bay Point. "We are here for you. And we will not forget," President Obama had said. "We will follow up to make sure that you get all the help you need until you've rebuilt."

In an executive order, Governor Christie instructed insurance companies to relax documentation and other requirements usually asked of homeowners, and to expedite the payment of claims. The DEP commissioner, Bob Martin, signed an order allowing approvals of permitting requirements for the repair and replacement of "critical public infrastructure such as roads, bridges, bulkheads and culverts." In a statement, Martin said, "For emergency repairs, we cannot let bureaucracy get in the way. . . .

We want our communities to go and do needed repairs and replacements without worrying about the permit process."

Mike, Kate, and other Bay Point homeowners took Christie and Martin at their words. Mike and Kate moved a camper trailer from the marina to the lot on Cedar Creek, where he began rebuilding an existing shanty that would become the bungalow. Seeing that the Paris Road rancher was just as destroyed as Mike's parents' home had been after the 1980 storm, Mike and Kate finally decided they would never again rebuild directly on the bay. Mike began repairing the damaged pump house, and Kate got in touch with the electric company to restore power.

In an email chain to club members, Ted Anders, who owned a home near the end of Paris Road, relayed information from conversations he'd had the day before with government officials. "The likelihood is that the DEP will be removed from the process on many different repairs and the township may not require certain types of permits," Anders wrote. Two days later, after attending a township meeting, he reported: "The permit process and DEP red tape has been radically erased. Members may begin rebuilding ASAP as long as it is within the existing footprint." Anders expressed optimism, noting that he thought Bay Point was on the road to recovery. The township and its mayor, Anders wrote, "stressed to me that if Members encounter any issue with any government office or agency as they rebuild and repair, they should contact the township immediately. The Bay Point community has the right to rebuild without infringement."

But as Mike and Kate dove into recovery, it seemed the state, with its "Stronger than the Storm" mandate to rebuild the Jersey Shore in time for the 2013 summer tourism season, had completely forgotten about the Bayshore. Six months after Sandy, Bay Point was still in ruins. The township had removed those homes that had been deposited on Paris Road by Sandy's surge, but other homes, including Mike and Kate's rancher, remained, deteriorating a little more each day, still awaiting removal, which the state had at first promised it would handle but later reneged. Vandals and looters were regularly showing up in the middle of the night, stripping bare the abandoned second homes of Mike and Kate's neighbors. One of the homes had been set on fire by an arsonist, causing a neighboring home to also be damaged. Fearing for their safety, Mike and Kate had set up the three security cameras on their property so they could monitor who was coming into town.

When Cumberland County Health Department inspectors showed up to Bay Point in April of 2013, Mike and Kate knew things were about to get worse. The septic tanks of every home were in disrepair. The inspectors noted broken lines and unsealed lids. When they shined their flashlights down into tanks whose lids were missing altogether, they saw a mixture of bay water and sand. While these all constituted violations, there was no way of telling whether the violations were the result of neglect over the years or damages from Sandy. Most homeowners in Bay Point hadn't returned—or couldn't return—to their homes, so whatever sewage had been in the tanks immediately prior to Sandy had long been flushed out into the bay.

At eight in the evening on Saturday, April 13, after a week of daily visits from the health department, the Bay Point Rod & Gun Club held their regular monthly meeting as they had always done. Members were resigning left and right—that night alone, Ted Anders reported that he'd heard from four members who had decided to leave the club. Anders volunteered to send a letter to the club's remaining members, telling them "that they may resign from the Club in good standing if they choose not to rebuild or sell their properties."

A little over two weeks later, on the first of May, the health department sent out official notices of violation. Homeowners were instructed to take immediate steps to correct the problems the inspectors had cited. They had one month to respond with their intentions for their properties—that is, if they intended to remain or retreat—and six months to obtain the proper permitting and install an upgraded septic system, which, due to the complexity of the rules governing septic systems in wetlands environments like Bay Point, could cost upward of $30,000. If nothing was done before the six-month grace period, the health department would begin issuing $2,500 fines. Mike and Kate were issued multiple notices of violation—for both the still-under-construction bungalow next to the camper on Cedar Creek, as well as for the Paris Road rancher, which was "caving into Bay," in the words of one health department inspector. It didn't make any sense to Mike and Kate why they would be issued a violation for a home that had been abandoned and was awaiting demolition.

Mike and Kate did not dispute that the bungalow on Cedar Creek might have a noncompliance issue, but they were confused by the aggressiveness with which the health department was now pursuing the problem. As far as they were concerned, they were acting on the advice of Christie and Martin, who were still imploring Sandy victims to rebuild "without worrying about the permit process." At this point, there seemed to be no choice but to live in violation of the regulations, because, in a sense, there were no regulations, since they seemed to be under reconsideration or eliminated or relaxed or put on hold—no one seemed sure which. Mike told a health department inspector that he and Kate intended to eventually move from the trailer into the bungalow and get it into compliance, but he first needed clear direction from someone.

The homeowner whose abandoned home had been destroyed by arson wrote the health department in shaky handwriting that suggested defeat. "Our house is completely gone from Hurricane and fire and is completely gone," she simply wrote. And yet, she too had six months to comply.

On April 29, exactly six months after Sandy, New Jersey finally received its first batch of money from the federal government—$1.83 billion. Christie marked the occasion by holding a ceremony at a seafood restaurant in Monmouth County, on the northern Jersey Shore, with HUD secretary Shaun Donovan. "We've got to be responsible with this money," Donovan told the governor and others in attendance. "And we've got to make sure it's spent right."

On May 16, Christie traveled to Sayreville, a blue-collar Central Jersey community along the Raritan River that had lost nearly three hundred homes from Sandy's surge, to announce the creation of the $300 million Superstorm Sandy Blue Acres Program. "We will not force any of these residents to sell their homes or force any towns to participate in buyouts," Christie told a crowd of seven hundred. "I'm not going to buy one home in a neighborhood and leave the rest of the neighborhood standing. You all need to get together as a neighborhood and say, 'We're ready to go.'" In a statement announcing the program, Martin said, "We understand this is a very personal and difficult decision to make for people who were decimated by Sandy and may have also suffered damage in previous storms, but who still love where they live. But for those who choose the buyout option, we promise to work diligently to move the process along as quickly as possible and to minimize government red tape and bureaucracy." Whereas the state's original Blue Acres Program, which began in 1995, had been a backwater initiative within Green Acres, the Superstorm Sandy program was suddenly front and center in New Jersey's open space policy moving forward. It was given thirty-three dedicated staffers, some of whom were broken up into what were internally nicknamed "tiger teams" that would "target" clusters of homes in Sandy-impacted communities. Along with Sayreville, Bay Point and Money Island were Blue Acres' first targets.

With the support of Lawrence Township's mayor, nearly every homeowner in Bay Point had begun the process of applying to Blue Acres by the summer of 2013—even Ted Anders, who'd been so hopeful that Bay Point could rebuild. Mike and Kate, however, refused to leave.

Mike began drinking alone. His work on the bungalow next to the camper stalled. Because there was so much confusion at both the state and local level, especially now that everyone else in Bay Point was ready to sell out to Blue Acres, it was proving impossible to get the right permits to continue construction. In the maddening limbo, Mike's drinking worsened. Never one to sit still and stay inside, he was now beginning to spend whole days in the camper. On other days, he'd get Kate to drive him to Delaware, where the alcohol was tax-free. He drank a gallon of vodka a day, sometimes more. There seemed little Kate, Katie, or Mikie could do to pull him from the darkness he'd so uncharacteristically fallen into. "Those were the toughest months," Kate later told me. "Dark days, man," Mike would often say. "Dark days."

IF IT WASN'T TOO COLD, Mike made his way down the stairs of the pump house and continued walking down Paris Road. The township had finally removed his and Kate's rancher, along with the other homes that had been washed off their foundations, but not until ten months after Sandy. Mike's brother Walt's home, a stout two-story that had managed to sustain little damage in Sandy, still stood. It had a deck off the second-floor bedroom that looked out over the bay. After Walt's, there was another gap, and then a strange little structure that stood a full ten feet out in the bay, even at low tide. It sat cartoonishly high on pilings, marooned out there over the water for years. It was the shed—Mike's onetime man-cave before it became his and Kate's honeymoon suite. Improbably, it too had survived Sandy. The shed's door had long been blown open in some forgotten storm and, from the road, Mike could see inside just a little. There was a warped counter and cabinets, their doors open and gradually falling off rusted hinges.

There were other homes still standing along the rest of Paris Road, all of them in different stages of decay. But the next one after the shed was the one that could jolt Mike into a different time—a time that, after all that had happened to him and Kate since Sandy, was almost too difficult to contemplate as once being real. Ray Sileo's home, which had long since been bought by someone else, stood tall out in the bay, looking as good as it did the day Mike and Kate danced on its sprawling deck, maybe even better. Its siding was true cedar shake, and time had only made the shingles a more stately, textured gray. The home's hundred-foot pier still stretched toward the horizon, as if reaching for the thin, distant line of Delaware's shore, nine miles across the bay.

"That home is *built*," Mike once told me. "That's why Sandy never touched it." He credited Sileo's decision to fortify the home's piling foundation with steel plates as the reason why it had survived. Kate had installed those plates. On each corner of the deck were lamplights whose glass had clouded over the years since its owners had abandoned it. There hadn't been any power past the pump house in years—there weren't even any wires connected to the house. But in those evenings when the sun burned blood orange on the surface of the bay, and reds, purples, pinks, and blues drained across the sky, those lamps would catch the light and glow as if they were pulsing with electricity.

Mike and Kate had seen the phenomenon a thousand times, but the brightness, the way the light beamed from the lamps' glass—it was easy to be fooled. Indeed, visitors who witnessed the glow often commented that the house must be haunted. In those moments, and on those morning walks, even when the lamps were still and dark, Mike often thought about that night up there on that deck, thirty-two years ago. Sometimes, he could even feel the hangover the next morning, and the excitement that bubbled inside him when Kate showed up to go fishing with him. Would these memories remain as vivid after the state tore the home down, and there was nothing left in its place but the bay and its ever-advancing brown waves?

EIGHT

"THE WINDOW IS GETTING SMALLER."

THROUGHOUT THE WINTER AND SPRING OF 2017, I began attending the monthly meetings of the Cumberland County Planning Board, as well as those of the Board of Freeholders, in Bridgeton and quickly discovered that the wounds Sandy had inflicted on the Bayshore, and those of the state's Blue Acres buyout initiative that followed, remained raw among local legislators. In one freeholder meeting, Bob Campbell's wastewater plan came up for discussion. "This project has to succeed," one freeholder said. "Either something's done, or . . . [the DEP] will come in and take [the Bayshore] down one house at a time." Another freeholder interjected. "Their enforcement is becoming almost threatening," he said.

Among the county Planning Board members, the Bayshore communities' inability to rebuild came up invariably. In his opening remarks in one meeting, Planning Director Bob Brewer held up a copy of a study by Rutgers University's Walter Rand Institute for Public Affairs, which compared the southern New Jersey region with the rest of the state, in terms of health, income, crime, education, and other social indicators. The study's question was, "Is South Jersey getting its fair share of public goods?" The answer was no. The study concurred with another study, done by Monmouth University, on the notion that South Jersey was "the state's Rodney Dangerfield"—an allusion to the comedian's signature line about getting "no respect." Brewer shook his head. "The rest of the state is just oblivious to the fact that we even exist," he said, before turning over the floor to public comments. An elderly woman, wearing a bright red sweater and with gray hair dyed a soft brown, approached the podium and begged the board to do something about this. "You guys need to save South Jersey," she said. "We're just dying on the vine here."

After the meeting, I spoke to Brewer and his assistant director, Matt Pisarski, at a conference table squeezed between offices and cubicles full of various county employees busily typing at their desks. Brewer had prepared several color printouts for me to look at, including zoomed-in satellite images, taken the previous summer, of a diner in Cumberland's easternmost township of Maurice River, as well as a couple of boat launches scattered throughout the Bayshore. The diner's parking lot was full of cars, and the launches lined with trucks hitched to boat trailers. This was all proof, Brewer told me, that the Bayshore had potential as a tourism destination. Along with the satellite images, there was an "activities map" that he had drawn himself on an 8x11 sheet of copy paper. He called it "my happy little map." It was done in colored marker—sweeps of green gave way to waves of blue—the bay—into which a big yellow and orange sun was setting. The map was crowded with items representing over fifty attractions and amenities along Route 553—Main Street. There was boating at Money Island; shore birds at Sea Breeze; oysters and music at Bivalve; my mother's family's wharf, Husted's Landing, in Fairton; and hiking, bald eagles, bait and tackle, crabbing, hunting, scenic views, open space, sandwiches, gas, and an ATM scattered along the fifteen-mile, two-lane road.

It was indeed a happy, optimistic depiction of the Bayshore's potential—if only it were realistic. Brewer unfurled another map that had been buried beneath the printouts. It showed Cumberland's forty miles of Bayshore coast with a long red border traced around it. "That's all protected," he said. "It'll never be developed." Then he pointed to three tiny, oblong borders within the protected zone: Fortescue, Gandy's Beach, and Money Island. Collectively, the three hamlets encompassed just three and a half miles of Bayshore coast, yet, as Campbell was always quick to mention to anyone who would listen, they made up the majority of Downe

Township's tax base. "The state can't provide for something to happen in these little areas?" Brewer asked, incredulously.

Brewer and Pisarski did not share Campbell's opinion that the tree huggers were the enemy. They actually felt quite the opposite. On his days off, Brewer sometimes drove down to Port Norris to walk a nature path that followed the banks protecting Bivalve. The path was part of a $100 million, 14,500-acre Estuary Enhancement Program completed in the 1990s by PSE&G, the energy company that had built, in the 1970s, two nuclear generating stations along the bay in neighboring Salem County. He would stroll through the marshland, admiring the herons standing along the ditches, and the trunk of an ancient cedar tree that sat, preserved, just beneath the surface of a salt pond. Pisarski also volunteered at the Cumberland County Eagle Festival, which was put on by one of the area's most ardent environmental and open space advocacy groups, a nonprofit called Citizens United to Protect the Maurice River and Its Tributaries.

What Brewer and Pisarski did share with Campbell was the opinion that the Bayshore had long been unfairly treated by the state and the DEP. I had grown up with Pisarski's younger sister, so he and I had been catching up before the meeting. I had told him that I'd returned home—or, at least almost home—to Ocean City. Now, in our conversation with Brewer, Pisarski used Ocean City as an example of the Jersey Shore as a whole to illustrate what he, Brewer, and every other county official saw as a gross imbalance in attention and resources between the Bayshore and the Atlantic coast. "They're not taking a block in Ocean City and demolishing it," Pisarski said, referring to that town's own severe flooding problems, which were often worse and more frequent than those in Fortescue, Gandy's, and Money Island. "They're building up, so that it stays exactly the way it is. On the bay side, it's just the opposite. They're using Blue Acres to say, 'Okay, we can't maintain this, you guys can't live here anymore and we're going to buy you out.'"

Pisarski had pale skin, and his cheeks were flushed with frustration. I could see his sister, whom I hadn't seen since I moved away over fifteen years ago, in his round face and blond eyelashes. Pisarski was trying to parse his words carefully so as to not fully criticize the DEP's dismissive position toward the Bayshore, given that he was the county administrator for the

Farmland Preservation Program, another statewide open space initiative under Green Acres. "From the state's position, they are saying to themselves, well, how much should each state resident pay to provide a coastal lifestyle for folks along the waterfront," he went on. "It's a tough question." Brewer listened, shaking his head. He was equally agitated. "Our Bayshore was neglected for fifty years," he said. "Time just passed it by."

BOTH PISARSKI AND BREWER POINTED OUT, however, that after Sandy the state had brought some positive things to the Bayshore that might otherwise not have come. This was in no small part because of the advocacy of Campbell and the other members of the Delaware Bayshore Long Term Recovery Committee. Brewer, modest to a fault and, like Pisarski, prone to blushing, had also been an integral part of the group, serving as the chair of its Intergovernmental Relationships Subcommittee, though he'd never mention it himself.

In 2013, the group's advocacy had attracted the attention of New Jersey senator Cory Booker. That December, the then freshman senator visited Fortescue, where he stood inside the still-wrecked Charlesworth Hotel and marveled at the realization that there was a place in his own state where one could watch the sun set over the water. "I don't think the rest of New Jersey realizes the urgency" of the Bayshore's situation, he had said, according to Amy Ellis Nutt, a Pulitzer Prize–winning reporter for the Newark-based *Star-Ledger* who had been writing a series of articles about the Bayshore, which she called New Jersey's "forgotten western shore." Four months later, Booker returned to announce that he had gotten Cumberland included in HUD's Distressed Asset Stabilization Program, which immediately identified six hundred eligible households—a number that nearly equaled the total number of eligible families across all nine Atlantic coast counties that had immediately received funds from the Sandy Disaster Relief Act. "That so many were eligible really speaks to the problems these people face," Booker told a crowd assembled on the steps of the Cumberland County Courthouse, according to Ellis Nutt. "Cumberland County is just not on people's maps, so for us the big difference was forcing Cumberland County into the conversation in Washington." Ellis

Nutt later told me that, on her reporting trips to the Bayshore, she had had the same experience as Booker. "It was a whole environment that I was unaware of, and that there were clearly people, much fewer people, but suffering the same severe results," she said. "A place where it was going to be exceedingly difficult to recover, if they could at all."

But Booker's HUD grants paled in comparison to the hundreds of millions in recovery money that was at that point rushing into the Jersey Shore. Meanwhile on the Bayshore, where there was virtually no state or federal funding for large-scale reconstruction initiatives, the Delaware Bayshore Long Term Recovery Committee was left to conceptualize and pitch projects that would never wrest the Bayshore communities from their chronic, and now accelerated, decline. For example, one of the group's project proposals was a "Bayshore Resiliency and Sustainability Education and Outreach" campaign to better inform Cumberland County residents on issues like sea level rise, sustainable development, coastal erosion, and resiliency. Other initiatives were a "Bayshore Eco-tourism/Business Improvement Task Force," a "Bayshore Marketing and Destination Plan," and a "Maurice River Rails-to-Trails" walking and biking path. Under the Christie administration, which wasn't overly interested in "green" initiatives, especially if they dovetailed with climate change, most of the projects had little chance of ever being funded. "We've had how many different groups of people down here," Pisarski said. "They all make the same recommendations, which is, you need to have restroom facilities and accommodations for tourists, and yet, in order to do that, we've got to make massive utility and infrastructure investments. None of their studies are saying, well, here's the money to do that."

It was this kind of sustained, wheel-spinning bureaucracy that had made Cumberland's political landscape so complex, creating a milieu in which an ideological hodgepodge of individuals like Brewer, Pisarski, Campbell, Mike and Kate, and Tony were all united in their frustration toward the same government agencies. It seemed to me that this kind of political environment was endemic to rural, low-income American towns where it wasn't realistic to stand staunchly on one side of the aisle or the other, because every decision made at the local, state, and federal level almost invariably affected a family member, a friend, or a neighbor. "Nobody wants to commit to the multi-million-dollar projects the Bayshore needs, even though there are ways to work with the USDA and some of these other federal groups," Brewer said. "But nobody wants to take that on right now, and, unfortunately, the window is getting smaller and smaller, because as Blue Acres continues and nature takes its course, the numbers, the cost benefit, which wasn't there to begin with, gets worse and worse."

AFTER THEY'D CONCLUDED their inspections of Bay Point in April of 2013, the county health department had shifted its focus that summer over to Money Island and observed not just the same gross septic violations, but myriad other environmental issues that went beyond its purview and into that of the DEP. That July, at the suggestion of DEP commissioner Bob Martin, a two-day fact-finding tour was organized, which included Campbell, county freeholders, health department inspectors, and DEP officials. Noah Hetzell, an officer at the county health department who was a part of the tour that cloudy, humid day, later described seeing dumpsters scattered across the island, still full of debris. Homes frozen in a state of ruin. The day they chose to visit was unfortunately timed—as Hetzell and a few others made their way back up Nantuxent Drive, along the oyster docks, the high tide reached its peak, and they had to wade through shin-high water to get back to their vehicles. The DEP's inspectors cited Waterfront Development, Coastal Wetlands, Tidelands, and CAFRA violations in the form of unpermitted fill, bulkheading, and dock construction. "How do you rebuild?" Hetzell wondered aloud to me, recalling the inspection and the subsequent regulatory hurdles that Money Island's residents faced. "How do you start from scratch?"

One possible solution to Money Island's predicament could be found in the example of Bay Point, where the mayor and nearly every property owner had been in support of selling out to the state through the Superstorm Sandy Blue Acres Program, then just two months old. But by the time Christie had announced in December of 2013 (not long after Senator Booker's visit to Cumberland County) that Blue Acres had secured $4 million from the USDA to complete the state's purchase of thirty-three Bay Point homes and vacant lots, Campbell had already steeled himself for a fight to keep Money Island from suffering a similar fate. He introduced a special resolution authorizing the township to petition "Governor Chris Christie and the New Jersey Department of Environmental Protection to halt the state's plan to implement a Hurricane Sandy–related buyout program in the Bayshore communities and redirect the fund to rebuild the communities."

Neither Christie's office, nor Martin's, heeded Campbell's petition. Instead, in July of 2014, Martin made his first-ever visit to Money Island to take a tour with Campbell and other officials. In a letter memorializing his visit, Martin made clear his plans for Money Island:

> The Township has requested the State's support to protect these homes into the future. However, the costs associated with correcting these violations and fortifying the shoreline against continued erosion and storms exceed the value of these homes. It is not feasible for the State to invest public funds to sustain an area that does not meet a simple cost-benefit analysis. However, as we discussed, the State is interested in pursuing the purchase of any homes where the owners are unable or unwilling to effect the necessary repairs. DEP's Green Acres program is a voluntary homeowner buyout program for which the State needs the support of the municipality. The Township must advise whether it will support DEP's purchase of these homes from willing sellers. DEP has already received request from some property owners who wish to sell their homes. . . . To provide a sustainable solution, we are offering to purchase the homes on Money Island West (Bayview Road).

After Martin had made his decision, Pisarski made a creative, last-ditch attempt to save Money Island. "The question that was raised at the county level," he told me, "was, is there a vernacular architecture that is unique to these Bayshore communities that could potentially be lost?" This was Pisarski's specialty—his 1999 graduate thesis at the University of Pennsylvania, where he studied historic preservation, was titled, "One-Room Deep Domestic Architecture of Cumberland and Salem Counties, New Jersey." In its opening lines, Pisarski wrote, "Of all the examples of material culture, architecture proves to be the most complex and meaningful object, representing social status, place and lifestyle. Shelter, at its most basic is home for the human species, something without which humans would not survive. But buildings are more than shelter; it is a building's ability to communicate that lifts it beyond most objects."

Pisarski had found hope and an ally in Andrea Tingey at the state's Historic Preservation Office. In the 1980s, with money from the National Park Service's Historic Preservation Fund, the state surveyed and inventoried the historic structures of all but two of its counties. Cumberland, along with Gloucester, also located in South Jersey, were the pair left out. Noticing that Cumberland had now been iced out of the list of counties to receive emergency funding in the wake of Sandy, Tingey and a team of three other preservation officers were able to use National Park Service funding their office had received through the Disaster Relief Act to initiate an extensive survey of Bayshore vernacular architecture—structures that might have been already listed as historically significant had the county been surveyed in the 1980s. "We spent a lot of time in the field along the oceanfront with FEMA, doing assessments on areas where we did not have cultural resource concerns, and recovery work could move forward without any further regulation from us," Tingey told me. But on the Bayshore, she continued, "we recognized that it was an area that was very vulnerable . . . an area where we weren't getting information through our regulatory system." She went on, "You can't protect it if you don't know about it."

Tingey and her team drove nearly every Bayshore road with GoPro cameras and photographers in the backseat of their cars, turning heads and getting lots of stares from locals. One day, they stopped to eat at the Landing and ran into Campbell, who saw their DEP vehicle and wanted to know what they were up to and if it had to do with Blue Acres. Kinney Clark, a GIS (Geographic Information Systems) specialist who was a part of the team, was struck by how much the Bayshore resembled coastal South Carolina, where he had grown up. "I felt like I was at home when I was there," Clark told me. Mostly, it was the landscape that was familiar to him, but the rural culture was as well. "I think one of the first impressions I had was that there was really interesting history about how these places came to be, and how they've evolved over time," he said. "And now that they're being bought out and sort of let revert back to nature, it makes it even more important that we get this documentation compiled so that we know what the cultural landscape was like for this period of time, in the eventuality that they all disappear."

In the end, Tingey and her team were unable to get any structures in Money Island listed as worthy of historic preservation, nor was Pisarski. The first saltbox shanties of the 1940s had long been washed away by hurricanes and other nameless storms, or neglected and left to fall to the ground, or demolished to make way for newer homes. Few had ever really had enough money to build a structure that could withstand the relentlessness of the elements, and there certainly wasn't any money to do so now. And, besides, the township, the county, and the state had failed to sufficiently enforce environmental regulations in Money Island, Bay Point, and elsewhere on the Bayshore—and residents had failed to sufficiently care, if only because they didn't have the money to do so.

In a letter addressing Pisarski and the county's request to have at least some of Money Island's remaining structures preserved, Robert Lore, a FEMA branch director, concluded that nothing in the town was eligible for listing in the National Register of Historic Places or New Jersey's State Register. Lore called Money Island "New Jersey's smallest, most rural and remote community" that was once "a verdant salt hay farming outpost." Even though his plan had been defeated, Pisarski had won a small victory in that what was left of Money Island had at least been documented before the excavators moved in and nature retook what it had been trying to retake since the day the county laid Bayview and Nantuxent Roads, over a half century ago. "Even if they are subsequently demolished," Pisarski told me, "we'll at least have a written and photographic record."

Aside from Tingey's study, Money Island was conspicuously missing from studies the state conducted after Sandy. They had given Downe Township the money to construct a new bulkhead on Bayview Road, which had been accomplished in large part through Tony's pestering the township after Roger Mauro, the former marina owner, had tried to run him down in 2006, but the project had taken ten years to complete. The more it dragged on, the more the bulkhead was hit by storms that further destroyed the road and bridge, causing the project's scope to expand. It had taken a $130,000 grant from the state's Department of Community Affairs to get the project over the finish line. After this saga, it seemed clear that the DEP wanted nothing to do with Money Island ever again.

Speaking with Brewer and Pisarski, I mentioned Tony's big aquaculture plans and his belief that they were the answer to reviving Money Island. Brewer chuckled. He knew of Tony, and he knew he had a penchant for grandiose ideas, but hadn't known about this latest one. "How many times can DEP tell you no, or say, 'Where's the twenty-thousand-dollar application fee?'" Brewer said. "You do the cost benefit analysis and you say, 'I can sell salt water taffy on the boardwalk and make more money.'" Nevertheless, Brewer seemed to respect Tony's tenacity as much as he was confused by it. "He had dreams and visions," he went on. "But they're slipping away."

NINE

"SAVE THE BAY."

NO ONE IN MONEY ISLAND had been more affected by the DEP and county health department inspections than Tony Novak. Every one of his marina properties had been cited for violations of county health codes as well as various state land use and riparian regulations, which carried threats of daily fines worth tens of thousands of dollars and a permanent injunction restraining him from continuing operation of the marina.

But in the nearly five years Tony had been receiving these notices of violation, the state had not moved to enforce them, instead opting to give him time to get the marina in compliance. Similar, though less severe, warnings were being sent to other Money Island residents whose properties had been deemed to be in violation during the post-Sandy inspections. The years of inaction had done nothing but embolden Tony and his neighbors—everyone seemed to simply shrug off the DEP letters that periodically showed up in the mail. The way Tony saw it, the state was just trying, through threats, to scare Money Island residents into selling out to Blue Acres. For some of his neighbors, these threats were working—by the spring of 2017, most homeowners on the Bayview Road portion of Money Island were negotiating with Blue Acres case workers. Tony, however, was standing his ground.

He had no other choice. The truth was that when he had bought the marina property in bankruptcy court in 2012, he had done so with the intention of turning around and either selling or leasing it to the state, which, Tony had hoped, would wipe out the property's outstanding violations and invest in its rehabilitation. But the response to Sandy had changed everything. It shifted Money Island under the purview of Blue Acres, which only purchased residential, not commercial, properties that had been damaged in the storm. Tony had applied to Blue Acres anyway, but had been denied. Not one to be discouraged, he'd shifted his energy toward his aquaculture plans. While the state delayed actual enforcement, instead only sending reams of threatening letters, he worked to secure an investor, like Cape May Salt Oyster Company, who he hoped could take the state's place in rebuilding the marina. But that plan had collapsed, too: in addition to Money Island's desperate state and its constantly flooded roads, the marina's myriad violations had convinced the company to turn its back on Money Island altogether and set up their FLUPSY barge in Port Norris, along the docks in Bivalve. This one had stung, Tony had told me, but it wouldn't stop him. He'd just have to find another investor.

One afternoon in early May, I made the drive from Ocean City to Money Island and met Tony in the sunroom of his cabin on Bayview Road. He was wearing dirty blue jeans, black sneakers, and an untucked polo shirt with a rumpled collar. He was also in a sour mood. That morning, he and Bruce Muenker, the marina's manager, had been out in the little aluminum boat that Tony called the marina's "maintenance boat," trying to move some docks around. The boat's engine had started making a loud clanking sound. "I'm no expert," Tony told me. "But I know that when an engine is clanking, that's not good." The bad engine, however, was just the tip of the iceberg. The real problem was that he had recently received more notices of violation from the DEP, which outlined the same laundry list of violations and threats of thousands of dollars in daily fines if things were not corrected immediately. One of the latest violations was for Muenker's camper. "I don't care what they say," Tony said. "I'm not kicking Bruce out. There are some things I just won't do."

He asked me if I didn't mind waiting a few minutes while he typed a letter to State Senator Jeff Van Drew's legislative director, Jonathan Atwood, who remained the senator's liaison for Bayshore residents fed up with the DEP. Tony was Atwood's most regular disgruntled correspondent. He leaned close to the screen of his old laptop, looking down through the glasses perched at the tip of his swooping nose, and typed loudly.

While Tony worked, I read through a document he had recently created in response to this latest round of violations, titled "Why Save Money Island?" "Sea level rise will force tough public decisions in the years ahead about which of New Jersey's working waterfronts to keep, and which to abandon," he had written in the document's introduction. "The decision to support Money Island NJ as a valuable multi-use resource for the businesses and residents of New Jersey should be one of the easier public policy decisions for our state's officials." He'd gone on to outline ten reasons why this was so, one of which featured Campbell and every Bayshore waterman's favorite statistic: the roughly $10 million—or $60 million, when applying the government's sixfold economic multiplier—worth of oysters offloaded annually in Money Island made it one of the state's most productive seafood ports. If Money Island could be metamorphosed into an aquaculture hub, Tony believed, millions more could be made.

After Tony had sent off his letter, his phone rang. It was his old friend Doug Rice, who had stumbled upon Money Island in the 1980s and bought the cabin we were now sitting in. Rice had recently suffered a stroke and was unable to return to his job as an accountant, so Tony was giving him odd jobs at the marina. Rice, no more of a waterman than Tony, was supposed to be looking around for boats to make up a rental fleet that would be debuted that summer. He'd recently bought one, but the problem was that the motor, according to Tony, was a piece of junk. "If the engine has duct tape wrapped all around it, that's probably not a good sign," Tony said after hanging up with Rice. "But I'm no expert."

By now, I was thoroughly perplexed by Tony. He still had a nice home and life in the Philadelphia suburbs. Nearly every morning he wasn't in Money Island, he met a group of successful businessmen at a coffeehouse in Manayunk, a trendy neighborhood just a few minutes outside of Center City. He had started visiting the coffeehouse not long after Roger Mauro had tried to run him down in 2006. Because the slow recovery from the head injury he'd sustained in the incident had caused him to lapse on his CPA recertification, he needed to find a place to study. He became a regular at a table by the window, where he would sit alone and pore over tax and financial books. Each morning, the businessmen gathered at a table next to Tony's, and they eventually got to know each other. One man owned an eyeglasses company; another was a scaffolding supplier for huge projects in the city. "Brilliant guys, and they're all worth a fortune," Tony once told me. "I'm the poorest guy in the bunch." He told the men about Mauro, the head injury, his troubles with the DEP, and his aquaculture plans for the marina. The men loved his crazy stories about Money Island, but their interest in the place stopped there. None of them had ever made the drive to South Jersey to visit Tony at the marina. Tony envied their success, but he didn't loathe it, because he fully expected his fortunes to turn any moment now. He'd once had money; he knew what it tasted like. And yet his heart seemed to be in the impoverishment that had befallen the marina, Money Island, the Bayshore—places that had never welcomed him as his wealthy Manayunk friends had. How could he so happily be moving between these two worlds—both of which had never completely accepted him, and he them?

Perhaps the answer lies in the details of his childhood growing up on his father's "gentleman's farm." Tony's mother had died from cancer when he was eleven years old, and because he was the oldest of four siblings, much of the responsibility for maintaining the farm's day-to-day operations had fallen on him. Although, at first, he knew nothing about growing Silver Queen corn or raising cattle, pigs, and sheep, Tony dived into the challenge. As a teenager, to get the corn harvested, he paid his little brothers a penny an ear. He struck deals with neighboring farmers to borrow some of their land to grow more corn. He joined 4-H to learn how to take care of livestock. "He was always into conservation," Tony's father, Nick, later told me. "I think he took Money Island on as a project—'save the bay.'" His brother John agreed. "He always will take on something that's monumental, something daunting," he told me. "And Money Island is unfortunately a daunting, never-ending problem that massages Tony's brain."

While Nick and John and the other siblings occasionally visited Money Island, they preferred Nick's home in Stone Harbor, on the Jersey Shore, where the beaches were wide and breezy and void of bugs. Tony, on the other hand, never cared for his father's beach house. He didn't like sitting

idle in the sand, or the fact that, in the large Jersey Shore towns like Stone
Harbor, second-home residents rarely got to know each other. One of the
first things that turned around his opinion of Money Island back in the
early 1990s, when he first started visiting, was the way everyone walked
up and down Bayview Road and Nantuxent Drive, filtering in and out of
each other's homes.

Tony talked incessantly about community, and he mourned its loss in
Money Island and throughout the Bayshore. And despite all his efforts—to
raise awareness through his various websites of the threat that sea level rise
posed to Money Island, and achieve his relentless dream of resurrecting
the place through state funding or some phantom angel investor—they
had done nothing but anger his neighbors, who just wanted Money Island
to stay the way it always had been. With every blog post about rebuilding
a new dock or sign of apparent interest from an investor, Tony had only attracted increased attention from the DEP, who in turn kept finding more
and more violations. "They blame the sea level rise on me," Tony had once
told me of his neighbors. "I'm an outsider, no matter how long I live here."

I looked around Tony's sunroom. The floor was carpeted in Astroturf.
In one corner was a telescope, a pair of binoculars, and a pair of white
rubber boots, the kind the commercial crabbers and oystermen wore. The
sun, now slipping west, poured buttery light through the windows, across
Tony's desk, illuminating dust particles floating in the air and the pile of
notices of violation from the state. Over the door that led into the cabin
was a sign that read "Life's Better at the Beach."

"Why still do it?" I asked him. "Why not just leave and go back to
Philly for good?" The cost of the permitting needed to get the marina in
compliance with the law was several times what the property was worth.
What investor would want that?

"I've already lost all of my home equity, my life insurance, my retirement plan," he said of his investment in the marina. "There's nothing
more that the DEP, or life, can do to me that hasn't already happened.
So why am I here? Because I don't have a lot of great options in life, and
I'm trying to make the best of what I do have." He stopped, buoyed himself, and found the Panglossian bearing that had guided him this far, and
would continue to do so, I was sure, forever. "There's no doubt we're

making progress," he said. "And I do think I have something positive to offer."

SPENDING TIME WITH TONY caused me to become increasingly conscious of the fact that I was more like him—an outsider—than the Bayshore native that I once was. I hadn't picked up a fishing rod in years or ever learned to drive a boat. I'd never even eaten a bay oyster. I began considering moving back to the Bayshore, from Ocean City, to see if I could do it again—live there, return home.

After leaving the monthly Planning Board meeting in Bridgeton one afternoon, I made my way toward Money Island. The route was the same as the one my father, brother, and I took on those predawn summer mornings in the 1980s and '90s, when we fished the bay most weekends with my uncle. The drive took me past the worn, Victorian duplexes of Bridgeton and the towering, ornate county courthouse, its first iteration built in 1752 and whose stone steps Senator Booker stood on in December of 2013, when he finally delivered Cumberland a sliver of federal relief money. I crossed the Cohansey River, at this point just 150 feet wide, which cleaves the city, giving its footprint the rough outline of two lungs. I drove past the old lumberyards, the last vestiges of the industry that gave Bridgeton its start, in 1686, when a Quaker settler established a sawmill on the banks of the Cohansey.

From here, the city crumbles away. A couple of miles of more run-down homes. An abandoned chicken processing plant. A bar, called the Toadfish, now closed but once a vibrant hangout for kids when I was in high school. The Cohansey Golf Course, also closed and overgrown—it was bought by the state, through Green Acres—where I had worked as a cart boy one summer. Past the house where my father grew up, and where his father and sister still lived. The Sunoco gas station that once was my great-grandfather Smith's general store. Bartone's bait and tackle shop, where we would stop on those summer mornings to pick up squid, bottom-fishing rigs, lead sinkers, and ice. The whole way, the marshland is never more than a couple hundred yards away, looming like a green and yellow sea in the spaces between the trees and tired architecture.

At Bartone's, I turned off Route 553 and on to Back Neck Road, which leads to the place where Philip Vickers Fithian stepped off the ferry that September day in 1773, on his way to Governor Reily's cabin at the edge of the marshland. Not far from where Fithian had disembarked, I passed my aunt and uncle's home, which was also the home where my mother grew up. I passed the entrance to Husted's Landing and turned on a side road that led back toward Money Island, through lowland patches of woods, where, when I looked closely, I could see some of the banks that the 2010 USDA report called "orphans." Turning back onto 553, I glanced over at the Old Stone Church, built in 1680, and today the oldest existing congregation in the Presbyterian Church in America. Buried across several rows, beneath the arthritic limbs of an old elm tree, were several generations of both sides of my family.

Past the church, heading east toward Money Island, the landscape opened into farms and homes with wide, flat lawns and large vinyl-sided garages with barn stars. In downtown Cedarville, I passed a stretch of Victorians less regal than those in Bridgeton and Port Norris, but no less worthy in the context of historical fortitude. These homes have been patched, painted, and expanded with screened-in dens, porches, and garages, but have not surrendered the tall, squared-up stance that defined the proud permanence of their age. Their tired facades have not been devalued by time, but by things like the recently completed Dollar General store nearby, whose large asphalt parking lot imposed a benign, culture-less liver spot on the face of a place that was once better than this.

Another couple miles down 553 and I'd entered Newport, where, at the intersection with Baptist Road, there's a two-pump gas station that is the opposite of the Dollar General. It's a tangible piece of the past where, in fact, the elderly attendant will ask, "How's the windshield; need washin'?" He'll check your oil, too, and talk about how the crabbing or the fishing or the oystering has been out on the bay. He wears overalls most days, and every day, a tweed newspaper boy hat.

I turned right on Baptist, passed Methodist, then turned left onto Newport Neck Road, which follows the zigzag of the original road that led to John Munyan's Flax Farm. Along the way are houses on lots so low that their septic systems cannot be buried and are instead set on top of the yard, covered by earthen mounds with PVC ventilation pipes poking out. Some of the mounds are simply planted with grass, others are creatively concealed by retaining walls and pruned shrubs.

Beyond the high ground, entering the marshland, was where I detected the first indication of spring. Although the trees remained bare, the foxtails and *Spartina* meadow betrayed a strain of chartreuse creeping up from the base of their stalks. With each additional degree in temperature, another centimeter of dull yellow would be replaced with life. The air was warm enough to put my window down, and it was so quiet that I could hear birdsong and the swish of the foxtails in the breeze. The road, of course, ended at Money Island Marina, where a southwest wind rolled unimpeded off the bay in lazy, soft waves. The bay, warming up, looked less viscous, more effervescent. Breaking the quiet was the groan of a diesel engine. Coming in from the bay was the *John C Peterson*, a seventy-one-foot, wood-hulled former schooner that had been built in 1927. The boat skirted just a few feet past the marina's docks, then made a hard left turn, following the narrow, awkward line of what was left of Nantuxent Creek's channel. I could hear the faint bang of Bruce Muenker's hammer. He was no doubt fixing what another winter had tried—but once again failed—to destroy. There was hope in these days, or at least possibility.

Oyster season had recently begun. When I had met with Brewer and Pisarski, we had talked about how many of the traditional oystermen were resistant to aquaculture and the companies, like Cape May Salt, that were introducing it, little by little, to the Bayshore. "It's the horse-and-buggies versus the horseless-carriage-type deal," Brewer had said. "That's progress. There's always a transition." On the other hand, multigenerational oystermen, like Steve Fleetwood, who operated the busiest loading dock in Money Island, had called it "smoke and mirrors." Fleetwood managed the largest packing house in Bivalve and wasn't interested in deviating from wild-caught oystering—after all, he'd managed to survive the slim years of the 1990s, when the bay's oysters were stricken with yet another disease that nearly wiped them out. He acknowledged that aquaculture worked well in other places, but still wasn't convinced it would work in the Delaware Bay. "People think it's a damn golden cow," he'd told me.

Nevertheless, he'd recently felt compelled to begin integrating aquaculture into Bivalve Packing's operations.

Muenker appeared from the bait shack, smoking one of his rolled cigarettes. From a distance he looked frail and tired, but as he got closer, he actually seemed spry. His T-shirt sleeves were rolled up in the greaser style, and his thin arms were sinewy and tanned. I hadn't been around for a few weeks, so I asked him how business had been. "Not too busy," he said, "but we've been busy." He sort of just floated away, uninterested in talking, to fiddle around with whatever it was that needed fixing.

I left the marina and drove the mile down Money Island Road to the turnoff that led a short distance across the marshland to Gandy's Beach. I had arranged an appointment to look at an apartment in a duplex whose decks, at high tide, reached out over the bay. When I first called the listing's real estate agent, she seemed baffled that anyone would want to rent on the Bayshore. She double-checked to make sure we were talking about the same place. Who would want to move *from* the Jersey Shore *to* the Bayshore, she wondered? I said that I'd grown up here, but that didn't make her any less incredulous.

It was sunset. A beautiful evening, not much color left now but a deep, cobalt blue in the sky. The surface of the bay was glass. Tiny, even ripples of swell moved in from the horizon all the way to their terminus beneath the house. I first walked to the second-floor deck, where a sliding glass door revealed a young woman inside. I knocked on the glass. The woman was confused, said the apartment I was looking for wasn't hers. Try downstairs, she said. I had startled her and she watched me carefully as I walked away. Downstairs, I found the real estate agent and the duplex's owner, who wore a black leather jacket that smelled of cigarette smoke. We began the tour of the house, which had two bedrooms, a small kitchen and living room, and a warped deck that stood over the water. Whoever the current tenants were, they had a child. One room was awash with dolls, stuffed animals, and other toys. The carpet throughout the house was the industrial kind—thin, coarse, torn at the edges. The floor was uneven, due to the house's foundation shifting in the disappearing earth.

At the end of the tour, the real estate agent asked me if I wanted to sign a lease. She had the papers splayed out on the kitchen table. I could see the blank lines where I would have to put my name. It had now almost been two decades since I'd had a Cumberland County zip code. Earlier, I had been ready to do this. Now, I hesitated. The home's owner, sensing my change of heart, seemed disappointed. He couldn't keep his eyes off the floor. I walked out of the house and back into the night. It was completely dark now, silent but for those perfect little waves sweeping in and out beneath the house. I couldn't do it. My original home, a place that had given me nothing but good memories, boundless experiences—and I couldn't come back. In between those memories and now, I knew that "home" had succumbed to a disease it contracted a long time ago—from the day it was born, really. As its son, I should have wanted to return to see it heal. But the best I could do was just pass through as a visitor, like so many of my peers who had also long since left.

PART THREE

RESILIENCE

TEN

"I KNOW WHERE IT IS AND WILL ALWAYS RETURN."

"GRAB A BEER," Kate said. It was a muggy June day, the air like sludge and the gnats plentiful and vicious. Kate pointed to a cooler sitting next to her fold-out chair on the corner of the front porch. Parker nosed my arm as I reached in to grab a Miller Lite. Mikie's young daughter, Mae, was occupied with some shells she had picked up from the little beach next to the bungalow. The beach was full of horseshoe crabs attempting to bury their eggs in the sand. Seagulls, terns, and the occasional red knot were bombarding the crabs, however, making meals out of the eggs. Mae's cheeks were flushed and her hands and feet were smudged with mud, and every once in a while a gnat would bite her. But she simply swatted them away and went on playing, completely content with being here on her mom-mom and pop-pop's porch. "She's our little bay girl," Kate said, smiling. We walked around to the back of the house, where a large supply shed sat up on another deck, next to a fish-cleaning station. The back deck led down to a pair of floating docks, where Mike and Kate kept their boats tied up. Kate pointed to a boat across the creek, moving on the distant horizon. "Mike's out tending the pots," she said.

Mike was busy moving the aluminum skiff between the buoys that marked the locations of the crab pots he and Kate had scattered around the mouth of Cedar Creek. Pulling the fifteen-pound, dog-crate-size wire-mesh cages from the mucky seafloor was not easy, but Mike's big arms pinwheeled quickly and effortlessly. Since he'd quit drinking two years ago, he'd shed nearly a hundred pounds. Back when he was drinking, his body breaking from the stress of living in the camper and trying to build the new bungalow on his own, pulling pots became almost impossible. Though he would never be able to pull over a hundred pots a day like he used to when he was young, pulling the few dozen that he and Kate had out in the creek these days was still impressive—a workout that would exhaust any healthy person, old or young.

When they crabbed together, which was most of the time, Mike and Kate had a system for tending their pots. As Mike drove up to a buoy, Kate would grab it with a mooring hook. Mike would then put the boat in neutral, walk up to the bow, take the buoy line from Kate, and haul in the pot. Once he had it up and resting on the gunwale, Mike would open the pot's hatch and empty the catch—a good haul was a dozen or more—into a wooden hopper Mike had built to hold two bushels, or about 150 crabs. As Mike worked the last crabs out—at least one always remained stubbornly clamped onto the mesh—Kate would rebait the pot with a rancid bunker—the local name for the baitfish menhaden—from a plastic bucket next to the hopper. Once they'd rebaited and fixed any damages to the mesh, Mike would walk back to the helm at the stern, moving the boat along until he felt they were over a good spot. At that point, Mike would say, "Okay, Slim," and Kate would toss the pot into the water, where it would sink slowly back to the shallow bottom. Between pots, Kate would sit on the bow with a Miller Lite in one hand and look contentedly at the landscape. Mike could deftly maneuver most any piece of machinery, but his command of a boat, what with all the water's nuances, bordered on the artistic, just like his and Kate's system for tending pots.

Crabbing was one of the things Kate loved most in the world, but I could see that it wasn't bothering her too much to not join Mike today, since missing out only meant spending more time with Mae. The three of us went inside to sit in the air-conditioning. Mike had recently turned sixty. For his birthday, Kate and the kids had chartered the *Bonanza*, a "party boat" that ran one-day fishing trips out of Fortescue. They hadn't caught many fish, but they'd had plenty of fun. Sixty years was an enormous milestone for Mike, given that since December of 2013, when Blue Acres secured the funding to buy out Bay Point and thus ensured the place would be a ghost town, a lot of people around the Bayshore didn't think he was going to make it much longer, including Mike himself.

As Kate and I talked, Mae was busy flipping through a Winnie-the-Pooh book, whose cardboard cover and pages were brittle and discolored. The book had been Mikie's, when he was Mae's age. Kate explained that the book had been in the chest that had vanished during Sandy. The chest had been spotted a year later, far out in the marshland, by a salt hay farmer. When they opened it, Mike and Kate discovered that its contents had mostly survived. The photos inside, and the Winnie-the-Pooh book, were pretty much the only keepsakes salvaged from the storm.

Mae had dropped the book and was on to something else to play with. I picked it up, finding the edges of its pages undulated as they moved toward the book's spine, in a way mimicking the floodwaters that had permanently cast them this way. The book was no different from the bungalow's faded, water-worn deck outside, or the warped floating docks down on the creek. Or the creases in Mike and Kate's foreheads, or the sunspots on their arms. Everything in Mike and Kate's life, I realized, had been altered by the tendrils of salt and sun and water. No wonder Mike had wanted to seal the interior of the bungalow with resin—the bar and those walls were the last thing they owned that hadn't been infiltrated by water. It might have taken years, at nearly the cost of Mike's life, but the bungalow had turned out to be a nice, cozy place. The kitchen had plenty of room to cook the oyster pies and crab quiches and beef stews that Mike and Kate loved to make for their many friends who were always stopping by to check in. The long bar, where everyone naturally gathered, was perpetually cluttered with Mae's toys, or apples that someone had recently dropped off, or a marine map of the bay. And, of course, there was the bedroom, with an actual bed for Mike to sleep in.

After a while, Mike slid the skiff alongside the dock and tied it off. Kate and I walked outside to meet him. It hadn't been the most productive morning, but Mike had been able to get about a bushel out of his traps. He got busy sorting the "jimmies" from the "sook," as the males and females are called. The keeper "number ones" and "twos" from the throwback "number threes." Mike complained about the meager number. "They were too busy trying to have sex," he said. The triangular aprons on the sooks' bellies were purple and clustered with bright orange eggs. The real prize that every crabber is looking for are soft-shells, but there were none in Mike's haul today. There were, however, a few shedders, which would be great to use for catching weakfish. There were also a few bay-brown, prehistoric-looking fish that had gotten into the pots. Technically, they were called toadfish, but we called them "oyster crackers," because of their powerful jaws, which the fish uses to eat crabs and other crustaceans. Watching Mike pull them from the hopper and throw them back into Cedar Creek, I thought about my days fishing the bay as a kid. If you caught an oyster cracker, that meant you were being lazy and not bouncing your sinker and bait off the bottom enough. I could still clearly feel the tap of the sinker on the bottom, as it reverberated up the monofilament line, through the rod, and into my hand. I recalled the careful process of removing the hook from the oyster cracker's mouth, so as to not get a finger bitten or jabbed by the sharp spines on its gills.

Mike usually sold his catch to one of the seafood stores nearby, but since he hadn't gotten much, he wanted to know if I wanted them. If I did, he said, I could have them, but it was up to me to clean them, which I could do at the cleaning station up next to the utility shed. A small surge of panic rushed through me. Up to that point, I had only talked to Mike and Kate about my past fishing and crabbing and hunting on the Bayshore. This would be the first time to prove that I actually was who I said I was. While Mike went in the house to take a shower, Kate threw me a pair of rubber gloves and handed me the bushel basket. If I pulled their backs off, she said, she'd spray out their innards with the hose. Pulling the backs was the hard part, since you had to reach into a basket of angry crabs with powerful pincers.

There was no doubt that Delaware Bay blue crabs were some of the most aggressive crustaceans on the planet. Anyone who grew up on the Bayshore understood the wrath of a caught crab, and just how painful it was to have a finger caught in their pincers. I took a deep breath and jammed a hand in the basket teeming with angry crabs, hoping memory would save me from looking like I didn't know what I was doing. I managed to pull one out, after a few misses. Removing a crab's back shell should be done with a single pull—simply grab one of the pointed sides on the back, pull up and off. But if you don't have a good grip, you can break it in two. That's what I did my first try. Kate saw—I could tell—but was nice enough to pretend she didn't. Each successive grab got easier until I was moving as fast as I once had all those years ago.

"You mind pulling off the eyes, too," Kate said. What she meant was the mouth of the crab, which looks like a series of tiny mud flaps. Apparently, she didn't like doing that. Then she asked, "Are you counting how many we got?" I hadn't been. "That's okay," she said. "We can just go back and count the dicks here," pointing at the crabs' aprons, which she had also peeled off and kept to be used for minnow bait. I went on throwing the shell backs into the water below the cleaning station, which had Parker in a frenzy. He swam below, from one shell to the next, barking and looking like the happiest dog on the planet. Kate and I fell into a comfortable, pleasant rhythm, until I felt like it was only a few days, and not years, since I'd last cleaned crabs. Until I almost felt like I'd never left the Bayshore at all.

IN THE SUMMER OF 1974, my mother and her two best friends bought an old, plywood-hulled boat from a local rescue squad with the intention of becoming commercial crabbers. They bought a five-horsepower motor to put on the boat so they could take it out to the last bend of Back Creek, near the old cabin that my father and uncles used for duck hunting when they were young. My mother and her friends were a rare sight among the predominantly male crowd hanging out at Husted's Landing. They spent the muggy days out on the water, unbothered by the bugs desperate to torment them. They tied pieces of raw chicken onto hand lines and collapsible metal traps and pulled up crab after crab from the shallow, muddy bottom. They sometimes forgot to bring a basket to hold the crabs, so they'd drop them on the floor of the boat, letting them scuttle around. My mother and her friends didn't seem to mind—one crab after another would dart toward their feet grabbing at their toes and ankles, and often managing to get hold of a good chunk of flesh. The business didn't go well, because the guys at the wharf would steal their crabs, or they'd miss phone calls from people wanting to place orders. On one occasion when they did deliver crabs to a customer, they accidentally dropped the bushel basket on the floor of the customer's kitchen, allowing the crabs to escape and scatter throughout the house. Sometimes, they eschewed work to spend the warm days on the sandbars throughout Back Creek, swimming and watching all the different species of birds fly past.

That Christmas, my father bought my mother a new boat, a fourteen-foot fiberglass dory, which would be much better for exploring the shallow creeks and ditches. "I looked upon that boat as another woman would a brand-new kitchen filled with the best appliances in the world," my mother wrote in an essay she submitted to a *Reader's Digest* "First Person" contest the following year. "It wasn't until I was married and away from South Jersey a few years, that I really knew where my heart belonged," she wrote of the creek and marshland.

When they got married in August of 1970, both of them just twenty-one years old, my parents moved to Athens, Georgia, to attend the University of Georgia. My mother majored in education and my father in landscape architecture. After graduation, they left on a road trip for California, camping along the way. It was the first time either one of them had traveled west of the Mississippi. On the way, they stopped at a commune for artists, students, and vagabond hippies in the Arizona desert, called Arcosanti, where the eccentric Italian architect Paolo Soleri was envisioning a kind of futuristic utopia. They slept in a tent and learned that desert air turned freezing at night. They camped next to a man, clearly high on something powerful, who traced the constellations with his fingers. They shared bathrooms and showers with people who sometimes decided to walk around in the nude. Other young people in the commune had only come because they had trust funds to burn. All of this was foreign to my parents—they had come simply because they wanted to build something new that the world had never seen before.

My father's job was to move wheelbarrows full of dirt and my mother's job was to straighten bent nails. Other times, they carried twenty-five-pound bags of concrete between job sites. The work was not difficult for them—when they were both twiggy kids, they had worked in the onion fields of my maternal grandfather's farm, near Husted's Landing. They had worked alongside African American day laborers from Philadelphia and migrant workers from Puerto Rico, who offered them a glimpse at life beyond the Bayshore. Some of the kids at Arcosanti were just like my parents; others weren't particularly ambitious. These kids' intoxicated ruminations were too eccentric for the dirt-under-your-nails life my parents knew and loved back home on the Bayshore. In short, they'd come to Arcosanti to work, unaware that others had come to find utopia, not reality. They lasted two weeks, then drove on to California, where my mother's brother—who looked a lot like Mike—was stationed at Travis Air Force Base. In San Francisco, my father interviewed at an architectural firm and got the job, but he didn't take it. It had been a few months and they were starting to miss home. They turned around and drove back to Cumberland County. My sister was born two years later, then my brother, and then me. My parents never did leave again, nor did they ever want to.

As kids, my brother, sister, and I used my mother's dory to do what she and her friends had done in those summers in the mid-1970s. In a narrow ditch that wound from the Cohansey River to a dammed irrigation pond just behind our house, we often went crabbing. We, too, would forget to bring a basket or cooler or container of any type to hold the crabs we caught. We learned early on where to hold a crab without getting pinched: at the base of its swimming leg on the back corner of its body. How to identify their sex by the shape of their aprons on their white bellies. And that the quickest way to release a pincer once it had seized upon a finger or toe was to simply rip it from the crab's body. In learning these things, I came to see myself in the overall hierarchy of the marshland, where we—the humans—were on top. I carried that sentiment over to the fish in the bay, the ducks in the ditches and salt ponds, and the whitetail deer and wild turkeys in the woods. So, naturally, I became a hunter.

My mother was never comfortable with this perspective I had developed, which held that there are humans, and then all the other animals. In fact, the first summer that my mother and her two friends had the new dory to explore Back Creek, they had a change of heart. They discarded their crab traps for a camera and a pair of binoculars. The graceful flight of the blue heron sent chills up and down my mother's spine. The gulls seemed to laugh at her and her friends. In searching for different types of marshland vegetation, they'd sink up to their waists in mud. My mother had written that essay for the *Reader's Digest* contest in the fall of 1975, at the beginning of her lament for the coming winter. "I can visualize the terns crashing into the water to catch a meal," she wrote. "I can hear the sound of the water lapping against the sides of the boat as we anchor in the middle of the creek. I feel part of that salt marsh, and know that its resources are not valued enough by man."

I had stumbled upon the essay, which an editor from the magazine had sent back with detailed, encouraging line edits, while looking through an illustrated copy of *Paradise Lost* that my parents kept on the bookshelf in our home. The essay might not have meant much to me during the years I lived away from the Bayshore, but now it seemed to offer the answers I'd been looking for about my own return home. I had lasted much longer out in the world than my parents did, but in the time I'd spent with Mike and Kate, and with Tony in Money Island, I'd surprised even myself with how long I could simply sit, stare, and marvel at the marshland that formed the backdrop of all of our lives. I was no longer the hunter I had been as a kid, though I could feel those urges trying to surface from deep within me. Their return was doubtful—I was now also more comfortable holding a camera than a crab pot or fishing rod or shotgun. "No, paradise isn't far away, nor in the future for me," my mother had concluded in the essay. "I know where it is and will always return."

KATE, MAE, AND I had been sitting on the porch for a while when Mike finally came outside, freshly cleaned. He wore a pair of jeans that were too big—they were bunched at the waist and cinched by a leather belt. He was still losing weight and regaining strength, though he still suffered from back pain and numb hands, especially after an hour or two of pulling pots. Also, the chicken fat injections that he'd been getting from the doctor weren't working as well as they had been at first. He sat down next to Kate and handed her a tube of ointment. Kate lifted up the back of Mike's T-shirt and gently worked the ointment into a sore on his shoulder. "Now,

I've got shingles," he said, shaking his head. "You'll find out what it's like when you get older." Despite the aches, Mike was smiling.

Down on the beach next to the house, the birds continued to harass the horseshoe crabs that had piled up on the sand, fighting for a place to lay eggs. "Guess I ought to go down there and turn them over," Kate said. It was a joke. She was referring to how, in recent years, after the drastic decline in the Bayshore's horseshoe crab and red knot populations, and the state's subsequent ban on all harvesting of the crabs, more and more environmental groups and tourists were showing up to walk Bayshore beaches and turn over those crabs that had been flipped upside down by the waves and were thus unable to right themselves. There was even a group of "experts" who taught volunteers how to properly right the crabs without hurting them.

None of the crabs on the beach needed flipping over, so Kate's sarcasm was clear. The DEP, Blue Acres, and all the environmental organizations with which they partnered, with their deep pockets and dreams of returning the Bayshore to open space again, seemed to only have the crabs and birds in their plans. These volunteers would drive hours from Philadelphia or Princeton to flip a few dozen horseshoe crabs over, or donate a chunk of their income to fund others to do so, but most of them would walk or drive right past Mike and Kate. Or worse, they'd have the nerve to knock on the door to lecture them about sea level rise and the need to retreat from Bay Point. "Why can't we both live here?" Mike asked no one in particular, as he remained hunched over. "I know these people have educations, but do they have life experience?"

It was only four days before, on June 12, that news had broken that President Trump had called the mayor of Virginia's Tangier Island, which sits in the middle of the Chesapeake Bay and, according to the Army Corps, is shrinking by about fifteen feet a year because of the same combined forces of erosion, subsidence, and sea level rise impacting the Bayshore. Tangier had recently been thrust into the national spotlight after CNN aired a story on the island's plight and, in the piece, Tangier mayor James Eskridge had pleaded with the president for help. "Donald Trump, if you see this, whatever you can do, we welcome any help you can give us," Eskridge had said, then later added, "I love Trump as much as any family member I got." The kind of help Eskridge was hoping for was the kind of help Campbell was looking for—infrastructure. A seawall to be exact. Eskridge, like Campbell, and presumably President Trump, did not believe in sea level rise and credited Tangier's rapid wasting away to the forces of erosion alone. In the surprise phone call, according to Eskridge, the president had told him not to worry about rising sea levels—that Tangier had been there for hundreds of years and it would be there for hundreds more. "Like the president, I'm not concerned about sea level rise," Eskridge had told the *Washington Post*. "I'm on the water daily, and I just don't see it."

The Trump-Eskridge story had outraged America's climate-change-believing populace, and the media had taken a patronizing tone in covering the story. Eskridge was, predictably, illustrated as the backward rural American who put his deep belief in God before any kind of scientific consensus. Little space was made for explaining the complexities of relative sea level rise, which would have shed light on Eskridge's view that it was erosion—as George Hammell Cook had proven in his 1855 Bayshore study—that was drowning Tangier. Eskridge's assessment wasn't wrong, just one-sided. Mike, and presumably Eskridge, understood that things were changing—they just couldn't understand why it seemed to be the experts' word against theirs, which was based on a lifetime of observation. Mike, Kate, and I talked about President Trump's conversation with Eskridge, and his promise to help Tangier build the $3 million seawall that the Army Corps had said would be necessary to save the island from being inhabitable by 2050. "I think he's an idiot," Mike said of President Trump. "But I voted for the person that I thought would help me." Mike suspected he was already seeing that help. "I feel like the DEP's backed off since he got in," Mike said. After years of what he and Kate felt was harassment by the state, Trump's unorthodoxy was a welcome change. "I'm not leaving," he said. "I got nowhere to go."

If you didn't stop to hear Mike and Kate's story, it might have been hard to conceive of anyone wanting to live in Bay Point these days. You might have thought that going anywhere was better than staying in this nowhere. It was an isolated place, and since the early '70s, it had dealt with theft and vandals, who began breaking into and tampering with the barge, which by then was beginning to fall apart as the beach and marshland around it continued to erode. It was in the 1990s that the club decided to install the security cameras on Bones Batten's property. But it wasn't until after the Blue Acres buyouts that scarier, more severe things started happening, like the arson incident in the spring of 2013 and nightly break-ins of the abandoned homes. Mike told me of a man who had shown up recently claiming he was from the DEP and that he'd been sent down to remove all the cabinets from the homes before the demolition occurred. "Don't touch that second-floor porch on my brother's house," he told the man. I looked over toward Paris Road, where Walt Nelson's place stood, looking like a perfectly functional home. Mike had been trying to figure out how to salvage that balcony for years, but he knew he'd never be able to get to it now that it was owned by the state. Apparently there was a brand-new Jacuzzi in a house near the bridge—the owner had bought it just before Sandy and never had a chance to install it. "That sucker ain't never been used," Mike laughed. "All kinds of people've been trying to get that thing."

The only thing new in Bay Point now, other than the Jacuzzi, were the white "No Trespassing" signs that Fish and Wildlife had stapled to every front door. Since Fish and Wildlife managed much of the existing open space surrounding Bay Point, it would take over management of the land gained through the Blue Acres acquisitions. The signs were a small bit of proof that demolition would be coming soon, as was the fact that the power company had recently come to take down the wires past Mike and Kate's. "When they come for the wires," Mike had told me not long after the power company's visit, "you know it's for real."

The afternoon was getting on, and Kate was getting nervous about having everything ready for a surprise baby shower that she and Katie were throwing for Mikie's wife, Mae's mother. She had recently found out she was pregnant with a boy, who would also be named Michael. Looking for an activity to do while the girls celebrated, Mike and Mikie planned on taking the *Katie Ann* across the bay to Leipsic, Delaware, to eat crabs. "They do everything different over there," Kate said, referring to Delaware's fishing regulations. "They can keep a sixteen-inch flounder, but we can't. What's the damn difference? It's the same water." Mike nodded, then shook his head. "You know they crab off the stern over there?" he said, smiling. "*Hill*billies."

I left Mike and Kate on the porch to deliberate the frustrating regulatory differences between New Jersey and Delaware. It was late afternoon and still hot. The sun shone white and the foxtails and *Spartina* meadow were fully green. As I drove out of Bay Point, I tried my best to swerve around the mud crabs scuttling back and forth across the pavement, but there were so many it was impossible not to run over some. And somewhere in my heart, I'd uncovered the hunter that I thought had died in me long ago. I agreed with Mike and Kate that they were being treated as lesser creatures than the horseshoe crabs and birds that filled the world just outside the bungalow, and the old hunter in me felt that to be backward. And yet, I couldn't help but think that the mud crabs were just the most obvious sign at the moment that the marshland would eventually overtake the road and, eventually, Mike and Kate's property too. Maybe I had that thought just because Mike and Kate had brought a part of me back that I'd once cherished but forgot existed—and if they left, that part of me would disappear forever.

ELEVEN

"AREN'T WE A PART OF THIS?"

ACROSS THE MARSHLAND, rumors were beginning to circulate that some of the remaining homeowners on Money Island's east side had given up on "No Retreat" and were ready to sell out to Blue Acres. I had heard this from various people at the meetings of the Downe Township Committee, the Cumberland County Planning Board, and the freeholders, but no one who had told me lived in Money Island. When I mentioned the rumor to Tony one day while we were sitting in the sunroom of his cabin, he said it was true. "Ten of those out of the sixteen"—meaning, the remaining homeowners on the east side—"are on their way out," he told me. "Probably all of them I guess, in various stages."

The east side was all that was left of Money Island, as far as a community was concerned. If that remaining cluster of sixteen homes, wedged on the narrow strip of high ground between Nantuxent Drive and the creek, were to go, there would be nothing left in Money Island but the oyster docks. It seemed obvious that the DEP, beginning with Commissioner Bob Martin, wanted nothing to exist in Money Island except the docks, which these days were the only profitable thing, along with the oyster packing houses in Bivalve, left on the Cumberland County Bayshore.

The homes on the east side were fortunate enough to be set back from the bay, thus spared its ruinous waves during storms. They also had the benefit of occupying the town's highest ground. A cluster of ten homes located there still had healthy cedar and swamp maple trees and shrubs

growing in grassy yards. All of the homes had spacious docks with nicely
kept fishing boats tied up at their ends. One home once had an above-
ground pool in the front yard; another home, a recently remodeled two-
story with a concrete-paved drive and decorative brick facade, had just
been purchased by a man who had used the Blue Acres money he'd received for his destroyed Bay Point home to buy and remodel this one in
Money Island. When I first began talking to Tony and Campbell about the
buyouts on Bayview Drive, neither one of them thought that the east side
of town would ever fold.

WHEN BLUE ACRES began discussing buyouts with Bayview Road homeowners in 2014, it only exacerbated the divide in the community. Because negotiations between the program and homeowners are private and
not shared with municipal governments, or other residents in the neighborhood, any whisper of one resident's talking to Blue Acres, even if it
was a just routine call from one of the program's case managers, had the
potential to whip up a frenzy of rumors that quickly spread throughout
town—and then the township, then Cumberland County in general. In
a place like Money Island, where the DEP had maintained a constant,
menacing presence for the last several years, Blue Acres was contributing
to the ripping apart of any semblance of trust between neighbors. Therefore, to be the first homeowners to give up and call Blue Acres to tell
them you were ready to sign over your house to the state was a decision
guaranteed to leave you vulnerable to criticism from your neighbors, as
well as Campbell.

To make matters worse, Blue Acres had gotten off to a terrible start in
Downe Township. On November 12, 2015, the program held a "kick-off
meeting" at the municipal building for those Money Island residents who
had been "accepted into the buyout program"—meaning they had expressed interest in selling, but hadn't yet committed. For many of the
residents, it was less an expression of interest than it was surrender. It had
been three years since Sandy, and there had been little recovery on the
Bayshore. No one had had the time to devote hours each day calling their
elected officials to plea for help, or scour the Internet looking for grants

that would require more paperwork. If they had flood insurance, they'd gotten some money—but most had no insurance at all.

Given the various factors behind the Bayview Road section of Money Island sustaining the most damages in Sandy, its greater vulnerability to flooding in general, and multiple residents' interest in selling out to Blue Acres, the program had targeted homes only in that section of town. Comparatively, the homes on Nantuxent Drive were in decent shape—not to mention less laden with land use and environmental violations. "Only households who receive this letter should attend this meeting," the notice for the kick-off meeting read. Residents of Nantuxent Drive, then, were excluded from attending.

Nantuxent Drive homeowners Jim and Carol Giles, however, hadn't known they weren't invited. At 7 p.m. that evening, Jim and Carol, along with a group of other Nantuxent Drive residents, showed up to the municipal building only to be denied entrance by Blue Acres and other state officials in attendance. "We got there and the state wouldn't let us in because, 'Oh no, you're not part of it, we're only dealing with the people on the other side; if you don't have a letter from us, you're not allowed in here,'" Jim had recalled to me. "And, I said, 'I don't see how you can keep me out of my municipal building!'" At the time, he and Carol had been staunchly against the buyouts and supported Campbell's No Retreat campaign. Being residents of such a small community, they believed they deserved to know what was transpiring on Bayview Road. "Aren't we a part of this?" Jim remembered angrily asking the Blue Acres officials. "How can them buying that side not have an effect on us?" (Despite repeated requests, the DEP did not provide comment on the meeting.)

Exactly two months later, on January 12, 2016, a Blue Acres official emailed Campbell to inform him that three face-to-face offers had been made to Bayview Road residents and that three other offers were also in the works. Despite Jim and Carol's opposition to the buyouts, the official also noted that Blue Acres had received seven additional applications from homeowners on Nantuxent Drive, "which as you know, is outside of [the] Blue Acres target area." A little over two weeks later, on January 29, the DEP sent out a press release officially announcing that Blue Acres had expanded into Downe Township. "The Blue Acres Buyout Program is committed to fulfilling the Christie Administration's goal of moving residents in flood-prone communities to safer ground," Martin said in the release, "so those families can enjoy their homes and live without fear of additional flooding and damages."

It was shortly after the DEP's announcement, in February of 2016, that I had returned to Money Island for the first time since Sandy and met Tony. As he had done a few months later with the Cape May Salt men, he had showed me around Money Island, describing his near-death run-in with Roger Mauro in 2006 and praising the new bulkhead on Bayview Road that had been constructed after the incident. Both the road and the bridge had been damaged by a nor'easter that had recently blown through. The "No Retreat" stickers on the windows and doors of Money Island's homes had already started to fade. Tony had taken me to a spot on the road where someone had spray painted "Kiss my ass." The message, he said, was intended for Blue Acres.

Even then, any sense of community in Money Island seemed to have already died. What neighbors were left, on both sides of the town, barely spoke to one another anymore. Residents drove in and out, often passing each other without even a glance. It was as if they were holding on to their homes, and their properties, out of sheer spite—spite for those who had chosen to sell out to Blue Acres, and spite for the state for failing to lend them a hand. Hardly anyone took their boats out on the bay anymore, and fewer still hung around at the marina. The wide, sandy beach that once existed on the bay side of town had all but gone completely underwater. As far as I could tell that day, those who were left simply sat in their homes, waiting it out to the bitter end.

JIM AND CAROL GILES, it turned out, were the reason for the rumors now circulating about the east side's selling out to Blue Acres. By June of 2017, they had gotten ten of the remaining sixteen east side homeowners to sign a petition they had drafted and sent to Blue Acres, stating that the group was ready and willing to enter into buyout agreements. It was, Jim and Carol admitted to me, a complete reversal from their position on the night of the November 2015 kickoff meeting. But in the years that had passed since that night, every homeowner on Bayview Road had sold out to Blue Acres, and there was no indication from the state that any further help was coming. Not even the oystermen had been able to convince the state to dredge Nantuxent Creek, which was getting shallower and shallower every year as silt filled its channel. "It's devastated us," Jim told me. "Nobody does anything anymore. You don't see anybody anymore. It's not the kind of place it used to be." Jim and Carol were believers in sea level rise, and the way they saw it now, the bay would consume Money Island before the local, state, and federal governments could ever come together on a plan to fortify the place. "When even the muskrats are having to go up the cedar tree," Carol said, "you know it's time to evacuate."

Jim and Carol's home was a cinderblock one-story built in 1950—one of the last remaining original homes in Money Island. In 2000, when they still lived in Woodbury, a middle-class South Jersey suburb near Philadelphia, they saw Money Island for the first time, after their son's football coach invited them to moor their boat at his house on Nantuxent Drive. "When we first came here, you couldn't find a place," Jim said. "Somebody had to die for you to get an opportunity to buy." So, in 2002, when they heard that a Money Island homeowner was considering selling, Carol wrote her a letter, telling her they'd buy it. When the homeowner wrote back, telling them she was willing to sell, Jim and Carol bought the home sight unseen. "It's like going back in time," Jim said. "This was a place of beauty, it was a place where everybody wanted to be." In 2003, Jim and Carol moved to Money Island full-time, and got to work remodeling and expanding the home top to bottom, from the roof to the windows, insulation, and hardwood floors. "I did everything to make sure this place was bulletproof," Jim said. "If you're going to live here in this environment, you have to be bulletproof."

It was a handsome home by any measure, with its original beams and huge stone chimney. When I visited Jim and Carol, we sat at a high-top table next to a pair of sliding glass doors that opened up to a small backyard shaded by a few trees and shrubs. Beyond that was a spacious dock that reached out over Nantuxent Creek. On the other side, the bank of the creek rose into hundreds of acres of *Spartina* meadow. An old tree, faded to gray from the weather and salt water, protruded from the bank's mud.

Gulls twirled in the air above the oyster fleet in the distance. After spend-ing so much time with Tony, walking his different properties, like the dilapidated trailer at 228 Nantuxent, I now found myself having trouble remembering I was still in Money Island. Jim and Carol's home was ex-actly what Matt Pisarski had so desperately tried to save when he'd made his last-ditch effort to have some of Money Island's structures preserved as historic vernacular architecture.

When Sandy hit, Jim was in the middle of adding a Florida room to the house. After the storm, he and Carol resolved to stay. They cleaned up the property, finished the Florida room, then took care of the damages, which included ripping out the floors and replacing the plumbing. All the lumber was pressure treated, all plumbing materials were stainless steel, all the in-sulation under the floor was water resistant. "I spent twenty-five thousand out of my own pocket in addition to what they gave me for insurance, because we wanted to be here," Jim said. "Our stance all along was, let's fortify, save the Bayshore. We wanted to live here the rest of our lives."

Jim's voice continuously rose as he explained all the work he and Carol had put in after Sandy. Then he deflated and went quiet. "You can't fight the water," Carol said, shaking her head. Her father had always told her that, if she ever bought a house by the water, she should make sure it had lots of vegetation. In 2002, she told me, the property had cedar, white pine, and swamp maple trees, some of them around fifty feet high. "We lost seven in Sandy," she said. They hadn't been lost from the wind or surge, but gradually, from saltwater intrusion. "There's your indicator," she said. Jim was exasperated. "I can't live here anymore," he said. "I can't live with this constant pressure of, if I don't take a buyout, is the state go-ing to regulate me out of here?"

Nothing about the years since Sandy, however, seemed to infuriate Jim and Carol more than Tony. It was Tony, they said, who was the reason for the demise of Money Island. In recalling their first years as full-time residents of Money Island, Jim said, "Everybody got together three, four times during the summer. There would be barbecues here and there. It was just such a sense of camaraderie and celebration of neighborhood." Nantuxent Drive residents would walk over to the homes of Bayview Road residents to hang out on the beach. Bayview Road residents would walk over to the homes of Nantuxent Drive residents to hang out on their docks. "Everybody got along," Jim said. "When all of that really stopped was when Tony showed up."

The trouble, according to Jim and Carol, began with Tony's prolific blogging about sea level rise and the township and state's disinterest in addressing the impacts it was having on Money Island. Tony's more recent desire for the state—and, when that didn't work, for a private investor—to buy the marina properties had lately been his favorite blogging topic. And, as Tony himself had told me, his habitual posting about improving the marina in order to attract these phantom investors, which invited ever-increasing scrutiny of the community by the DEP, infuriated Jim and Carol more than any of Tony's past writings about climate change. All the attention that Tony had brought, and was trying to bring, to a place that had been founded on the desire for being forgotten, was not sitting well with his remaining neighbors. "He likes to believe that he talks for Money Island," Jim said. "But he doesn't speak for any of us."

To prove that he wasn't lying, Jim reminded me that on the Fourth of July, Tony planned on having a barbecue at the marina, as he had been doing for a few years now. Nobody from the neighborhood intended on showing up, Jim told me. "Nobody talks to this guy," he said. "Nobody."

TONY HAD ALREADY TOLD ME about the Fourth of July community barbecue, and, even before talking with Jim and Carol, I was wondering what kind of turnout there would be. That many of the residents in Money Island did not like him was not news to Tony, or something he had tried to keep secret from me. He talked often about his sometimes contentious relationship with Steve Fleetwood, the Bivalve oysterman who rented one of the marina's docks, and their disputes over details like rent and the unending costs associated with repairs and upkeep.

Tony had scheduled the community barbecue for July 1 because it fell on a Saturday. It was a hot, stagnant afternoon on the bay. The air was vibrating with hungry greenheads that drew blood with every bite. I arrived early and found Muenker in his usual spot behind the desk in the bait shack, rolling cigarettes. A teenager who Tony had hired for the summer was busy out on the marina dock, cleaning crabs and clams. Tony was anxiously bouncing from Muenker in the bait shack to the young man on the dock. He pointed to a battered crab boat and told me if I stuck around, the captain would be giving people free rides around the creek mouth.

With everyone too busy to talk, I milled around the dock. It was in great shape, as good as anything my mother's cousin had ever had at Husted's Landing. At its edges were Tony's aquaculture tanks for his nascent shedder crab business, which was struggling. Crowded in the center were a few picnic tables shaded by umbrellas. At one table an older couple was sitting, swatting greenheads and watching Tony zip about. Their names were Ed and Peg and, though they didn't live in Money Island, they kept their boat at one of the marina's slips during the summer. The slip was out on Nantuxent Drive, next to the oyster docks. The fishing on the bay had been lousy, they said, and half the time they couldn't get to their boat because of how bad the road flooded. "Does anyone live in those houses over there?" Peg said, pointing to the Bayview Road side of town. "I don't ever see anyone coming in or out of them."

As I sat and talked with Ed and Peg, Steve Fleetwood showed up with a box of oysters, which he was giving to Tony on the house, as he did every year. He and Tony immediately jumped into a conversation about the DEP. "One of their people were here yesterday," Tony said. Fleetwood asked what for. "The usual issues," Tony said. Fleetwood nodded knowingly. He stroked his white handlebar mustache with his thumb as he listened to Tony speak. He wore dark sunglasses, and when he finally removed them and perched them on his baseball cap, there were razor-edged tan lines running from the corners of his eyes to his temples. Fleetwood, like all the watermen, was disheartened by the Blue Acres buyouts in Money Island, but his position was unique, given how closely he had to work with the DEP and other state agencies in order to operate Bivalve Packing, the largest oyster operation on the Bayshore. He listened to Tony, nodding politely, but said little. I detected a slight, guarded respect between the two men. Both understood how hard it was to maintain a fishing operation on the Bayshore these days, and if you were trying—well, at least you were trying.

Fleetwood didn't stick around for the party. By then, around twenty people were sitting at the picnic tables on the dock. A handful of people were down on the floating docks, sitting in fold-out chairs and casting lines into the creek, hoping for the odd perch to bite. One woman was walking her dog in the marina parking lot. She told me she had, just by chance, seen a mention of the barbecue on Facebook and decided to make the twenty-minute drive over from Millville, where she lived, to check it out. She seemed amazed that such a place existed just a few minutes from home. But the greenheads were torturing her dog. "He's never experienced bugs like this before," the woman said.

Tony then announced that he would be giving a demonstration on how to prepare a soft-shell crab for cooking. Almost the entire party gathered around him as he pulled a soft-shell from a nearby cooler. The woman with the dog leaned in to take pictures. Tony grabbed a pair of scissors and said, "Clip off their faces and that does it." That subdued the crab so it was more easily cooked on the frying pan. I had never seen Tony look so proud. He was clearly in his element. Then someone in the crowd asked him how to tell when a soft-shell was ready. It should have been a softball for any aquaculturist, but Tony faltered. He racked his brain for a few seconds but couldn't come up with an answer, so he called out to the crabber who'd brought the boat for the day. "When the females have pink on their bellies, that's when they're good for eating," the crabber said. "Ah," Tony said. "When the females have pink on their bellies." I looked around the crowd that had gathered to watch Tony's demonstration. Other than Bill and Paula Bowen, an elderly couple who lived on Nantuxent Drive, there wasn't a single Money Island resident there—unless you counted Muenker, but since parties made him grumpy, he had cloistered himself in the bait shack, glued to his captain's chair.

After Tony was finished and the soft-shell crabs were cooking, I sat with Bill and Paula at one of the picnic tables. The sun was almost directly overhead and it was nearing a hundred degrees without a hint of wind. We marveled about how the weather swung in such drastic directions. Bill talked about a deep freeze in the 1970s, when people drove their cars out onto the bay. Near us, tables were stacked with banquet tins full of steamed crabs, clams, barbecued oysters, corn on the cob, hot dogs, hamburgers, and all kinds of grilled vegetables. The *Martha Meerwald*, built in 1909, slipped out of the creek and into the bay, on its way to Bivalve for repairs. "Worked on her when I was a boy," Bill said. We talked about how the watermen preferred the old boats over the new. "They hate the feel," Bill said of the modern steel-hulled boats.

Jim and Carol Giles, of course, were nowhere to be found. Nor was Campbell. Like Jim and Carol, I had once been suspicious of Tony's motives for buying the marina only to turn around and attempt to sell it to the state or an investor who could then turn it into the aquaculture hub Tony truly believed it could be. But I questioned the assertion that he wanted to see the town—or even the neighbors who disliked him—go away. Tony was in fact desperate for the camaraderie and celebration that Jim and Carol talked about. His only downfall was that he craved to be the voice of a community that did not crave a voice. He wanted Money Island to be a prominent place on the map—he had even added a pin for it on Google Maps. It had been his dream to save a rural community ever since his college days, when he had written in his school newspaper that they only needed "a little help, in the form of professional advice and financial assistance."

Instead of Money Islanders, most of Tony's guests were from his other life, his more cosmopolitan life—the life that I, along with his father and brothers, worried he should have stuck with. Once, when I was talking with Mike and Kate about the demise of Money Island and Tony's attempts to revive the marina, Mike offered an answer as to why Tony had so far been unsuccessful. "He's not from here, you know?" Mike said. "He just don't know our ways."

TWELVE

"TREE CITY USA"

IF YOU DIDN'T LOOK BEYOND CUMBERLAND COUNTY, it was easy to conclude that Blue Acres was not welcome in the rest of the towns the program had targeted after Sandy. In fact, the truth was the opposite. Inevitably, there was initial local resistance to the idea that the state was interested in eliminating whole neighborhoods, some of which had homes that had been in families for generations, but rather quickly residents fell in line and sold out. Certainly, no other elected official in New Jersey had declared the introduction of Blue Acres buyouts in their municipality a "line in the sand," as Campbell had. Nor had they distributed bumper stickers declaring "No Retreat."

Nowhere had the buyouts been more publicized than in Sayreville, the working-class Central Jersey town where Christie had announced in May of 2013 that Blue Acres had been infused with $300 million from the Sandy Disaster Relief Act. Sayreville was one of the first towns that Christie had visited in the days after Sandy, along with New Jersey rock icon Jon Bon Jovi, who had grown up there. "Some of the people I met that day have been in my mind for the last nearly seven months," Christie had said at the event. "I saw and felt emotion that day that I saw and felt in very few places across the state; really tough, gritty people who had just been beaten down and needed some help."

I too had a vivid memory of Sayreville from the days after Sandy. It was only a fleeting moment, but it had been seared into my mind, because it was in Sayreville where I first saw Sandy's destruction. I had jumped in a van with volunteers who were heading for Staten Island, to help hand out toiletries and other household goods in the town of Tottenville, whose Raritan Bay–adjacent neighborhood had been slammed by an enormous storm surge. As we drove north on the Garden State Parkway, there had been little evidence that a catastrophic hurricane had just passed through, other than downed tree limbs and the caravans of out-of-state utility trucks that had begun pouring into the Jersey Shore and New York to aid in the recovery effort. But as we approached Cheesequake Creek, a tributary of Raritan Bay on the southeast corner of Sayreville, Sandy's wrath suddenly came into stark relief.

Where the Parkway passed over the creek, there was a marina just to the east. On normal days, the marina was accented by a line of sailboats and powerboats neatly slotted into floating docks, but on this day, it was as if a bomb had exploded beneath them. The boats had been tossed far back onto high ground, as far as I could see. Huge sailboats lay on their sides, their keels jammed into the soggy earth, masts bristling in grotesque directions. Several boats were neatly stacked on top of each other, and others were wedged in a stand of trees on the other side of the lot. It had occurred to me at that moment that I had never seen such destruction from a hurricane, and I remember having a physical reaction to the sight not unlike the surge of terror one experiences when witnessing a horrific accident. I was also perplexed. The marina, and Sayreville as a whole, were far back from the Atlantic coast—how could the surge have gone so far inland? This was before New Jersey had fully absorbed the fact that some of the worst of Sandy's damages occurred in back-bay and riverine communities, not just on the Atlantic coast.

What I was seeing, however, was just the beginning of the surge's impact on Sayreville. On the other side of the borough, the Washington Canal, a nearly two-hundred-year-old bypass built to expedite transport between the South and Raritan Rivers, had peaked at fourteen feet above its normal level at the height of Sandy. The canal sat just a few hundred feet from Weber Avenue—a perfectly suburban street lined with shady pine, birch, and crabapple trees, where cul-de-sacs were punctuated with basketball hoops and the spacious, bicycle-cluttered front yards of modest one- and two-story red brick or vinyl-sided homes. Before Sandy hit, the neighborhood was already struggling—the previous summer, Hurricane Irene had roared through, causing severe flooding. Now, every one of the seventy-five homes on the block had been impacted by Sandy's catastrophic surge.

When Christie announced the creation of the Superstorm Sandy Blue Acres Program in Sayreville, residents of Weber Avenue had been among the large crowd cheering. It was a ceremonious beginning to the program— one that made it easy to presume that it would be welcomed throughout the state's Sandy-ravaged communities, not loathed like it would be in Money Island. Within two months of Christie's visit, $29.5 million had been allocated to begin targeting 129 homes in Sayreville, most of which were on Weber Avenue and neighboring MacArthur Avenue. In part because of its residents' positive interest in Blue Acres, Sayreville had been chosen as the first community to be targeted.

I WANTED TO FIGURE OUT why Blue Acres had been so accepted in Sayreville, so on a scorching day in July, I drove the two hours north up the Garden State Parkway, from Ocean City, to meet with Art Rittenhouse, the town's unofficial spokesman and commissioner of the borough's Shade Tree Commission. Appropriately, Rittenhouse was waiting for me in the Sayreville Borough Hall parking lot, under the cool, outstretched shadow of a sprawling red oak that had been planted on the borough's centennial in 1976 and officially named the "Liberty Tree." He didn't get out of his minivan but instead wound down the passenger-side window and told me to hop in.

"It's terrible out there," Rittenhouse said after I shut the door. He cranked the air-conditioning to high. He was in his early seventies, uniformly round, and immediately cheerful. Instead of turning toward me to talk, he went on casually looking forward, as if we were old friends taking off on our usual drive. "I do these tours because I'm semi-retired," he said. I noticed the American flag printed on his T-shirt, and that his baseball cap, pulled tight over his forehead, read, "Tree City USA." Sayreville, Rittenhouse told me, had recently been honored as a Tree City

USA community by the Arbor Day Foundation. In addition to heading up the Shade Tree Commission, Rittenhouse was the chair of the
Sayreville Republican Party. He'd worked hard canvassing the town in
the run-up to the 2016 presidential election. As we left Borough Hall
and passed homes with "Make America Great Again" signs still pegged
in their front lawns, Rittenhouse allowed a gratified smile, then began
talking about Blue Acres. His sister-in-law had sold her Sandy-ravaged
home to the state through the program, and had been happy with the
$250,000 she received.

Weber and MacArthur Avenues were less than a mile away from Borough Hall, but almost the entire drive was slightly downhill, toward the
Washington Canal. The neighborhood we passed through was tidy, unremarkable blue-collar suburbia, until we stopped at a traffic light just
before MacArthur. All of a sudden, there were a few homes elevated at
an awkward height. You expect to see elevated homes along the coast,
where the surrounding landscape is one of sand dunes or marshland, not
densely packed, tree-shaded ranchers in the Newark suburbs. Rittenhouse
pointed out that they had been raised after Sandy, since this part of the
borough was included in FEMA's adjusted flood maps. As we drove along
MacArthur, there were more homes that had been recently elevated. At a
restaurant that Rittenhouse said had been closed since Sandy, we made a
left onto Weber Avenue, the street closest to the Washington Canal.

What I saw made it difficult to envisage the tight-knit neighborhood
street that Rittenhouse described it as once being. Almost all of that was
absent. There remained only one basketball hoop, half covered by a tangle
of tree branches and shrubs at the cul-de-sac of an empty street named
Beekman. Concrete driveway entrances all along Weber led into empty,
overgrown nothingness. There were about twelve homes still standing
along the street, although some of them were vacant, their Blue Acres
settlements yet to be finalized for one reason or another. Rittenhouse
guessed that most of the remaining homeowners in the neighborhood
were now considering selling out to Blue Acres, much like the residents of
Nantuxent Drive were in the wake of the Bayview Road exodus. Perhaps
sensing my preoccupation with how abandoned the whole place looked, so
long after the demolition had occurred, Rittenhouse answered the ques-

tion I'd been pondering. "By the end of the year," he said, "there'll be trees planted all along here."

Rittenhouse was referring to a rehabilitation and resiliency project, headed by Rutgers University, which would revitalize the now-vacant lots. Up until this point—summer of 2017—Blue Acres was steadily moving toward its goal of acquiring thirteen hundred properties statewide. The program had made nearly nine hundred offers, almost seven hundred of which had been accepted. In Sayreville alone, 148 properties had been purchased. And, statewide, almost five hundred homes had been demolished. One problem was that, once demolitions were over, some municipalities were on the hook for the upkeep of their newly acquired open space. Like Lawrence Township, Sayreville had struggled to find the funds for maintenance. Open space also meant increased areas of opportunity for unsavory behavior. For many residents who decided to remain in these now-gutted neighborhoods, a once safe place could be dangerous—not just because of the gaping holes left by uprooted homes, but by the heightened risk of vandalism and theft that comes with large parcels of abandoned property. With each additional acre of unkempt open space, the need for a solution was becoming more dire.

Indeed, Sayreville's collaboration with Rutgers was the first attempt at revitalizing a Superstorm Sandy Blue Acres Program acquisition—a full five years after the storm. It had been two years since the last homes on Weber and MacArthur Avenues were demolished, but still nothing had been done. It wasn't until 2016 that Rutgers had released a final report laying out a plan that would take into account both public access and flood resilience. The forty-two-page report's primary objectives were to "protect the safety and health of the Borough residents by encouraging homeowners to relocate permanently to higher elevations" and to "restore the natural function of the floodplain to promote storage and infiltration of stormwater in appropriate areas, particularly during significant storm events." Rittenhouse was excited about the project, which he reiterated would be starting very soon, once funding was secured. The borough had estimated that the project would cost about a half million dollars, and they were hoping to pay for it with a hodgepodge of grant money—from the federal government, from the DEP, and from various nonprofits. Once all the funding and permits were secured, the borough expected the project to take four or five years to finish—which would make its completion just under a decade after Sandy. (By the winter of 2019, no work had begun on Weber Avenue; instead, one home that had been abandoned after the initial buyout had caught fire and remained standing, a half-incinerated blight beside a handful of weary holdouts.)

Sayreville was the kind of New Jersey municipality that embodied the benefit of the United States' great strides in environmental regulation over the last half century. In the early 1800s, it and much of the rest of Middlesex County became key farming communities because of their proximity to New York City. By the middle of that century, steamboats crowded the Raritan River, competing to transport passengers and goods—namely apples, peaches, pears, and other fruits—to Manhattan and Brooklyn, which were just twenty miles away by water. But by the turn of the century, Sayreville had remade itself into a brick-making hub. As Rittenhouse and I drove along MacArthur, he pointed out an old apartment building built by the Sayreville-Fisher Brick Company in the early part of the twentieth century. Sayreville-Fisher bricks, he said proudly, could be found in the Empire State Building, the Statue of Liberty, and the Brooklyn Bridge. The company, he went on, had "pretty much built the town." Owens-Illinois, the glass giant who'd fueled Cumberland County's industrial boom years in the 1950s and '60s, had also had an enormous plant in Sayreville.

Through the first half of the twentieth century, Sayreville, and Middlesex County as a whole, had evolved, like much of the New Jersey cities and towns adjacent to New York City, into a community overrun by industry and the pollution that came with it. In Sayreville, no material or chemical was too toxic or terrifying for the factories that lined the banks of its rivers. They produced insecticides, electronic parts, film, detergents, lead-based paint products, and nuclear materials, piling the wetlands with industrial waste and New York City trash.

In 1983, the EPA finalized its first Superfund National Priorities List, revealing that New Jersey had the most toxic waste sites in the country. It continues to have the most toxic waste sites, and Middlesex County has the most in the state. In the 1820s, a passenger on a steamboat traveling along the Raritan River wrote of the shoreline's "broad green salt meadows that stretch off like soft carpets until they meet the clay beds and tangled woods of the Jersey Shore." By the 1970s, that same shoreline was an industrial wasteland, accented not by blankets of salt hay meadows but smoke stacks and mountainous, toxic waste–laced dumps. The Raritan River and Bay—which once had some of the most profitable oyster beds in the state, behind the Bayshore—were effectively dead. When the bottom dropped out of domestic industry in the United States in the 1980s, Sayreville began a slow, economically painful transition into a commuter community. The collapse of industry was no different here than it was in Cumberland County, but Sayreville's advantage was its interconnected, rather than isolated, place in the Northeast Megalopolis. As New York City ascended economically, so too have the hundreds of small communities whose residents make up a significant percentage of its workforce.

Rittenhouse was keen to show me the rest of Sayreville, which, he said, was undergoing a revitalization that had in part been sparked by Sandy. On Jernee Mill Road, he pointed out the Owens-Illinois factory, which now housed a logistics company. We passed the Starland Ballroom, where, in the early 1980s, Jon Bon Jovi, who at that point was still just John Bongiovi, met Richie Sambora. The windowless brick venue, which had been shuttered for nearly a year after being flooded by Sandy, was set back from the road, behind an enormous, empty parking lot. A digital sign advertised upcoming shows by Modest Mouse, the Descendents, and Skid Row. Rittenhouse talked about another blazing hot day, in July of 2013, when Jon Bon Jovi came to Borough Hall to present a check for a million dollars to Christie and his wife, Mary Pat, who was overseeing the Hurricane Sandy New Jersey Relief Fund. "My wife was born and raised here," Rittenhouse said. I asked him if he was as well. He was not; he was from nearby Sussex County. "Sparta High," he said with reverence.

Beyond the Starland Ballroom and the old Owens-Illinois plant, signs of Sayreville's revitalization began springing up everywhere. Jernee Mill Road formed a loop around the borough, and as we dipped farther from the downtown district, the scars of Sayreville's industrial past gave way to stately maple, oak, birch, gum, and walnut forest, much of which was now preserved through Green Acres. It was midday now and the temperature had neared a hundred degrees. We passed Old Bridge Chemicals, and then a pasture and stables carved into the woods, where a few horses had gathered under the shade of a stand of trees. "Can't blame them on a day like this," Rittenhouse said. Not far back in the woods—I would later learn, since Rittenhouse didn't mention it—was the Red Oak electrical power plant and another hazardous waste cleanup site where the chemical company Hercules Incorporated had allowed the insecticide DDT to leach into the groundwater.

We drove on, rounding our way back toward town, past the Shri Dwarkadhish Temple, which occupied a former YMCA building. It was one of the largest Hindu temples in New Jersey. Three miles down the road, past a September 11 memorial, Rittenhouse turned into another enormous parking lot, this one to service the 138,000-square-foot Faith Fellowship Ministries megachurch. Just behind the church was a vast construction site along a wide bend in the Raritan River. Here was where one of New Jersey's most egregious Superfund sites once sat—in 1934 the land was purchased by National Lead, which spent the next half century producing paint pigment and dumping PCBs, titanium dioxide, and "technologically enhanced naturally occurring radioactive material" into an adjacent lagoon.

The site had been abandoned in the 1980s, but in 2014 the EPA ordered the company, now called NL Industries (increased scientific understanding, in the mid-twentieth century, of the adverse health effects of low-level lead exposure, especially in children, must have made the company's original name problematic), to pay $79 million to clean up the lagoon. When the project began, the EPA, DEP, and the real estate developers who'd bought the land learned they'd underestimated how wildly polluted the site was. In some areas, a ten-foot-thick layer of an "acidic paintlike substance" had been found—one of the developers likened it to quicksand. When complete, the estimated $2 billion project would be home to The Pointe, a 418-acre retail complex, featuring a two-hundred-thousand-square-foot Bass Pro Shops retail outlet along with a movie theater, office spaces, a hotel, and apartments. The state was even picking up most of the tab for an entirely new interchange that would connect to the Garden State Parkway, which ran directly past the site.

Rittenhouse and I eventually parked at the Ken Buchanan Riverfront Park, about a mile upriver from Weber and MacArthur Avenues. A power plant towered from the shoreline just a few hundred yards away. A few people, despite the scorching sun, stood on a walkway at the river's edge, casting fishing lines into the brown, glassy water. Rittenhouse still had the air-conditioning turned to high, and neither one of us was interested in stepping outside the minivan. The park was new, and it lacked any shade trees. Rittenhouse pointed across the river, toward huge earthen hills, some of which made up the Kin-Buc Landfill, once a state-approved dumpsite for industrial and municipal solid and liquid wastes. It was one of the earliest sites on the national Superfund list. "There we have the local mountains," Rittenhouse laughed.

I couldn't wait to leave. The only moment I did not feel hemmed in by the crush of suburbia, industry, asphalt, concrete, and toxic waste was the brief moment driving through the patches of Green Acres open space on Jernee Mill Road. Since its inception in 1961, the Green Acres program had preserved nearly seven hundred thousand acres statewide. There was no doubt that places like Sayreville, where the natural environment was for a time nearly purged by the insatiable appetite of industry, were on a gradual path back to some vague semblance of health. I guessed 2.5 million square feet of retail space was better than a forty-acre, lead-laced lagoon.

Ironically, the Bayshore's isolation, and the decades of inattention from industry and the state, had saved it from the overdeveloped fate its residents feared most. The question facing the state now was, could it continue to keep the Bayshore the pristine, shining example of conservation without also keeping its residents locked in an unending state of economic disadvantage? In a densely populated state like New Jersey, where precious acreage is increasingly being chewed away by the rising sea, would the concept of conservation, as it is understood in the traditional sense—the restoration of the natural environment and wildlife—and applied under the Green Acres mandate, have to be reimagined in a way that preservation didn't necessarily mean denuding the landscape of all human habitation?

The problem wasn't Blue Acres or any of the other open space programs under Green Acres—the problem was encapsulated in the aggravating phrase I had heard repeated constantly by everyone I talked to about the Bayshore's crumbling in the decades before Sandy and its collapse after: "cost benefit." So long as the federal government, New Jersey, and other coastal American states went on allocating funding for protection against sea level rise on the basis of communities' contributions to government coffers, "retreat" would always be the solution for those communities that couldn't meet the cost-benefit formula, and "remain" would always be the solution for those communities that could.

I was reminded of a conversation I'd had with Larry Hanja, a DEP spokesperson, who had been sympathetic toward Campbell's "No Retreat" campaign but nonetheless careful not to offer an opinion, according to the rules under which Blue Acres operated. "[Mayor Campbell] would love to see sewer lines built out there, wide beaches and dunes—something similar to what's going on on the ocean side," Hanja told me. "But the fact of the matter is you can't justify it through cost-benefit analysis." He was correct, of course. Under such a rubric, you could no longer justify the entire Bayshore. But that didn't answer the question of why one group of people and the land they lived upon was not as important as another, especially when the land that both groups were living upon was sinking equally fast.

THIRTEEN

"I'M JUST A DUMB FISHERMAN."

IT WAS JUST ABOUT 5 A.M. when I came around Pete's Corner, as old Bill Bowen called the last bend on Newport Neck Road before the pavement straightened out into a narrow line the rest of the way to Money Island. I was surprised to see that in the distance, the streetlights on the Bayview Road side of town were still working. In the predawn blackness, the roofs of the abandoned homes were stained orange by the lights' glow, which accentuated the dried salt clouding their windows and the cracks and gaps and sags in their exteriors and decks. In the other direction, however, along Nantuxent Drive, there was life on the water. The bright white of the oyster fleet's spotlights, mounted on their towers, hovered like dislodged stars above the darkness of Nantuxent Creek. It had been a good season out on the bay, and there were still a few months to go.

Just past Tony's trailer at 228 Nantuxent, I turned into the tiny dirt parking area between the road and Bivalve Packing's dock. A young waterman who had arrived early was sitting in his truck, scrolling through his phone. His face was cast in a soft blue. A few minutes later, the captain, Steve Fleetwood Jr., pulled up next to us. Although I had gotten to know his father during the past year, this was the first time I met Steve Jr. He was stockier than his father, who was lean and tall, and he didn't possess the gruffness that his father sometimes had when first meeting someone. Rather than taking some time to warm up to you, Steve Jr. was immediately accommodating, exuding the good ol' boy openness that I'd come to know and cherish as I had been rediscovering the Bayshore.

I followed Steve Jr. into the small wheelhouse of *Kelly's Pride*, a former crab and scallop dredge boat that Bivalve Packing had picked up from a Chesapeake outfit about ten years ago. At thirty-seven years old and forty-one feet, she was one of the newest and smallest oyster boats working the Jersey side of the bay. Steve Jr. told me to make myself comfortable as he got busy organizing the day's paperwork he had to fill out for the DEP. As he got ready, the young waterman I'd seen waiting in his truck came sleepily aboard, along with three other older watermen who seemed unbothered by the raw hour. They tossed day bags stocked with snacks, drinks, and cigarettes down inside the cabin below the helm, then slipped into their white-bibbed oilskins. After Steve Jr. made the call to a DEP dispatch line notifying them that he was heading out—as every oyster boat captain was required to do—the crew untied the lines and we pushed off. Sunrise was still an hour away.

We moved smoothly through Nantuxent Creek's narrow, shallow mouth, just a stone's throw away from Tony's public fishing docks, so as to stay in the channel. While the young waterman climbed down in the cabin to catch some sleep on the ride out, the three other crewmen sat at the galley table next to the helm, sipping on thermoses of coffee. Steve Jr. was quiet, focusing on moving us gingerly through Nantuxent Cove, the narrowest part of the channel. It had been a long time since the cove had last been sounded, and the channel markers were no longer accurate. Apparently, resetting them was not high on the priority list of the DEP's Bureau of Coastal Engineering, which was in charge of setting and maintaining the state's aids to navigation. Anyway, neither Steve Jr. nor the rest of Money Island's watermen followed the markers—they knew the route by heart, with a little help from sonar. Getting grounded on the hard-packed sand of the cove was an expensive endeavor, no matter if you were heading out or coming home, although coming home could be particularly devastating: if you were stuck with a load of oysters on a hot summer day, and weren't able to move for a few hours, you'd probably have to dump your catch due to spoilage. When I remarked to Steve Jr. how much of a risk I thought it was for Bayshore oystermen's businesses that the channel wasn't properly marked, let alone dredged, he just shook his head and smiled. "We're used to it," he said, without breaking focus on the darkness ahead.

From the cove channel, the Bayview Road side of Money Island was about two hundred yards off port. All three men at the galley table turned, instinctively it seemed, to look out the window at the passing shoreline and its broken row of homes. They called upon their individual memories of the vibrant neighborhood that had once stood there. The conversation then turned, as it so often did on the oyster boats, to the fate of Money Island and the role that the DEP played in that fate.

It had now been almost two years since Blue Acres announced it had targeted the Bayview Road side of town, yet all the DEP had done to the homes was affix No Trespassing placards on their front doors. Even if the DEP had regularly issued public information to Bayshore residents not directly involved in the buyouts, few residents, especially the men aboard *Kelly's Pride*, had time to keep up. So, facing a constant vortex of local rumors in lieu of concrete information from the DEP, most watermen saw only what was before them when heading out into the bay for work every morning: an inaccurately marked channel that the state would never get around to approving for dredging, and a neighborhood that, instead of being converted to an attractive parcel of open space, had been bought and abandoned, allowed to fall apart piece by piece.

For the watermen, the more pressing question was not the fate of the Bayview Road side of Money Island—that was now clear—but what was going to happen to the Nantuxent Drive side. Despite its remoteness, despite its flooding, despite its residents' feuding, Money Island's commercial fishing fleet was still landing $10 million in oysters, plus tens of thousands more in blue crabs, annually. Because of the state's strict, FDA-mandated "time to refrigeration" requirements—in place to curb the spread of *Vibrio*, a naturally occurring bacterium in shellfish that can cause food poisoning—it wasn't possible in the summer months to run a load of oysters from the productive upper bay beds to Bivalve before the temperature onboard got too high. So Money Island, located between the upper bay beds and Bivalve, was the only port to land their catch before it spoiled. Instead of installing refrigerators on the ancient boats, which would be both costly and take up precious deck space, the majority of the oyster companies, like Steve Fleetwood's Bivalve Packing, simply had refrigerated trucks drive from their packing and processing houses in Bivalve and elsewhere on the Bayshore to Money Island, where they would wait for the boats to come in and offload before midday. "If Money goes," one of the watermen, a burly guy named Bill, said, "where do we go?"

Bill wanted to know what everyone thought about the state buying up the Bayshore because it wanted to profit from the sea of oil, or maybe it was natural gas, that people said was beneath the marshland and bay seafloor. I was familiar with this conspiracy theory, as well as others, and first heard it from Mike. He'd often told a story about how his father would come home after fishing up Cedar Creek and talk about seeing flames burst from the marsh mud. Mike's father might have been seeing things, but then again he might have not—the marshland's constant anaerobic decay of plant material produces carbon, which if trapped in the mud can ferment into a pocket of methane. A well-placed cigarette or piece of metal heating in the sun, for example, could be enough to ignite the pocket. The methane, of course, was what gave the marshland its pungent, yet oddly sweet, smell.

Not quite a conspiracy theory, but nonetheless another example of the perception that the state did not have the best interests of the Bayshore's residents in mind, was the long-simmering desire of a succession of Trenton legislators to build a bridge across the bay, from Delaware to somewhere along the Bayshore. This trepidation had roots in the earliest days of Money Island and Bay Point. In 1961, Democratic gubernatorial candidate Richard J. Hughes promised that, if he were elected, he'd build a six-and-a-half-mile, $97 million toll bridge that would span from Bombay Hook Point, Delaware, to Sea Breeze. Later, in 2000, six Drexel University civil engineering students, who called themselves Millennium 6, proposed a thirteen-mile bridge-and-tunnel project that would span from Kitts Hummock, Delaware, to Fortescue. Though nothing had come of either proposal (even though Hughes was elected governor in 1962), the state's keen interest in the bridge, like the secret knowledge of oil and gas reserves, had become lore in the Bayshore communities. Because the state would never have the support of the Bayshore communities to buy the land needed for the bridge, the theory went, they were instead doing it underhandedly, through Blue and Green Acres purchases. "You know why the state wants to buy all the land?" Campbell had once told me. "So they can build that bridge."

Next to Bill sat a fidgety, leathered man named Johnny. He nodded his head as Bill told familiar stories about people seeing bursts of flames from the marsh mud. "Could be," Johnny said with a voice made growly by a lifetime of smoking. "You never know what these bastards want." Another waterman, a quiet man named Joe, only nodded his head. He preferred to continue looking out the window, which now pointed south as Steve Jr. motored toward Shell Rock bed, eight miles up the bay. The sun had crept above the horizon now, a brilliant pink smudged by the purple-blue haze of what would soon be a hot, breathless morning.

It was an unmistakable summer sun, but also a special one. Later that day, the entirety of North America would experience a total solar eclipse, an event that hadn't occurred since 1979. For weeks, there had been intense buildup in the media and among friends of mine in Ocean City for the eclipse. Reporters were stationed in the best locations to witness it, the safety glasses to view it had sold out, and even US treasury secretary Steven Mnuchin and his wife, the actress Louise Linton, were flying to Kentucky on the taxpayers' dime to watch the damn thing. On the *Kelly's Pride*, everyone shrugged when I asked about their plans for the event. Bill said, "Oh, is that today?" The rest of the guys had to work their other jobs. In that moment, I could feel the remoteness of the Bayshore, but also its roughhewn authenticity. It felt insulated and safe. As we eased over Shell Rock bed, the shore of Delaware sat three miles away, its marshland and trees appearing as a wavering, steel gray line above the glassy surface of the bay.

At just after 6 a.m., Steve Jr. dropped the *Kelly's Pride*'s dredges into the water. We were slightly south of the Ship John shoal and lighthouse, where I'd spent countless hours as a boy, fishing for weakfish and striped bass, and where Steve Jr.'s grandfather had been the last keeper before the light became fully automated in 1973. A horn on the lighthouse let out a

deafening blare every couple of minutes that would have been almost impossible to endure for anyone who hadn't experienced it before. The crew
was too busy to be bothered by it—or, more probably, they didn't even
hear it anymore. For me, the sound induced a flood of memories. When I
was a boy, on those summer nights when the wind blew from the south,
I sat in my bedroom with the windows open and listened to the horn's
faint blare. Fishing Ship John was always the most intense because, in the
early 1990s, it was one of the most productive areas of the bay. During
the summer weakfish runs, boats would anchor so closely together around
the lighthouse and shoal that fishermen could—and sometimes did—jump
from boat to boat when hooked up on a big weakfish that had decided to
take off. The best way to catch a big weakfish was by casting heavy lead
lures, which required a much higher level of talent and fitness than simply
dropping a baited hook to the bottom and waiting for a bite. Those who
could cast the best caught the most, and those who caught the most were
noticed by all the fishermen nearby. I had been a decent caster when I was
young, but all that I learned had been forgotten in the years since I'd left
the Bayshore and more or less quit fishing.

Now, there wasn't a single boat in the vicinity of Ship John. The lighthouse's coat of crimson paint had faded—a tired version of the color I
remembered from my boyhood. It had been years since anyone had caught
a big weakfish or striper out here, and, now that catch limits were so strict,
few fishermen wasted their time or boat fuel to make the trip. That these
fish hardly existed in the bay bothered me. I knew I had been a part of
the problem. In those days of abundance before the collapse, near the end
of the 1990s, we would race to Ship John after school to catch the last
few hours of light, and still fill up our coolers with dozens of mature fish.
Standing on the deck of the *Kelly's Pride*, seeing the bay completely void
of a single fisherman on what was otherwise a perfect summer day for
fishing, I wondered how many of those fish were wasted. I could remember our freezer at home sometimes overflowing with frozen fish fillets, a
lot of them never to be eaten. There was plenty of disagreement between
Bayshore watermen and conservationists about open space, sea level rise,
and anthropogenic climate change, but almost everyone agreed that too

many fish had been taken from the bay for too many years. "We didn't need all them fish," Mike had told me one day.

The 1990s were just as devastating for the bay's oyster stocks. Since 1957, the year the outbreak of the MSX parasite caused the collapse of the industry, small, slow gains had been made on the oyster beds—just enough to keep the industry breathing. The 1990 season had been one of the best in years, but late that summer, the researchers at the Rutgers University Haskin Shellfish Research Laboratory in Bivalve—an expansion of the original lab run by Dr. Thurlow C. Nelson, who had helped discover MSX—identified in Delaware Bay oysters another parasitic disease called Dermo, which some scientists think has migrated north from southern waters, where it originated in the 1940s, with the gradually warming ocean. In the 1950s, Nelson and his fellow scientists at the shellfish lab had found trace amounts of Dermo in bay oysters, due to the then-commonplace industry practice of importing Chesapeake Bay seed oysters. But they'd never seen an outbreak like the one that came a few decades later at the end of that bumper season of 1990. In response, the state closed the entirety of their lease grounds between 1992 and 1994, effectively shutting down the Bayshore oyster industry.

In an effort to jumpstart the industry, the state legislature passed, in 1996, a resolution that established a task force to oversee oyster fishing in the bay. That same year, the Delaware Bay Shellfish Council, which is made up exclusively of Bayshore oystermen, including Steve Fleetwood, who has served as council chairman several times, agreed to impose a per-bushel tax on themselves in order to create a fund for the transplantation of oyster shell, or cultch, each spring, just prior to the beginning of the season. The council, together with the tax, not only went a long way toward improving the health of the bay's oysters; it also helped bring together what had become, since the 1957 collapse, a fractured operation in which oystermen worked for and with themselves, not as a union. With forward-thinking watermen like the Fleetwoods, the Delaware Bay oyster industry was finally gaining strength again.

Steve Jr. stood at a console positioned on the starboard side of the deck, where he could steer the boat, operate the dredges, keep an eye on his location via a GPS screen, and watch his crew sort the catch. Shell Rock was one of the bay's most productive beds—in all it spanned almost fifteen hundred acres and held some seven hundred million oysters, about a quarter of the bay's entire stock. The harvesting of oysters from Shell Rock, as with all the state-owned beds, was regulated through annual quotas that were based on the previous year's harvest and the deliberation of the Shellfish Council, which made the final decision on quotas for each of the bay's eighty license holders in an annual meeting, held at the Haskin Lab. Bivalve Packing held a third of the quota, the most of any oyster outfit operating on the bay.

Today, Steve Jr. was working a roughly ten-acre-size quadrant, moving the *Kelly's Pride* from one end to the other in a zigzag pattern, much like a groundskeeper would mow a football field. Steve Jr. controlled, via hydraulic winches, the two dredges, which were three-foot-wide chain-link scoops that, when deployed correctly, raked the bottom enough to scoop up the layer of oysters sitting on its surface. Steve Jr., like all the oyster captains I'd watched work the bay, made this process look deceptively easy. It was not. Steve Jr. had to work the dredges independently, staggering them so that while one was up, the other was down. For the dredge that was up, Steve Jr. had to smoothly swing the boom it was connected to into a hopper attached to the gunwale, which would trip a latch at the base of the dredge and release the oysters into the hopper. As he swung the empty dredge back out over the water and released it, he would then direct his attention to the other side of the boat and repeat the same process with the other dredge. The oysters falling into the aluminum hopper had the metallic sound of a jar of coins being poured onto a hard floor.

For the crew, the work was no less difficult. Running from each hopper was a conveyor belt that moved fast, pulling the contents of the hoppers past the crew whose job it was to sort the good, or "market," oysters from the dead oysters, the shells and blue crabs and horseshoe crabs and all manner of other bottom refuse. Often, the dredge would pick up a piece of wood from the hull of a centuries-old wreck, or a colonial-era glass bottle. On another trip, I'd watched as a crewman sifted a piece of a clay pipe from a dredge full of empty shells and mud. The belt moved fast, so a crewman had to instantly know when he was looking at a good market oyster. "You got to be quick but clean," Steve Jr. told me as he simultaneously worked the dredges, watched the GPS, and slipped a glob of chewing tobacco underneath his lower lip. Dredging a healthy bed like Shell Rock was made more difficult by the fact that the oysters came up in clumps of two, three, and sometimes four. Not only did the crewmen have to identify which of the clump was a good oyster, but they then had to separate them by knocking them against the metal edge of the belt. Without the right angle, or with too hard of swing, you'd risk breaking a good oyster. Not once did this happen with Steve Jr.'s crew—one or two swift cracks against the belt's edge and the clump fell perfectly apart. While it meant additional hassle, seeing oysters coming up in clumps was a welcomed sight because it meant that the bed below was healthy and not overfished. At the crew's feet were red plastic bushel baskets, which, once filled, had to be lifted up and carried over to one of six nearby huge metal cages that could hold roughly a ton of oysters each.

On Bivalve Packing's bigger boats, like the 60-foot *Howard W. Sockwell* and the 56-foot *Peter Paynter*, built in 1910 and 1899, respectively, the sorting process was much more automated. On the *Peter Paynter*, which was working beside us, the captain, who happened to be Joe's uncle, didn't have to worry about manually directing the dredges into the hoppers. Nor did the crew have to sort or separate, since the boat was equipped with two huge tumblers that resembled old-time birdcages tipped on their sides. The *Peter Paynter* was the larger, at 55.8 feet, and had just turned ninety-nine years old. Both the *Howard W. Sockwell* and *Peter Payner* had once been proper schooners, meaning they were originally built with fore- and aft-rigged sails. Their wooden hulls, wide and low, were perfectly suited for the shallow, choppy waters of the Delaware Bay. The *Peter Paynter*'s size and more advanced equipment meant that she could harvest more oysters than the *Kelly's Pride*—indeed, not long after dawn she had two cages full before *Kelly's Pride* had one—but Fleetwood preferred the *Kelly's Pride*. "My dad doesn't like all that equipment because it tends to chip the oysters' lips," Steve Jr. told me. Chipping, he said, could cause them to die faster, not to mention make them look less appealing to buyers, who had to satisfy picky consumers in the upscale oyster bars of New York, Philadelphia, and Washington, DC.

The unpredictability of the size and shape of wild-caught Delaware Bay oysters was what, the Fleetwoods thought, made them so special. Each oyster was like a fingerprint—no shell, nor the meat inside it, was the same. Aquaculture, on the other hand, involved coddling the oysters from seed, which ultimately produced a more uniform, market-friendly oyster. For example, Cape May Salt tend to their cages on a regular basis to wash and tumble the oysters, which allows them to form the scooped-out bottom shells, or cups, preferred by restaurants that serve the oysters on the half-shell. By contrast, fishing the bay's natural beds, Steve Jr. said, was like "picking wild raspberries"—you never knew what each dredge would turn up.

Like his father, Steve Jr. preferred wild-caught oysters to aquacultured. But the truth was the wild-caught ones often didn't sell as well in the high-end markets, because they were often too big, or their shells too dirty-looking. I'd heard several oystermen complain about how particular the patrons of high-end oyster bars had become. "You can't get more *organic* than this," Fleetwood had told me one afternoon as we stood in the cavernous refrigerated warehouse at Bivalve Packing's headquarters. He'd reached into a cage of upper bay, perhaps Shell Rock, oysters that had been dredged that morning and grabbed one to show me. The Bayshore oyster industry, he said, was being pushed and pulled by "people with fancy degrees that've never gotten their hands dirty on an oyster boat." He rotated the oyster in his big, calloused palm. The oyster was probably too large and unshapely to be served on a bed of ice next to a lemon wedge in a boutique Manhattan restaurant. "But what do I know?" he went on. "I'm just a dumb fisherman."

The morning quickly took on a quiet, smooth rhythm. Every dredge, it seemed, produced at least a couple dozen high-quality oysters. The wind remained slack and the bay's surface, under the beating sun, took on the color of a well-worn penny. As the men worked, Steve Jr. and I got on the topic of family. He was just three years older than me, so we had briefly attended Cumberland Regional High School at the same time. He'd played baseball with two of my cousins. After a while, we figured that we'd been at the same parties and local bars together at various points in the distant past. At one point, when we were boys, we weren't much different from each other—I'd spent the warm days of my youth on the bay, in my uncle's boat, and the cold days deer or duck hunting. Steve Jr. had done the same—his father had him on the oyster boats as far back as he could remember. As he curled the bill of his baseball cap tight around his eyes and hurled a wad of tobacco spit overboard, Steve Jr. looked at the *Peter Paynter* not far away and told me about two pictures he had at home. One was of him as a boy, standing next to his father on the *Peter Paynter*, as his father drove it around the first bend inside Nantuxent Cove at Money Island. The other picture was of Steve Jr., now a man, running the *Peter Paynter* with his father, his hair and mustache now gray, standing next to him. "I grew up on that boat," Steve Jr. said.

How had our lives gone in such different directions? Maybe it was the road trip across the country that my parents took in college. It could have planted some kind of seed within them that would later cause them to encourage my siblings and me to leave the Bayshore to pursue career and experiential opportunities that our home could not provide. Steve Jr., on the other hand, was more than the recreational waterman that I had been. His great-great-grandfather had been a Port Norris oysterman. This was his destiny. Although I wasn't sure what mine was, I knew it wasn't this. I talked about the years I had lived in California and Australia and New York City, as a college student, magazine editor, and freelance journalist. While Steve Jr. had gotten married and settled down, I had vagabonded around the world, jumping from one odd job to the next. Standing next to Steve Jr., with his T-shirt tucked in, cleanly shaved, round face, and exceptional skill at running the boat, I felt like a child. "It's great that you got away and saw the world," he said, but without envy. A part of me wanted to hear him say, "I wish I'd done that." But he didn't, because he didn't wish that. The life I'd lived seemed to amuse him, but not much else.

The serenity of the morning was suddenly broken by Bill shouting for Steve Jr. to stop the boat. In the current, which Steve Jr. had said earlier was one of the strongest he'd seen in a long time, the port-side dredge cable had snagged the line of a nearby crab pot. We were now dragging some unfortunate crabber's pot behind us, which, with the extra weight, was causing the *Kelly's Pride* to list slightly. Mike, the young waterman, jumped up and, while straddling the moving conveyor belt, leaned out over the water to grab the line. Balancing on the gunwale, he then ran, half-smoked cigarette clutched between his lips, to the stern, where he began hauling up the heavy, wire-mesh pot. While Mike heaved in the pot, Steve Jr. carefully worked the boom toward Joe, who slowly began untying the line from the cable. With one hand on the wheel and another on the lever that controlled the boom, Steve Jr. kept the *Kelly's Pride* pointed into the tide so as to keep the boat from bucking in a crosscurrent. It was, in watermen terms, a scene of pure poetry—each movement from each man brought us one step closer to safety. Within a minute or two, Joe had worked the line loose and Mike had the pot up and sitting on the deck. Then everyone was back to work. "On a small boat like this," Steve Jr. said, "it's important that everyone gets along."

At just after 9:30 a.m., the crew had filled all six oyster cages. As Joe, Mike, Bill, and Johnny went about cleaning up, Steve Jr. went back inside the helm. "Now it's time for the fun stuff," he said. "Paperwork." There was a stack of Fish and Wildlife tags that he had to fill out and attach to each cage, so that they could be recorded. On the ride back to Money Island, Johnny cooked hot dogs and sauerkraut on a little gas grill, then stuffed them in slices of white bread. Eating a meal on the way in from the oyster grounds was a Bayshore oystermen tradition that went back as far as anyone could remember.

On my way off the boat, Steve Jr. handed me a nylon sack of oysters and told me to eat them before they spoiled. I left the dock and made my way over to the marina parking lot. The floating docks were empty and I didn't see Muenker or Tony hanging around. I pulled an oyster from the sack and grabbed a shucking knife I had just bought, walked down to one of the docks, and sat down. The moon was just beginning to pass in front of the sun, and it was as if the natural world was hushing itself—the wind barely registered, the bay lay smooth as oil, the birds sat still on the porch railings of Bayview Road's empty homes. The *Peter Paynter* emerged from the horizon and carefully made its way through the creek's channel. After it passed, its long, even wake reached the dock, causing it to buck gently and creak against its pilings. Several refrigerated trucks rushed into town and turned down Nantuxent Drive to meet the *Kelly's Pride* and *Peter Paynter*. The moon eclipsed the sun and the sky turned a light amber. It took me a few shaky attempts to crack open the oyster, and when I did its precious brine spilled out and over my hands. I cut the oyster loose and tipped it into my mouth. The meat was tender and dense and the same temperature as the bay. I swallowed and, through the saltiness, I could taste the sweetness of the marshland. I dipped my hands in the water to wash off the brine, moving them with the current, against the current.

FOURTEEN

"I THINK IT'S THE BUGS."

THE ONGOING SUCCESS of the 2017 oyster season highlighted what I was coming to see as the Bayshore's primary existential conundrum: Would the place crawl back from the brink of extinction on the backs of the watermen, or would its revival come from conservationists, who were putting their hopes in ecotourism, not industry, as the savior of the Bayshore?

With the state—through Blue Acres—whittling away at what was left of the bayfront communities, often through management partnerships with conservation organizations like the Nature Conservancy, Natural Lands, and Wildlife Preserves, it was clear that the state also preferred the expansion of open space and ecotourism over new infrastructure and seafood-based industry. Ironically, however, Sandy had made available more federal dollars than ever before for the kind of projects that local stakeholders like Pisarski, Brewer—and especially Mayor Campbell—had been desperately hoping for.

After Cumberland County's failure to be included in the initial round of Disaster Relief Act funding, Campbell and the Delaware Bayshore Long Term Recovery Committee had managed to score victories in later funding rounds by proposing projects that innovatively balanced the Bayshore's dire need for infrastructure with the desire of conservationists—who held far more lobbying power than the local municipalities—to maintain the most natural bay shoreline as possible. Ever since the 1960s, when the Army Corps began conducting its national shoreline studies, Bayshore legislators and residents had gotten used to failing the federal government's thresholds for funding. But finally, in January of 2015, the Corps issued a Federal Interest Determination—in other words, a cost-benefit analysis— on the Bayshore's post-Sandy condition that determined "pursuing further study of the Downe Township study area is warranted."

In the following years, a disintegrating vinyl bulkhead in Gandy's Beach was replaced with a larger, stronger steel bulkhead. In Fortescue, some fifteen thousand cubic yards of silt and sand, a significant portion of which had been caused by Sandy, were dredged from Fortescue Creek and used to build a sand berm and replenish three acres of beach. In the surrounding Fortescue Wildlife Management Area, a "thin-spreading" pilot project was implemented in a ten-acre section of degraded marshland with the hope that, by adding an additional layer of sand, silt, and mud, it would augment its natural accretion, thus helping it to better keep up with sea level rise and provide Fortescue homeowners better protection during future flooding events. Campbell had been thrilled with the project, which he called in a DEP press release "an ambitious step in an attempt to restore the meadowlands along the Delaware Bay."

Even Money Island had been included in a tiny living shoreline project led by the Nature Conservancy and the American Littoral Society. The organizations had teamed up to install small "oyster reefs" on a section of beach at the end of Bayview Road, as well as a stretch of eroded shoreline on one of Tony's marina properties. The project, however, was so minor that it offered no benefit other than providing a space for living shoreline research—a few "oyster castles" and coconut fiber "logs" certainly weren't going to slow down Money Island's rapid erosion, which was only accelerating because of sea level rise. By 2017, even the enormous steel bulkhead in Gandy's Beach had done little to help the town's bayfront homes, some of which were now marooned out over open water, leaving the Army Corps no choice but to explore an even more ambitious project that was considering a network of jetties.

In Fortescue, however, the beach replenishment and thin-spreading projects were working—on summer days, the beach was busy with fishermen casting for flounder and weakfish, and in the creek, larger boats, like the *Bonanza*, moved smoothly into and back from the bay. The success of the projects had bolstered Campbell's campaign to next bring waste-water infrastructure to Fortescue and Gandy's, which he believed was far more important than dredge spoils and living shorelines. "In Fortescue and Gandy's, the empty lots that we can't build on because of septic issues will all be buildable again, and Downe Township needs those ratables really bad," Campbell told me. "Our three beaches pay 70 percent of our tax revenue. If the DEP takes another ten or twenty houses in Money Island, we'll have nothing left. We'll go bankrupt."

ONE OF THE CONSERVATIONISTS most involved in not only the Fortescue projects, but in the Bayshore recovery effort in general, was Larry Niles, a wildlife biologist who, since the 1980s, had worked for the state and, later, as a consultant to various conservation organizations working throughout the Delaware Estuary. Along with a partner, he had recently started a consultancy firm, called Niles & Smith Conservation Services. Sandy's opening up of funding opportunities to coastal resilience research on the Bayshore had been a boon for Niles's work, and he was determined to keep the momentum going.

Although he lived on the western part of the Bayshore, in Greenwich, he agreed to meet me one early afternoon in late summer, in Maurice River Township, on the other side of the county. One of Niles's latest sites of interest was Thompson's Beach, located in the township, where he was working with the American Littoral Society to try and get the state's permission to conduct a thin-spreading accretion project similar to the one implemented in Fortescue.

We met in the parking lot of a local Wawa—one of a regional chain of convenience stores and gas stations—that sat near the terminus of Route 55, the state highway closest to the Bayshore—or, at least, somewhat close. For years, the Bayshore townships of Cape May and Cumberland Counties had been asking elected officials for the highway to be extended south to encourage more tourism to both the Bayshore and New Jersey's southernmost shore points. Little traction had ever been made. (Though the subject would once again be renewed in the 2018 midterms, when Bob Hugin, a Republican challenging the US Senate seat long held by Democrat Bob Menendez, brought up the issue at a campaign stop in South Jersey. "Hugin's my guy," Bob Campbell would tell me. "He's going to get Fifty-Five done." The *South Jersey Times* was less optimistic. "Menendez is no more to blame for that than any other state lawmaker or member of Congress in a generation," the newspaper wrote. "Heck, we've been talking about finishing the last 20 miles of this road to the shore for 40 years.")

Niles had been at another meeting and hadn't had the chance to eat, so he ran inside for a hoagie sandwich and a bottle of Perrier water. He invited me to ride with him in his Toyota RAV4, his wife's car, for the ten-minute drive to the Thompson's Beach observation deck, which these days was the only human-built structure left there. On the drive, we got on the topic of surfing, which, I told Niles, was the reason I had left the Bayshore for California after high school. As it turned out, Niles's sons were both surfers, and one of them had also moved to California with hope of becoming a professional surfer. I had harbored such ambitions as well, despite being woefully lacking in the talent needed to succeed in the sport. Niles's son must have suffered a similar fate—he was now an investment banker in San Francisco.

He was wearing an olive-colored button-up made of moisture-wicking synthetic material, a pair of Ray-Ban Wayfarers, and a pair of slip-on boat shoes. His arms and balding scalp were tanned from his being outside regularly, working in the marshland. He had a kind of loaded smile, not unlike Campbell's, that suggested a keen rebuttal was brewing. His voice was deeply graveled and drawn out by a strong South Jersey accent. Pope Francis's 2015 encyclical on the environment, he said as we turned onto Thompson's Beach Road, was the most important environmental document we have. "For my entire career, all my work has been guided in that way," he said, referring to the pope's insistence that all life depends on healthy air and water and a stable climate.

The landscape before us quickly fell away. The *Spartina* meadows stretched for miles on each side of the narrow asphalt road, broken intermittently by stands of ghost forest, their bleach-white trunks reaching like arthritic fingers from the muck and shallow salt ponds. On the tips of several of the dead trees were osprey. "There are so many now," Niles said, leaning over the steering wheel and craning his neck so he could get a good look at the motionless raptors. "We can't even count how many."

Niles would know. He had been instrumental in saving New Jersey's eagle and osprey populations in the 1980s, when they were both endangered species. In 1981, there was only one pair of bald eagles left in the state, and they were located in Downe Township, in an area called the Bear Swamp, where one of New Jersey's last remaining old-growth forests still stands. In the early nineteenth century, many local landowners, like John Munyan and his sons, owned land in the Bear Swamp for logging, but a large section of the forest crowded with red maple, sweet gum, holly, and sour gum trees had somehow managed to survive being felled. In the 1930s and '40s, some forty pairs of bald eagles nested in New Jersey, many along the Bayshore, but the advent of the pesticide DDT, which caused the eggs of eagles and other raptors, like the osprey, to become too thin to support the weight of the birds, had decimated their populations.

A large portion of the backdrop of my childhood was the saga of the last eagles of New Jersey. We didn't know the exact location of the pair, because the DEP kept secret their location in the Bear Swamp, fearing that curiosity-seekers, hunters, or loggers would disturb the birds. So, as my brother, friends, and I traipsed through the woods and marshland around the Cohansey River, we often looked up in the trees, hoping to be the ones to spot the eagles. We never found them, though we were often fooled by the many turkey buzzards that circled in the warm air currents above, in their search for the fresh carcasses of deer, raccoons, and other creatures. The campaign to save the bald eagle pair in the Bear Swamp led in 1982 to a partnership between the DEP and Natural Lands, one of the region's largest open-space preservation nonprofits, to purchase some fifteen hundred acres of the Bear Swamp to be permanently preserved.

The restoration effort had pitted conservationists against local loggers, who continued to work in the Bear Swamp area, just as their ancestors had. At the time, Niles was the principal zoologist and head of the Bald Eagle Restoration Project, under New Jersey's Endangered and Non-game Species Program. As the face of the project, he became one of the main targets of growing local ire toward conservationists and the DEP, who seemed to be converging on the Bayshore from all angles—from the shoreline, which was disappearing at an ever-faster rate; from the woods, where the old logging culture was being vilified for disturbing the last two eagles in New Jersey.

Later in the 1990s, Niles became the chief of the Endangered and Non-game Species Program, where his focus shifted to horseshoe crabs and red knots. He had traveled from the Arctic to Tierra del Fuego, studying the red knot's migration, among other research. Now, as a consultant, Niles had expanded his purview beyond the birds and crabs to the ravaging effects that sea level rise, along with the lingering scars of several centuries' worth of salt hay farming, had left on the Bayshore marshland. This work had only served to further erode his reputation among Bayshore watermen. As we drove along, Niles thought back on his years working on behalf of New Jersey's most fragile animal species and the current ones focused on sea level rise. "I'm notorious," he said as we drove along. This seemed to rankle him only slightly. He perched both hands on the steering wheel and continued gazing forward, then smiled and shook his head.

IN PREVIOUS MONTHS of roaming around the Bayshore, listening to various watermen air their frustrations with conservation organizations, environmentalists, and the DEP, I had become aware of Niles's reputation. One afternoon a few weeks before our visit to Thompson's Beach, for example, I was looking at the last minute for a few dozen crabs to cook for dinner and decided to stop into a seafood store in Newport. It was getting toward the end of summer, and the heat was gradually becoming less oppressive. Though the oyster season was on its way out, this was prime time for blue crabs.

On a plywood desk that doubled as a checkout counter and a table for a small TV that was at that moment playing *Matlock*, there were two ripped pieces of butcher paper. One said "Be right back" and another "bonkers." It took a minute before it dawned on me that the word was a misspelling of "bunker." I heard some shuffling; at first I couldn't figure out where it was coming from, and then I leaned over the counter and found an old yellow lab curled underneath, completely unbothered by my presence. Elsewhere on the desk were containers of freshly poured lead sinkers for bottom fishing, and "splitter" leaders for fishing with multiple hooks. Across the shop's damp concrete floor were collapsible traps for recreational crabbers, and several freezers and refrigerators full of bait.

Eventually, a gray-bearded man named John emerged through the back door. He apologized for keeping me waiting. He and his family lived in a house behind the store and he'd been back there, since there wasn't much business on a weekday in late summer. When I asked him how the season had been, John grumbled. The crabbing had been hit and miss, as it always seemed to be—no one, not even biologists, could seem to figure out why the blue crab harvest ebbed and flowed as much as it did season by season. The oystering had been good though, and he'd been able to fulfill the quota he'd been given by the state, which was around fifteen hundred bushels. Our talk of catch limits led to a conversation about "the Gestapo"—that would be, of course, the DEP.

I'd only intended to pick up some crabs, but I could see John was ripe for a good dressing down of the department. "Do you want to talk more about that?" I asked.

He smirked, then sat down in his office chair, put his feet—which were in a pair of white rubber boots—up on the counter, and pulled two apples out of a paper bag. He bit into one. "You don't want to get me started," he said. The DEP, John said, was being run by a bunch of do-gooders who wanted nothing more than to regulate places and people they knew nothing about. "They want to save the world," John said. "But they never had to work a day in their lives, these people."

John was one of many Bayshore watermen who had once harvested horseshoe crabs during the spring mating season to be sold to commercial conch and eel fishermen, who ground up the crabs and used them as bait. For as long as humans had lived on the Bayshore, they'd viewed the docile, easily apprehended horseshoe crab as bait, fertilizer, or feed. The Lenni Lenape even used the crab's long, sharp tails as spear points. In the late nineteenth century and throughout the first part of the twentieth, Bayshore horseshoe crabbers constructed huge pens that could hold eighteen thousand crabs at a time. In 1870 alone, over four million crabs were harvested from the bay. By the 1990s, conch fishermen from as far away as New Hampshire were driving rental trucks down I-95 toward the

Bayshore in the middle of the night to load up on crabs and be gone by dawn. In 1996, with the population plummeting, New Jersey's Republican governor, Christine Todd Whitman, moved to restrict horseshoe crab harvesting, before the practice was completely banned on the Bayshore in 2006.

What frustrated John most, however, was that on the Delaware side of the bay, an estimated six hundred thousand horseshoe crabs a year were still being collected for their blood. Pharmaceutical companies pay huge sums of money—sometimes up to $29,000 per quart—for the fluid, because for virtually every drug to be certified by the Federal Drug Administration, it has to pass a test using Limulus amebocyte lysate (LAL), whose key ingredient is the horseshoe crab's deep blue blood. After the crabs are bled of up to 30 percent of their blood—it takes about four hundred crabs to make a quart—they are returned from their temporary home at one of just a handful of labs in the region to the Delaware beach they were scooped up at. The laboratories claim that the bleeding process does not harm the crabs, but researchers like Niles, who have studied the crabs on the Bayshore for years, are dubious.

To John, the fact that he and the rest of the Bayshore's watermen couldn't get in on the horseshoe crab blood trade—which, based on the price of a quart of lysate and the number of crabs collected annually by the labs, was theoretically worth at least $50 million—was yet another sign of big corporations and the legislators they lobbied sticking it to the lowly Bayshore waterman. As far as John could tell, there were plenty of crabs out there to go around. "I'll tell you what," he said. "I see more crabs out here than I ever did my whole life, and I been taking them since I was six years old."

Since the implementation of the ban and the subsequent increase in red knot populations, birders and other ecotourists had been showing up to the Bayshore during the spring mating season to flip over those crabs that had been tossed upside down on their journeys from the water to the beach. This incensed John. "These people," he said. "They come here with their double-brimmed hats, driving their Volvos and Subarus." He waved a hand in the air, as if he were shooing away flies. He was generalizing, but not much—indeed, the vast majority of these visitors did prefer the multi-pocketed khaki pants, vests, and floppy hats commonly worn by birders around the world. It was also true that when a Volvo or Subaru showed up, there was a good chance it carried a birder or volunteer horseshoe crab-flipper. Certainly, none of the oystermen or crabbers were driving such vehicles. I looked uneasily out the window next to John, which offered a clear view of my car—a Subaru Forester.

But what irked John most was what had happened in Fortescue. For years before Sandy, the recreational and commercial fishermen who kept their boats at the marina there—which was in fact owned by the state—had been begging the DEP to dredge Fortescue Creek for fear that one more storm would render it impassable. Watermen like John couldn't figure out why the project wasn't a slam dunk. It had taken Sandy, of course, to finally make the dredging and beach replenishment projects a reality. "I could've told you how to make a damn beach," John said. He went on to explain, deftly, the various environmental permitting hurdles that had to be jumped in order for the project to happen, and the many non-watermen stakeholders who'd been involved. "And here comes Larry Niles," he said. "A hero because he saved the eagles back in the 1980s."

NILES PULLED INTO a small parking lot for the Thompson's Beach observation deck and parked next to a young man from Fish and Wildlife who was collecting the trash. Two boat ramps flanked each end of the parking lot. Unlike his work with the state's endangered species, Niles told me, he wanted his new job of trying to combat the corrosive effects of sea level rise on the marshland to be at its core a human-centric mission. He was focusing on projects that could preserve the bayside communities rather than eradicate them in favor of wildlife. These days, he said, it was easier for him to speak his mind. Whereas in the past, when he had worked for the Department of Fish and Wildlife, he might have had to think twice before criticizing the state. But now, as a civilian, he had more leeway. "Conservation ultimately depends on the welfare of the people who live in these places," he said. "And all the failure on the bay has led the people who live there to believe there is no future." There was now a locked gate blocking off the rest of the three-quarters of a mile of dirt track leading to where Thompson's Beach once stood. Normally, Niles had a key to the gate, so he could drive the rest of the way to the water's edge, but he'd left it in his car back home in Greenwich. It was a warm but overcast day with little wind. I realized that his clothing—the synthetic button-up, sunglasses, and boat shoes—was what John from the seafood store in Newport would consider classic birder attire. Although the greenheads had died off, it was now the time of year for blackflies and gnats. One of the first, and most tried and true, tests to see if a person was from the Bayshore was to see how they handled the flies—if they were swarmed and bitten relentlessly, then they had the sweet blood of an outsider. Of course, it was just that we had grown to tolerate them. Niles had grown up in Bucks County, Pennsylvania, but had lived in South Jersey his entire adult life. Nevertheless, I couldn't help but wonder how he would react to the bugs.

Just as we stepped around the gate, a grayish-brown bird skirted across the track up ahead. "I think that was a clapper rail," Niles said. "It's rare to see them." We walked on, to a point where a nearby gut twisted toward the road, around a muddy stretch of marshland.

What we were looking at was a slice of the $100 million, 14,500-acre Estuary Enhancement Program completed in the 1990s by the energy company PSE&G. The company had purchased a 1,396-acre tract of marshland behind Thompson's that had been damaged by miles of banking. Like Fortescue, Gandy's Beach, Bay Point, and Money Island, Thompson's Beach had been a thriving bayfront community throughout the second half of the twentieth century, but had begun to fall into disrepair by the mid-1990s because the township—Maurice River—and the county were unable to stave off the rising water and erosion. When PSE&G destroyed the banks and dug new ditching to restore the marshland to its natural state, the road to Thompson's began to flood so much that the town's fifty-nine property owners could hardly get to their homes anymore. PSE&G offered Maurice River Township $1.2 million to raise and expand the road, but the DEP was against it, noting that the permitting alone would cost nearly $100,000. Instead, the DEP suggested the township should "consider alternatives"—in other words, sell the beach that the town sat on to the state, to be returned to open space. Unwilling to implement a tax hike to pay for the new road, the township sided with the DEP, setting off a years-long fight with two homeowners who refused to leave. Eventually, the township won by condemning the holdouts' properties.

While there was no positive benefit of the restoration project for Thompson's Beach, it had at first improved the *Spartina* meadow that surrounded the town. The banking, Niles said, had accelerated the land's natural subsidence because it had prevented the tide from regularly inundating the meadows, which brought with it the decaying plants, mud particles, and sand that was necessary for its natural accretion. But with the water levels rising, some sections of the meadow had not been able to keep up. Now, they were not much more than mudflats.

Niles hoped the project with the American Littoral Society would restore these stretches of overwhelmed meadow. He had proposed to the DEP a project to dredge mud from various nearby creeks that would then be thin-spread over the mudflats, which would give them the boost they needed to compete with the ever-increasing flood tides. An added benefit of the dredging of the creeks would be that they would become deep enough again for not just spawning fish but also recreational fishermen and their boats. The project, however, was still in the data collection stage—Niles and his business partner had been busy traipsing around the surrounding marshland, recording over four hundred data points that included elevation, vegetation height and density, underground biomass, and wildlife species composition. Building up the meadow was a precise process—if it was made too low, the mudflats would persist; too high, the invasive foxtails would take root and choke out both the *Spartina alterniflora* (cordgrass) and *Spartina patens* (salt hay).

The reason why the project hadn't happened yet was that Niles and Smith had been waiting two years to get some of the necessary permits from the DEP and the federal government. "Regulators have this mind-set that we've got to stop everything," Niles said. "Which means rich guy gets his way and poor guy doesn't." A case in point was the fact that Ocean City was at that moment in the conceptualization phase of a $2.75 million living shoreline project to restore a severely eroded, 150-acre island of uninhabited marshland, located in its back bay, called Shooting Island. The National Fish and Wildlife Foundation was providing a $2.6 million grant for the project, while the town would cover the rest. The idea was that by implementing thin-spreading and oyster reefs, Shooting Island would be restored to the area it was in 1930, which was twice the size it was now, thus providing a better flood barrier for Ocean City's densely populated—and severely flood-prone—bay side. Despite the city's and the project contractor's inability to provide data that could show just how much protection a revitalized Shooting Island would actually provide, since the concept of living shorelines is so new, the project was on track to be funded and given the green light within the next year. "There seems to be no problem with throwing millions of dollars on an Atlantic coast beach that can be lost overnight in a nor'easter," Niles later told me. "But no, we can't spend two hundred thousand dollars on the Delaware Bay."

In 2010, prior to the Fortescue project, Niles and Smith did a comprehensive study of all the restoration projects that had been implemented in the Delaware Estuary's tidal marshes and concluded that almost all of them had ultimately failed. "Many of them failed because the DEP denied or delayed permits," Niles said. In his opinion, there were specific reasons for why the environmental permitting process was so complex when it came to the Bayshore.

The first was political confusion. Niles brought up how Bob Martin had been appointed by Christie to lead the DEP in part to streamline the permitting process, yet that priority seemed to be carried out for select communities. Christie and Martin's promise to cut the red tape after Sandy was the most obvious example. While the state's richer local governments and their residents could afford the lawyers and consultants to guide them through the recovery process without making rebuilding and permitting mistakes that would ultimately cost them, the poorer local governments and their residents were often left to navigate the ever-evolving bureaucracies at the state and federal levels. "Leaders think they can just make things go fast," Niles said. "Higbee's restaurant (in Fortescue) can't get a bathroom because they can't hire a lawyer to guide them through the permitting process, but a corporation in Cape May can, because they can afford a lawyer." Bayshore land was not being defended, Niles said, because there was no consistent voice to defend the region before lawmakers in Trenton, many of whom did not know the Bayshore existed, let alone had ever visited it. And with the ever-increasing swing in partisan ideologies, the process of turning over the government's vast functions from one governor to the next had become dangerously fractured. "Each administration comes in and has a new vision for how things should work, so they dismantle the previous administration's work, rather than build upon it," Niles said. This, of course, was the circumstance that had infected Donald Trump's EPA, which had been thrust into a state of inertia under its new administrator, Scott Pruitt.

This led Niles to talk about a problem I heard often from Campbell, Tony, and several local and state government consultants. As political appointees like Martin wasted time trying to undo the policies their predecessors had put into place, midlevel managers went on working with their own individual agendas. Niles laughed when he brought up midlevel managers. "They all have their own ideas," he said. His point—and here he echoed Campbell, Tony, and others' points—was that someone in the DEP's Trenton office could be making consequential decisions without the issue ever reaching Martin's desk. Jersey Shore communities, on the other hand, with their economic and political might, had the ears of Martin and Christie and other powerful politicians. "The rich have the power to make sure that most of the money ends up in their communities," Niles said. "Why is there no money going to the Delaware Bay? Essentially, because it's poor. So, I think one way to address this is to start looking at it as an environmental justice issue." As for his own political leanings, Niles seemed as complicated as the system he was criticizing. "I'm a registered Republican," he said, "but I'm actually a liberal Democrat."

Eventually, we made it to the end of the track, where a wide beach spread in both directions, made with forty thousand cubic yards of white sand from a nearby silica mine. The static hum of crickets and other insects was so loud it nearly drowned out the lapping of the bay's tiny waves. An osprey rode the wind's current in the distance, while close by, a pair of ducks jumped out of a ditch, their flight much less graceful than that of the osprey's. All that was left of the town of Thompson's Beach were a handful of decaying pilings and a section of bulkhead from the last holdout's property, which now protruded out in the bay like a tumor on the otherwise narrow, pristine beach. Marsh grasses and cedar saplings were overtaking a tall stone chimney. Niles pointed out three eagles patrolling the sky over the marshland, noting that one was a juvenile. "He's still learning how to hunt," Niles said. It was midday now and hot, muggy. I could feel rivulets of sweat running down my torso and legs. The blackflies and gnats were closing in on us, but they didn't seem to bother Niles at all.

As we walked back, Niles told me that, despite all his travels, he still loved the Bayshore more than anywhere else. "It's like the 1950s," he said. "People wouldn't believe that this place exists as it does." But, he said, the Saint Lawrence River in Quebec, Canada, was a close second. He and his wife visited there often these days. He had always been impressed by how the preserved land there had been made accessible through public spaces, RV parks, and campgrounds. Scattered in between the open space was privately owned land. All of it, Niles said, seemed to operate in chorus with the natural environment, instead of against it. The state should have done what Canada did, Niles said. "The Bayshore is a cornucopia of natural resource wealth, but it's just being pressured down to the nub." We stood for a while, swatting more and more blackflies and gnats. They were becoming intolerable, even for him and me. "Actually," he said. "I think it's the bugs.

FIFTEEN

"WE HAVE GOBS OF PLANS."

AS IT DOES IN SPRING, the marshland is usually the first to remind the Bayshore that fall has arrived. Throughout the summer months there is a radiance in the stalks of the foxtails and *Spartina* meadows. In September, that green hue does not at first appear to be changing color, but simply stalling. But with the arrival of one cold night, or maybe two, a soft yellow overtakes the landscape, hinting at its impending hibernation. There is a stiffness in the way the stalks—now turning brittle in preparation for the freeze—move in the wind, which is itself changing, shifting ever so slightly, first toward the west and then the north. There are also the other, far more unnerving indicators—the hurricanes, spinning like great, loose gears across the Atlantic. And there was nothing subtle about the 2017 Atlantic hurricane season.

On my way to Bay Point one afternoon in early September, I stopped into the Landing for lunch. I overheard a few people there talking about Hurricane Irma, which had just reached Category 5 strength. The forecast for the storm's track had just been updated, and it was now projected to make a direct hit on the Florida Keys. The television above the counter was glued to the Weather Channel, which already had its meteorologists on the ground in towns throughout the Keys to build up the suspense of the impending landfall. "We're getting lucky," the woman behind the counter told me, as she handed me my BLT sandwich. We both watched an animated track of the storm. "Them people on the other hand . . ." She trailed off and smiled sympathetically. It wasn't that she didn't care about the destruction that was about to be visited upon the Keys—or the years of recovery that would follow—it was that she understood it all too well. When you lived in a place so drastically molded by the weather, what was always in the back of your mind was the next storm—we were lucky this time, sure, but next week could be our turn once again.

A map of the entire Atlantic came up on the television, showing other storms—potential hurricanes—farther to the east, marching from northwest Africa toward the Caribbean and the East Coast. In April, the Colorado State University Tropical Meteorology Project, which issues overall forecasts for hurricane seasons, had called for a total of eleven named storms and four hurricanes, but by August, it had adjusted its forecast to sixteen named storms and eight hurricanes.

Already, there had been catastrophic damage—in mid-August, Hurricane Harvey had intensified rapidly and moved unusually slowly off Texas's Gulf Coast, allowing it to generate an incredible amount of moisture. Houston had been inundated. Ultimately, Harvey produced an unprecedented 60.5 inches of rainfall in Texas. As the Landing's waitress and I watched Irma bearing down on Florida, officials were already claiming Harvey's federal emergency aid price tag could very well exceed that of Sandy's $60 billion. Texas senator Ted Cruz, who had been one of the chief delayers of the passage of the Sandy aid package—and ultimately voted against it, along with every other Texas Republican in Congress, except one—was now caught in an awkward game of political spin as he pleaded for swift federal aid for the post-Harvey recovery. MSNBC correspondent Katy Tur had asked Cruz, "A lot of people are pointing out that you voted against aid for Sandy . . . and saying you're asking for money now when you weren't willing to help the people in the northeast. What do you have to say to them?" Cruz dismissed the criticism as "political sniping," and reiterated his stance that the Sandy package had been full of pork. Rep. Frank LoBiondo, the usually quiet congressman who represented South Jersey, responded to Cruz in a tweet. "Despite my TX colleagues refusal to support aid in #SouthJersey time of need," LoBiondo wrote, "I will support emergency disaster $$ for those impacted." While an $81 billion Harvey package would soon quickly pass in the House, it, like the Sandy package, would be stalled in the Senate. By February of 2018, however, a $90 billion package would be passed, bumping Sandy back as the third-costliest storm in US history, behind Hurricane Katrina.

Looking at the television became, more than anything, aggravating. There was the Weather Channel, with its meteorologists breathlessly reporting the latest storm news from locations—harbors with bobbing sailboats, seawalls being battered by fitful waves, grocery stores with empty shelves—which served to further hype their reports. Katy Tur and Ted Cruz locked into an argument over aid. Every news channel with its own dramatic graphic and tagline for the storm. It all screamed of short-term drama and compassion. Of course I understood that what made hurricanes so irresistible to the news networks and their viewers was the images of destruction they promised. Here was an opportunity for correspondents and news anchors to speak from a "war zone" footing. A chance to proliferate the American mainstream media's obsession with "body count." A chance to describe a neighborhood "flattened," "decimated," "gone."

But in truth, the real pain came in the months and years and decades after the dramatic images of destruction had been forgotten by everyone. It was, like so many other things in life, the little decisions that inflicted the most pain—the political bickering that delayed a bill that in turn delayed the funding a rural, chronically cash-strapped municipality needed to rent a dumpster to clean up storm debris; that, ultimately, delayed a family's ability to move on from the trauma of losing a home or, in the Bayshore's case, an entire community. After every major storm, lawmakers would continue to posture and politicize out of existence American citizens, like Mike and Kate, whom they would never meet. The complete story of natural disasters like Katrina and Sandy and Harvey and Irma and Maria—which less than a month after Irma would devastate Puerto Rico—could not be captured in the dramatic images the news media plastered on televisions and in print in the days during and immediately before and after a catastrophic storm, but in the years after, when wounds became scars that would never go away. The evidence for such a fact could be found in the first sentences Kate ever uttered to me—when she could only call Sandy "the storm."

After lunch at the Landing, I made my way to Bay Point to see if Mike and Kate were around. Before crossing from Downe to Lawrence Township, I passed several yards bristling with yard signs for Campbell, who had decided to run for a seat in the State Assembly. This year was especially pivotal in New Jersey politics, given that Christie's final term was expiring. The Democratic candidate, Phil Murphy, was expected to win easily. Murphy's Republican opponent, the current lieutenant governor, Kim Guadagno, was irreparably damaged by her affiliation to Christie, who was leaving office as one of the most unpopular governors in New Jersey history.

Once thought to be presidential material, due in large part to his bipartisan outreach to President Obama in the wake of Sandy, Christie's standing had been destroyed by multiple scandals, including his mishandling of Sandy Disaster Relief Act money. In January of 2014, it was reported that a federal investigation had been opened to determine if Christie had improperly used relief funds from HUD's Community Development Block Grants program for "a marketing campaign to promote the Jersey Shore and encourage tourism." The firm the Christie administration awarded the $4.7 million contract to, it turned out, was politically connected and had featured Christie and his family in a series of "Stronger than the Storm" television ads that would run in multiple states, from New York to Washington, DC. (The marketing's broad reach was rather convenient for a potential presidential candidate.) Another firm, which bid half the amount to produce the campaign but hadn't proposed integrating the Christies in its commercials, was not selected for the job. The *Star-Ledger* called Christie's decision to "siphon off money that was intended for victims of Sandy to promote himself in a series of TV ads" a "new low." Christie pointed out that the campaign was approved by the Obama administration, and HUD, the agency tasked with investigating the case, ultimately found "nothing improper" about the campaign itself, but did find that New Jersey "did not procure services and products for its tourism marketing program in a manner that met the intent of all federal procurement requirements."

Even more consequential was the Christie administration's decision to hire some of the same private contractors that had gotten into trouble for their mismanagement of duties in post-Katrina New Orleans. In May of

2013, as Bay Point homeowners began turning en masse to Blue Acres to escape the psychological burden of having to watch their homes crumble into the water while the DEP and County Health Department struggled to find a solution for the Bayshore communities' recovery, the state hired New Orleans–based Hammerman and Gainer International, for $68 million, to process paperwork to determine homeowners' federal aid eligibility. The New Jersey law firm that HGI hired to handle its contract bid had recently made a $25,000 donation to the Republican Governors Association, which had contributed $1.7 million to Christie's 2013 gubernatorial reelection campaign.

Almost immediately, HGI ran into trouble. Homeowners and several advocacy groups working on their behalf complained of delays, misplaced paperwork, and claim denials. One advocacy group found, through an Open Public Records Act request, that three-quarters of those who appealed their federal aid denials, which had been processed by HGI, had wound up winning those appeals. The state ended up firing HGI, but the contractor hired to take HGI's place had also had a history in New Orleans—it had botched a $900 million contract to administer the Katrina recovery program. In 2014, the nonprofit investigative website NJ Spotlight published a scathing two-part story in which the reporters meticulously outlined these and many other egregious errors made by the Christie administration and its Sandy recovery team. "From the get go," NJ Spotlight wrote, "a smooth recovery was doomed."

After dropping out of the 2016 presidential race, Christie joined the Trump campaign with the hope of gaining a position in the next president's cabinet, but Trump ended up offering him nothing. Tellingly, there wasn't a single yard sign for Guadagno in Downe or Lawrence Township—even in the yard that once featured the "Hillary for Prison" billboard. Even more radically, in Cedarville, there was a lone sign for Phil Murphy.

As I made my way out of Cedarville, along Jones Island Road, the markings of fall slowly continued to appear, as if mimicking the easy-going pace of the community it was descending upon. The fields that ran along the last stretch of high ground, where Jones Island Road turned to Bay Point Road, were crowded with the Mexican and Central American farmworkers who now made up the vast majority of South Jersey's farming labor force, handpicking Sheppard Farms' final crops of bell peppers, romaine, and squash. In the distance, the patch of woods that made up the recently expanded, state-owned Nantuxent Fish and Wildlife Management Area had exploded into an autumnal firestorm of color. On the horizon, jammed in between the edge of the marshland and the brown line of the bay, was Bay Point.

I was surprised to see that there was no sign of the impending demolition, save for the numbers that state officials had spray-painted on each house. All summer, I had been hearing, along with Mike and Kate, that demolition would begin on the first of October. But there was no news that a bid advertisement had been issued by the state. As always, everyone was left guessing, which only fueled suspicions and conspiracy theories that the state was delaying the project further in order to force out Mike and Kate. "Who knows," Mike said when I asked him about the demolition. "I heard they weren't doing it anymore."

He and Kate were, as usual, sitting on their porch, Parker dozing at their feet. Mike was rubbing his arm and wincing. His shingles had cleared up, but now it was something else. "Nerve damage from all the labor I done over the years," he said. While it was mostly his decades crabbing, tonging, and working for the Delaware River Port Authority that had worn him down, the strain of building the bungalow on Cedar Creek, and the gallon of vodka a day in the years after Sandy, hadn't helped. Despite the pain, he continued to lose weight and feel stronger. He'd been sober for two years now. Kate, on the other hand, had already started on her cooler full of Miller Lite, and she offered me one. Mike wished he could join us, but he knew better. "I'm okay now," he said. "I'm done with it."

With Christie on the way out and the state government facing transition, Mike and Kate wondered what it would be like when Murphy took over the government. Mike wasn't too worried. "Can't get no worse than Christie," he said, laughing. He lifted a hand and waved in the direction of the abandoned homes on Paris Road.

As it happened, on September 18, the state's Division of Property Management and Construction, the department that handles the Blue Acres demolition contracts, held a pre-bid meeting at the Lawrence Township

Municipal Building, the same place where Blue Acres had held their kick-off meeting in 2013. After nearly four years, the state would finally begin the demolition of Bay Point. The advertised estimated cost for the job was nearly $2 million. For Mike and Kate, who had received an offer from Blue Acres of $12,000 for the Paris Road rancher, after insurance and other deductions, the demolition's price tag seemed unfathomable. Across Nantuxent Cove, in Money Island, the estimate for Bay Point's demolition could have paid for the bulkhead on Bayview Drive nearly five times over. These allocations were exactly what infuriated Campbell, Tony, Niles—everyone—on the Bayshore. There seemed to be plenty of money for retreat, but none for restoration.

SINCE MEETING WITH LARRY NILES, I had been thinking about his point that the ever-intensifying polarization of political ideologies from one administration to the next was only serving to tear apart any progress toward making the Bayshore a model of modern conservation, in which the answer was not always to choose between creating a space for either humans or nature, but to create one for both. But also, I couldn't avoid thinking about the Bayshore's inability to move forward into a future that didn't include the total annihilation of its bayfront communities and the fishing industry that defined them, and that that struggle had to do, at least in part, with the overabundance of conservation organizations vying for environmental accolades on the Bayshore. There were so many: the Nature Conservancy, Natural Lands, American Littoral Society, Wildlife Preserves, New Jersey Conservation Foundation, Partnership for the Delaware Estuary, Audubon, Ducks Unlimited, Cohansey Area Watershed Association. All of them grabbing at the land and its "natural riches," as Niles had put it.

So, in early October, as six different contractors bid on the Bay Point job, I decided to sit in on a "comprehensive conservation and management plan brainstorming session" hosted by the Partnership for the Delaware Estuary (PDE), a nonprofit organization designated as one of the EPA's twenty-eight National Estuary Programs. PDE works to bring together stakeholders to produce environmental data that could attract funding and influence legislation for the benefit of the entirety of the Delaware Estuary. The point of this session was to simply gather feedback from the Bayshore's general public for PDE's 2018 management plan, called the *State of the Estuary* report, which hadn't been updated since 1996 but was now required to be by EPA administrator Scott Pruitt, who wanted to gut the National Estuary Program.

The session was held in the folklife museum of the Bayshore Center at Bivalve, a small campus—founded in 1988 by a Money Island resident named Meghan Wren—that also included an art gallery and café, situated along the Maurice River in several of the original oyster shipping sheds and wharves and next door to Fleetwood's Bivalve Packing. Artifacts of the bygone oyster industry—photos of Bivalve's packing and processing houses surrounded by mountains of oysters, landscape paintings of the marshland, a scale model of an old bay schooner—crowded the walls and wood-slat floor. A space in the center of the room had been cleared out for a few rows of plastic fold-out chairs, where about twenty people, all representing different organizations, industries, and government entities with their own Bayshore-related environmental initiatives, had taken a seat. There didn't seem to be anyone from the general public. And, other than Meghan Wren, I did not recognize any residents of the bayfront communities. Barney Hollinger, a lifelong oysterman and former chairman of the Delaware Bay Shellfish Council who'd come out of retirement to help steer Cape May Salt's Bayshore aquaculture operation, was the sole representative of the oyster industry.

The chatter among the attendees and PDE's representatives focused on Trump's proposed federal budget, which called for deep cuts in EPA programs essential to Bayshore conservation efforts, in addition to the National Estuary Program. Despite their apprehensions about Trump's proposed budget cuts, the group was buoyed by the impending transition of the state government from Christie to Murphy, who on the campaign trail had been promising to realign New Jersey as a forward-thinking state in terms of climate change, renewable energy, and environmental stewardship in general.

Immediately after the session began, there was confusion in the room. If the point of the gathering was to collect new input from the "general public" on the state of the Bayshore, this wasn't the right crowd—virtually all the people in the room were entrenched stakeholders who regularly communicated their needs to PDE and who were hoping that, today, there would be a discussion of funding. One couple who in fact appeared to be from the general public popped in and stood in the back of the room, but soon left without a word. In the absence of fresh voices, the session devolved into an airing of the same old grievances that seemed to never be taken seriously by the state and federal governments. Hollinger pointed out that, for the Bayshore oyster fleet to continue working, Nantuxent Creek and Cove needed immediate dredging. He begged the PDE representatives to make the dredging a top priority in the 2018 *State of the Estuary* report. Wren reminded everyone that Christie had just announced a $20 million project in Barnegat Bay, on the Jersey Shore, which included stormwater infrastructure improvements, wetlands restoration, and ongoing water quality monitoring. When Christie announced the project at a park along the bay, he told the crowd how much the region contributed to New Jersey's $43 billion tourism industry. "Every time I see something about Barnegat," Wren said, "I think, 'Wait a minute, what about the Delaware Bay?'"

Eventually, a man named Ben Stowman, who was the land use director for Maurice River Township, spoke up from the back of the room. "Where's the funding come from for all these projects?" he asked. "Or is this conversation just about what you'll present to the DEP or the EPA, or whatever?"

"Yes," one of the presenters responded meekly. "And it's difficult to get everybody [at the DEP and EPA] to agree on the same thing."

"You're correct about that," said Stowman, who was wearing a baseball cap that read "LOVE WHERE YOU LIVE." He then commented to no one in particular, "Money's a big problem."

NILES HADN'T BEEN AT THE PDE SESSION, but a few weeks later, he came to another brainstorming session, this one called the "Delaware Bay Watershed Coastal Resilience Assessment," which was held in the same room at the Bayshore Center. This time, however, it was hosted by the National

Fish and Wildlife Foundation, or NFWF—everyone in the room pro-
nounced it, per its acronym, as "Niffwhiff"—which was the organization
that would soon give Ocean City a $2.6 million grant to begin the Shoot-
ing Island living shoreline project. The meeting was much larger, drawing
about thirty people, and the number of different stakeholders present was
dizzying. Along with those representatives who were at the PDE session,
there were others from the DEP, US Fish and Wildlife, The Wetlands Institute, Association of New Jersey Environmental Commissions, Getting
to Resilience LLC, Delaware River Basin Commission, Stockton University, NatureServe, and the National Oceanic and Atmospheric Administration—and, rather surprisingly, also in attendance was Campbell, who
had only heard about the gathering that morning and was not happy about
not being informed earlier.

The meeting progressed with much the same confusion as the PDE
meeting had, with stakeholders jostling for a few moments to explain to
the NFWF presenters why the foundation should fund their coastal resilience or restoration project over those of the other stakeholders in the
room. Niles, who was pushing for funding for a project that would dredge
the Maurice River and use the spoils to replenish the surrounding inundated marshland, spoke up and made clear his frustration about the overlap
in interests. Other stakeholders in the room wanted to do essentially the
same thing. "There are several perspectives on how to approach this, and
I think that's part of the problem," Niles said. "We have gobs of plans, but
we don't have any money." One of the presenters shook her head. "I'll say
right now," she said, "we have no dedicated funds to get these projects on
the ground now."

Another problem that quickly revealed itself was that NFWF's presenters didn't seem to have done their homework. As part of their display they
had printed, on a large foam-core board, a satellite image of the Bayshore,
with different colored boxes indicating different communities and their
"Asset Index," and along the coast of Downe Township, encased in a
light-green box was . . . nothing. It appeared that NFWF had forgotten
to note Money Island or Gandy's Beach, or hadn't known they existed altogether. Wren raised her hand to interrupt one of the presenters. "There
are some entire communities within the area of the light green," she said.

"Why are they discounted?" The presenter seemed stumped. He fumbled before saying, "Well, even though there may be some population in here, there probably isn't, uh, a lot of these other critical assets, critical infra-structure to create enough of a high-density ranking such that it would show up like some of these other areas." It was clear that the presenter had in fact not known that communities—Gandy's Beach and Money Island— existed in that area. "If there are blatant errors in the national data set," another presenter confessed, "this is the time to bring those up."

By then, Campbell was long gone. He'd spent his time in the back row shaking his head, snacking on a handful of cookies from the food spread NFWF had brought for the meeting. He'd left his napkin full of crumbs on the seat, along with one of the handouts NFWF's presenters had given everyone to take home. Before the meeting started, he and I had sat out on one of the Bayshore Center's docks overlooking the Maurice River and the center's restored schooner, the *A.J. Meerwald*. "I didn't get an invite," Campbell told me, frustratingly. "I guess they're going to talk about resil-ience, beaches, all that crap. But I came to see if they were going to talk about infrastructure." NFWF, along with most of the other participants in the room, had planned *not* to talk about infrastructure; what's more, they had planned to talk about how to avoid it. Campbell must have known infrastructure was nowhere near the agenda, but I could tell he relished being surrounded by so many tree huggers, making those who knew him squirm. Before he left, I'd overheard him introduce himself to someone who didn't know him—yet. "Nice to meet you," he said, smiling. "I'm the new governor."

Later, I pressed Niles about this idea that there were so many stake-holders invested in the Bayshore that they were actually a hindrance to progress. "I think that's true," he said. "Everybody has their favorite proj-ect that they're pushing, and each has their own political or inside connec-tions. Then somebody like NFWF says, 'We've got money for projects,' and everybody ends up getting sort of a piece, but it doesn't add up to a solution." Nevertheless, Niles told me, there was a larger battle to be concerned with, which was that industry, like the lysate labs in Maryland, now dictated much of the regulatory power. "They control the fisher-ies, they control agriculture. Look at what happened with the horseshoe crabs—in the beginning all the money that was being had was going to the local fishermen because they were going out and harvesting the crabs to sell for bait." Now, Niles pointed out, the lysate labs contracted just a handful of companies to collect their crabs, none of which were in New Jersey. "That's the big story of conservation," he said. "Our natural resources, the wealth of the land—they don't belong to rural communities anymore; they belong to industries." So, all these conservation organizations, he went on, were "truthfully, the only hope."

I'd left the meeting feeling more conflicted than ever. My Subaru Forester matched the other Subaru Foresters driven by the attendees. Like them, I had also come to accept that the answer to preserving what was left of the Bayshore's original places and culture would be one that included tough choices. To build up resilience, to bolster what was left of the Bayshore's high ground, would mean retreating from much of it. I believed the science that said human activities had accelerated climate change. I believed the water was rising. I thought it absurd that one even had to argue about its existence. I just didn't understand why it was so difficult to preserve what was left. Every fall and winter, many of the beaches of the Jersey Shore were chewed away by hurricanes and nor'easters, and yet every spring they were replenished with tens of millions of dollars' worth of dredged sand. Why couldn't Money Island be approved for a few barge loads of sand from the bay's shipping channel, which the Army Corps was at that moment dredging? (Most cuttingly, the channel spoils were going to the Delaware side of the bay, to replenish the beaches there.) I understood that the Bayshore provided for the state a fraction of the revenues the Jersey Shore did, but I still believed it was a tragedy that certain Americans—almost always low-income Americans—had become nothing more than numerals in a cost-benefit equation. No wonder they'd voted for a man who promised, if nothing else, to blow up the system.

TWO DAYS AFTER THE NFWF MEETING, I drove to Bay Point to see Mike and Kate and was surprised to see that Site Enterprises, the company contracted to do the demolition, had already set up fencing around the properties that had been bought out by Blue Acres. The fencing lined West Bay

Point Road, opening briefly at Mike and Kate's driveway before blocking off the road entirely just past their bungalow. They were not home and no one from the company was on-site. It was a cold, gray afternoon, the bay aggravated and brown.

As I was getting into my car to turn around and leave, a Lawrence Township truck pulled up next to me. George, the township's road supervisor, wound down the window and leaned toward me, asked me what I was up to. George had once owned a home in Money Island, and he recalled fondly the marina's prosperous days, before Tony had bought it. He whistled thinking about that time. "Drinking was the reason Money Island Marina failed," George said of Roger Mauro. "And I guess Bay Point Marina, too." The thought dredged up his anger about the buyouts. He mentioned an expensive footbridge in Downe Township that had been built by Natural Lands to provide access to a nature trail that quickly became impassable with almost any high tide. Some residents were fond of calling it the "Bridge to Nowhere." "Why couldn't that money go to propping up this here?" George asked, waving a hand at the now fenced-off homes along Paris Road.

"Anyway," he went on. "Are you for us—or the state?"

SIXTEEN

"THIS VIEW, WE SHALL SEE, PERSISTS."

JUST AFTER DAWN ON NOVEMBER 22—the second day of the Bay Point demolition—I sat with Mike and Kate at the bar. The temperature had plummeted overnight, causing a heavy fog to hang just above the bay, which was still clinging to its summer warmth. Outside, Site Enterprises had finished up with the remains of Bones Batten's house and was on to the next. Kate was already preparing oyster stuffing for the twenty-four-pound turkey she was going to cook for Thanksgiving dinner that weekend. Katie, Mikie, his family and in-laws, and two friends were planning on coming over. In addition to the turkey and oyster stuffing, Mike and Kate had to make green bean casserole, mashed potatoes, sausage stuffing, and homemade cranberry sauce. Kate had a Pandora country music station playing loudly through a pair of speakers over by the surveillance screen and television, though it wasn't enough to drown out the crunch of another home being torn to the ground a few dozen feet away. Kate handed me a cup of coffee as George Jones's "I Don't Need Your Rockin' Chair" burst out of the speakers.

A friend of theirs named Jerry walked through the door a few minutes later. Jerry had lived for a while in the camper next to the bungalow—the same camper that Mike and Kate had lived in for two and a half years after Sandy. I'd first met Jerry once back in the summer, after stopping by to see Mike and Kate, who'd gone out to the gym, which had become routine for them after Mike got sober. It had been a sweltering day, and Jerry opened the door of the camper shirtless and drinking a beer. He'd surprised me by wanting to talk about books. His favorite was William W. Warner's *Beautiful Swimmers*, written in 1976, about the watermen of the Chesapeake Bay who made their living harvesting blue crabs. "No better book on watermen than that one," Jerry had told me. I had since read the book, finding a multitude of similarities with the people of the Bayshore. A few lines had stuck with me more than most: "The watermen treated anything that floated, swam, crawled, or flew into their marshy domains as God-given and therefore not subject to the laws of mortal men. What the Lord provided, no landsman should tell them how to harvest. This view, we shall see, persists." I learned later that Mike had introduced *Beautiful Swimmers* to Jerry, along with James Michener's *Chesapeake*.

Today, Jerry had come to check out the demolition, and, more importantly, to see how Mike and Kate were holding up. Rather than devastated, as I, and perhaps Jerry, had expected they would be, Mike and Kate seemed unbothered by everything. In fact, they were both in buoyant moods. The demolition's state supervisor, Regina Bruno, had asked Mike if he'd be interested in helping Site Enterprises' crew lay booms around the houses that sat out on the water. (The state required the use of booms so that debris that fell in the water could be captured.) Site Enterprises had only a tiny aluminum boat to use and none of the crewmen had much experience running a boat or working on the water. In fact, right before they'd demolished Bones's house, I'd watched two of the Site Enterprises crewmen nearly capsize the boat trying to put the booms around the house. "Maybe the state'll throw me a couple hundred dollars," Mike said. "Get a little money back off this situation, you know?"

"You want these fine?" Kate asked as she began chopping an onion.

"Yes ma'am," Mike said. "Well, you know, within reason. Don't make them invisible." Mike went on. "Before the house went, I had pretty much an industrial kitchen," he said. "But we sort of lost everything." I'd come to understand that Mike and Kate regularly made offhand references to Sandy, and the struggle that ensued, like this. To them, Sandy was as common a subject as the weather was to everyone else.

Mike mentioned that Katie had recently bought him a dehydrator, along with a box of .38 Special bullets, using points she'd accrued with the outdoor retailer Cabela's. "We used to get a lot of points. Now we get negative points," Mike said, referring to how, after Sandy, he and Kate had plummeted into debt. He laughed, then recalled an experience with a particularly aggressive creditor. "One time they called asking for me and Kate said I was deceased. Next day we get in the mail a letter to the estate of Mike Nelson saying, 'Sorry about your loss.'" Now Kate and Jerry were laughing. "I don't worry about none of that anymore," Mike went on. "Donald Trump went through bankruptcy many times. Why can't I do it once?" He trailed off, got serious. He recalled the bailout of the auto industry after 2008 financial crash. "Billions and billions of our tax money went to all them. Now they're all billionaires again. We paid for that. So guess what? They can take care of me with a couple thousand bucks."

"That's one of the reasons I never really cared for Donald Trump," Jerry said. "Because I was in with that crew down there in Atlantic City, where he stiffed a thousand carpenters, plumbers, everybody."

"Not right," Mike said. "Not right."

"They worked for nothing because, hey, he decided to go bankrupt," Jerry said.

Mike didn't have a high opinion of Trump morally speaking, but he was sticking by him in the hope that the president's policies would ultimately lead to the easing of fishing regulations in the bay. He missed the old days when Bay Point Marina was alive with fishermen. He understood, of course, that those days would never return, but he at least wanted to keep living the life that he and Kate did right here on the bay. Already, under Trump, Mike said that the state's constant "encouraging" that he and Kate consider retreat was "easing up a little," though he wasn't sure if that was just because the state had gotten what it wanted with the Blue Acres buyout.

MIKE AND KATE quickly became friendly with Regina Bruno and the other on-site representatives for the state—Bill Byster, from the Division of Property Management and Construction, and Gary Parent, from Blue Acres.

Bruno, especially, seemed to understand better than her male counterparts how sensitive a matter the demolition was to Mike and Kate—just three days into the job, she gave Mike a hard hat and reflective vest so he could go wherever he wanted on the site.

Because Bay Point was in the middle of ecologically sensitive habitat, particularly for horseshoe crabs, the state needed Site Enterprises to finish the job by February, or they'd have to wait until the next winter, when they could work again without disturbing the wildlife. If that were to happen, new permits would have to be applied for and a new contract written, which meant the threat of the job being left half-done. And every day, the weather seemed to be getting colder and colder. With December came a steady, bone-chilling northwest wind that shredded the bay and made it impossible for Site Enterprises' ten-foot aluminum boat to lay the booms around the homes on Paris Road. To get the job done, Jimmy DiNatale, the owner of Site Enterprises, had decided to hire Mike, who could easily navigate the freezing conditions with his crabbing skiff.

There was also some pressure from the DEP to move quickly before Christie and Martin left office, because the Bay Point job would see Blue Acres reach, and then surpass, its five hundredth demolition. Bruno, Byster, and Parent had told Mike and Kate that they heard Christie and Martin might come down to mark the milestone, but no one had showed up. Nevertheless, that afternoon, the DEP did send out a press release titled, "Christie Administration Marks 500th Blue Acres Demolition with Removal of House along Delaware Bay." In the release, Martin said, "The Christie Administration is committed to making New Jersey more resilient to storms such as Superstorm Sandy. These demolitions will result in moving families out of harm's way in a very vulnerable area along Delaware Bay."

With the completion of the Bay Point demolition, Blue Acres was moving toward its goal of purchasing and demolishing thirteen hundred Sandy-impacted, flood-prone properties. The program had made nearly as many offers but, at that point, had acquired only 618 properties, some of which were in Money Island. Almost all the properties were located in inland townships, not on the barrier islands of the Jersey Shore. The borough of Sea Bright, located in Monmouth County, which encompasses the northernmost part of the Jersey Shore, had been the only oceanfront municipality to participate in Blue Acres. In the decade leading up to Sandy, 130 properties in Sea Bright had made multiple claims to the National Flood Insurance Program, totaling $7.2 million in payouts—more than any other town in Monmouth County in that period. Yet, Sea Bright's only willing seller to Blue Acres was the owner of an apartment complex, which sat on about an acre of land on the bay side of a stretch of the borough that was less than a hundred yards wide. If Sea Bright was any indication of the willingness of the rest of the Jersey Shore's property owners to retreat rather than rebuild, it seemed highly unlikely that the last several hundred properties to sell out to Blue Acres would be theirs. Certainly, none of the owners of the $1 million-plus, single-family homes in Ocean City were talking about Blue Acres—in fact, many residents of Ocean City who I talked to didn't even know the program existed. They didn't have to—their homes, and thousands more, had already been repaired, elevated, or completely replaced with billions of federal aid money. For those New Jersey homeowners, Hurricane Sandy was a distant memory. Shouldn't it have been that way for everyone?

MIKE LAUGHED WHEN I asked him about the visit from the bigwigs that never materialized. "I could've told them that was never going to happen," he told me. It was the next morning and the bottom had all but dropped out of the temperature—a steady northwest wind blew off the bay, leaving its surface furious. The thermometer topped out at eleven degrees. Mike needed to check the pump house to make sure the line hadn't frozen, but it was too cold to walk, so we jumped in his muddy, camouflage-paneled all-terrain buggy. Inside the pump house, Mike wound up the long cord of the construction light, from down inside the tube where the water pipe ran into the ground, to make sure the bulb hadn't blown out. The wind made a baritone sound as it barreled across the wide-open land-scape outside. There wasn't a single bird in the sky, not even the local eagles, which I'd come to expect to see sitting on the empty telephone pole across the road from the pump house—the pole that still had the "SLOW: CHILDREN AT PLAY" sign bolted to it.

Nearby, Bruno, Byster, and Parent were huddled in their individual cars, scrolling through their phones. The Site Enterprises crew was doing the same, in a big pickup truck parked next to the pump house. The problem was not the cold, but the wind. In the 268-page solicitation notice for the project, much of the content was dedicated to the handling of Bay Point's "asbestos-containing waste materials," as per regulations from the US Department of Labor's Occupational Safety and Health Administration (OSHA), the EPA, and the New Jersey Departments of Health, Labor, and Environmental Protection. In Bay Point, eighteen of the thirty-five dwellings had been classified, under federal regulations, as having "asbestos-containing material," meaning "all homes, sheds, decks and garages" scheduled for demolition were to be considered contaminated.

Additionally, the abatement process had to meet industry standards set by the American National Standards Institute and the American Society for Testing and Materials. Rubble was to be doused with water treated with a "wetting agent or surfactant." Workers had to wear air respirators. The truckloads of debris had to be covered and immediately transported to an approved landfill. In a place like Sayreville, where the wind was broken up by suburbia—and perhaps slightly by the "local mountains," as Art Rittenhouse had called the Kin-Buc Landfill across the Raritan River—demolition was easier. Out here on the bay, it was a nightmare. Not to mention that all the homes on Paris Road now stood out over the water, some even at low tide. Bruno, Byster, and Parent were constantly having to call off work when conditions became too windy.

Such was the case about an hour later, when the excavator closed in on Mike's brother's house. The wind was forecast to only get stronger, so the Site Enterprises crewmen wanted to try to squeeze in one more demolition before Bruno and her team shut them down. Down on the water, tangled around the pilings of the house, was the boom—overnight, in the wind and waves, it had been pushed out of place and rendered useless, but no one could go out on the water to fix it, not even Mike, on a day like today.

I went down and walked on what was left of the beach below the house. The marsh grasses were encased in a thin layer of ice, and globs of sea foam were frozen on the hard mud. A couple of brave gulls hovered over the water. They seemed pinned against the wind, unmoving. Eventually, the Komatsu excavator revved its engine and opened its claw wide. Within seconds, it was tearing a gaping hole into Mike's brother's home, just above the front door. The deck that Mike had wanted to salvage was soon splintered into pieces. The claw, and the pneumatic arm on which it was attached, knew no resistance. It was transfixing to watch the home become rubble, like watching the ocean or the sweep of a desert. The air suddenly became filled with pieces of pink insulation and other lightweight building materials. One of the Site Enterprises workers hurried around, futilely trying to pick up all the pieces fluttering down like snow, before they could blow off into the marshland. Dust and other unseen particles, combined with the frigid, lacerating wind, stung my eyes, causing tears to stream across my face.

Within minutes, Bruno and Byster had called off any more work for the day. The air continued to flutter with pieces of Mike's brother's home. When the demolition began, Mike had been sitting in his buggy, watching solemnly. I noticed now he was gone. If he'd left because he didn't want to see the house like this, it was going to be a long wait. With work done for the day, the home sat there at the edge of the bay, in plain view from Mike and Kate's bungalow—a half-devoured monument to the American Dream they'd had in their grasp just five years ago, before Sandy and the state took it away.

A FEW DAYS BEFORE CHRISTMAS, the weather warmed, and the Site Enterprises crew put in as many hours as they could before the temperature plummeted again. I arrived at Mike and Kate's just as they finished feeding the crewmen sausage and sauerkraut sandwiches. Mike had wandered out to the far end of Paris Road, to check out the latest demolition.

Kate told me to grab a beer and sit down at the bar, that she wanted to show me something. She opened her laptop and began scrolling through a photo album that Katie had made for her and Mike for Christmas. There were, of course, many pictures from Bay Point Marina—Mikie and Katie hoisting up big weakfish and flounder. Happy, inebriated moments from the many holiday parties and fishing tournaments. There were also several pictures from Mike and Kate's wedding. It wasn't so much their youth that struck me as it was the sight of them so dressed up, so formal—not the "baybillies" they loved to joke that they were.

When Mike returned later, he invited me to jump in the crab boat for a ride. A longtime friend of his, "a man named Pierce," had recently passed away, and his request was that Mike spread his ashes in Cedar Creek. Mike pointed to a narrow gut that spilled into the creek, not far from the house. "Mr. Pierce used to fish for perch right there," Mike said. "So that's where we'll spread him."

It was near dusk, and Bruno, Byster, Parent, and the Site Enterprises crewmen were heading out of Bay Point, one by one, until the island was empty save for Mike, Kate, and me. It was still warm, around fifty degrees, and the sunset was awash in fiery colors. The lamplights on the old Sileo house were glowing, as they did in light like this, and it was easy to see how so many people were tricked into believing the place was haunted by ghosts. Tonight, however, the lamplights' glow was especially poignant— as it happened, the current owners of the home had not sold to Blue Acres. Other than Mike and Kate's little shed, Sileo's place was the only structure left on Paris Road.

We paused for a while, about fifty yards off the point. In the far distance, toward Back Creek, an oyster tonger worked alone. Below us, Mike said, was where the barge once sat. Nearby, and also submerged, was the chimney of one of Bay Point's original homes. We seemed impossibly far out in the bay, nowhere near even the low tide line. On a stretch of riprap along the shoreline, where a home had existed a few days before, a blue heron stood, scanning the water for fish. I thought about the clamor of the first day of the demolition, how it felt as if the silence of Bay Point was being torn open in a way that would never heal. It seemed I was wrong— already the place was rebalancing itself, just as it had done after so many catastrophes. The entire ordeal that had befallen the community—Sandy, the buyouts, the demolition—"was something that happened and it was a tragedy," Mike said. "But I want to go ahead and live our lives and forget about it." He pointed out that, every day, this was their view. "What more you want in life?" he said. Now that Bay Point was effectively gone, Mike reckoned they could change its name. His vote was "Kate's Island." She sat next to him at the stern, wearing her old Bay Point Marina windbreaker, sipping a Miller Lite. She laughed, but she didn't disagree. Damn right this was her island, and it was breathtaking.

At the gut where Mr. Pierce used to fish for perch, the surface of the creek was a deep brown, satin smooth. As Mike spread Mr. Pierce's ashes, they sat on the dark, still water for a long while, before unfurling, like a puff of smoke, into the bay. Mike fretted that he forgot to say the Holy Trinity prayer before sending Mr. Pierce off. Kate told him to stop worrying, which set him at ease. "It don't matter how big we are," he said after a long pause. "We're all the same weight when we're burned down." He leaned over, shook out the remaining ashes. "Because we're mostly made of water."

"BUILD YOUR WINGS ON THE WAY DOWN."

IN JULY OF 2018, in the midst of the first heat wave of the summer, the news came that Campbell had received the funding to begin planning the construction of his wastewater project in Fortescue and Gandy's Beach. Less than a month after being confirmed by the New Jersey Senate, the DEP's new commissioner, Catherine McCabe, had taken up the project and authorized a $2.5 million grant. The USDA chipped in another $2.5 million, plus an additional $1.5 million low-interest loan. Suddenly, Campbell had $7 million dedicated to making his infrastructural dream one step closer to reality—he'd just need to find another seven in the coming years. "This is highly unusual for a place like Downe," Jim Rutala, the consultant who guided Downe Township through the grant writing and submission process, told me. "No one expected the money to come this fast." There was no mention of the project including Money Island, where the last of the Bayview Road homeowners had turned over their keys to Blue Acres. On the Nantuxent Drive side of town, more residents had joined Jim and Carol Giles in their decision to begin negotiations with the program.

On July 3, there was a ribbon-cutting ceremony for the wastewater project's funding in Fortescue, at the Charlesworth Hotel. The temperature was in the mid-nineties and there was little movement to the air. I made the drive from Ocean City around noon, at the height of the day's heat. Because of the holiday, the eastbound side of the road was streaming with cars heading toward the Shore. Heading the opposite direction, driving toward the Bayshore through the now-lush woods of Belleplain State Forest and the Peaslee Wildlife Management Area, I was, as usual, alone. I had been making this drive regularly for nearly two years now. I knew every bend and bump in the road. I knew where the wild turkeys and deer were most likely to cross. I knew when to look out for the dump trucks emerging from the dirt tracks that led to the silica mines hidden in the woods.

I made the usual pass through Port Norris. The oyster shell piles in Bivalve had been rancid for a while already, but the sweltering heat and dead wind caused the stench to hang thickly over Main Street. Growing up on the Bayshore, you came to love the kind of smells that few others did. It wasn't, of course, the smells themselves that I loved, but the images they evoked in my mind. The smell of the marshland or of fish rotting in the summer sun, could take me to exact days in my childhood. There was that afternoon with two grade school friends, around the same time I saw Money Island for the first time. We were carp fishing a creek that had been dammed off from the Cohansey River, just around the bend from the bank that had been built by Philip Vickers Fithian in 1766. It was low tide and, in order to get close enough to the water to cast our lines, we had, one by one, gotten dangerously stuck in the mud, all the way to our armpits. At the last second, we managed to pull each other out using the handle of our fishing net as a rescue line. I can't remember being afraid, though I'm sure we were. I only recall the scene after—the three of us sitting on the safety of the gravel bank, caked in mud that was drying into hard gray scales on our skin, simply trying to figure out another way to get our lines across that mud flat and into the water.

Fortescue was busy. The marina's slips were full of boats and the *Bonanza* was out on the bay with a full charter. On his "Money Island Marina Community" Facebook page, Tony had recently been posting photos of flounder, perch, and stripers that fishermen had been catching. The word around town was decent-sized flounder were back in the bay. The parking lot of the Charlesworth was full, as was the overflow lot next door. I had to park on the shoulder of New Jersey Avenue, a fair distance from the hotel. Before walking inside, I joined a sheriff who was there for Congressman LoBiondo's security detail, on the hotel's bayside deck. It was high tide, and the water sloshed gently against the bulkhead below us. In all the time that had passed between now and Sandy, and in the hundreds of hours I'd spent ping-ponging between Money Island and Bay Point over the last two years, I'd never made it back to the Charlesworth. The last time I'd stood on its deck was when it was buckled beyond repair from Sandy's surge.

The Charlesworth's main dining area was full—about sixty guests sat at dining tables covered with white tablecloths and decorated with red plastic cups and little American flags. On one side of the room was a table full of cheeses, breads, desserts, and other hors d'oeuvres. I recognized several of the regular attendees of the monthly Downe Township Committee meetings, enjoying the bacon-wrapped scallops and steamed shrimp that a waiter was serving around the room. Few in the crowd were below the age of sixty. State Senator Jeff Van Drew was also there, wearing a navy suit jacket over a dark T-shirt. LoBiondo sat at the table closest to the door, talking little. Campbell was bouncing from one table to the next. One of the township councilmen had set up his guitar and a microphone and was softly playing folk songs. He wore a shortsleeve button-up with a pineapple print. His guitar case was covered with stickers. One read "Our land is our future."

Campbell grabbed the microphone and welcomed everyone to the party. "When the administration changed from Christie to Murphy, we were concerned that there wasn't going to be the support with the new administration and the new commissioners that were appointed by the new governor," Campbell said. "But we were wrong. They've been totally supportive."

It seemed that everything was moving at a pace you would expect at the Jersey Shore, not here. By the end of the summer, Campbell said, the engineering plans would be completed and by winter, bids would go out and be awarded. "There's still a lot of balls in the air," he said. There were, of course, plenty of ghosts of infrastructure projects past lingering around Campbell's optimistic speech, and any realist in the room wouldn't dare dream that the project would be the savior of the Bayshore. There was the ten-year saga of the seawall on Bayview Road, which would soon be empty save for Tony and one other holdout's cabins. There was Sea Breeze and the faulty seawall the township had installed, which accelerated its fate to become open space. There was the Gandy's Beach seawall, built with Sandy money just a few years before, but already in need of reinforcement. There was Thompson's Beach, nothing more than a wide, sandy shore with a lone chimney among the foxtails. And, now, Bay Point, too. Campbell was careful not to mention Money Island in his speech.

I looked out at the audience and it wasn't all smiling faces—these weren't naive people. Arguably, there were few communities in America more experienced in the destructive confluence of catastrophic weather and indifferent government. Many of these people shared family names with the Bayshore's first European settlers, so it was in their blood to fear both of these forces equally. I felt their anxiety—a part of the Bayshore was the closest it had ever been to rebuilding since Sandy, and yet there was still so much more paperwork to fill out, permits to secure, stakeholders to please. I next looked at the politicians. Van Drew was unabashedly cosmopolitan in his suit and perfect tan. Campbell's work boots were still clean. LoBiondo was solemn and disinterested—he was one of many moderate House Republicans who had abruptly announced their retirement before the 2018 elections. None of this would be his responsibility after November. Instead it would be that of Van Drew, who was running to replace LoBiondo, and would later join a large number of candidates that year in successfully flipping House seats from Republican to Democrat.

But maybe this was actually it—in the end, it did all come down to water and sewage, which, LoBiondo pointed out in his brief speech, "aren't the sexy projects." Both he and Van Drew seemed particularly proud about the fact that local, state, and federal politicians, both Republican and Democrat, actually came together and got something done. It was true—at this point, in the summer of 2018, such a thing did feel like a miracle. For once—though nobody outside that room probably would ever know—the Bayshore was a leader, an example of America at its best.

"Every level of government worked to make this happen, and that's how it should be," Van Drew told the crowd. "It's so important to ensure that this part of a very precious environment, and a very precious heritage that we have, isn't forgotten. We live in a very urban state, a state that's very complicated, with a lot of powerful areas, and very often, quite frankly, they do like to forget about the folks that are a little smaller, a little quieter, a little bit more out of the way. But we're not going to let that happen. We're going to keep fighting, standing up for what's right, and make sure that people get their fair share, and that's what this is about today too, getting your fair share."

Weariness may have been the dominant feeling in the room, but there was hope, too. You could feel it in the laughs after Van Drew and LoBiondo's jokes about Campbell's calling them at all hours of the day to keep up the political pressure in Trenton and DC. You could see it in how much everyone dressed up for the occasion. It seemed to me in those moments in that room, with its blue-curtained picture windows and the light of the hot summer day spilling through, that we had all time-traveled to the Fortescue of the past, when people ambled on the boardwalk that followed the bay's edge and steamship passengers from Philadelphia crowded the beach and maybe it really was the weakfish capital of the world. Looking outside at the placid, almost-but-never-quite-blue bay, it was easy to forget the wreckage that remained along the shore, wrought by a storm that was now almost six years gone. It was more comforting to think of Sandy as just one in a long string of storms that had been survived than to think of it as it really was: a catastrophe bound to be repeated sooner than later. LoBiondo told the crowd that if they looked up the word "tenacity" in the dictionary, they'd find a picture of Bob Campbell. But that wasn't quite right. It wouldn't be Campbell—an outsider who, no matter how much credit he deserved, didn't truly have the Bayshore in his veins. It wouldn't be Tony, either. It was all the men and women in the room whose roots ran deep into the primordial mud upon which they'd built their lives. It should have also been me, but I had left and knew, by that point, that I too was an outsider.

WHILE THE PARTY WENT ON AT THE CHARLESWORTH, I ducked out and made my way toward Money Island to visit Tony. At the spur, I made a hard left past the faded "No Retreat" sign and onto John Munyan's century-and-a-half-old road. At the party I had spoken to Meghan Wren, the founder of the Bayshore Center, and asked her how Money Island got its name. There were so many origin stories. I'd heard the name came from Blackbeard and Captain Kidd, who had prowled the bay in the early eighteenth century, stashing bounty in nameless places along the shoreline, including Nantuxent Cove. "It's a spelling mistake," one Money Island resident had once told me. "Should be 'Muddy Island.'" A man standing next to Wren said his ninety-year-old grandfather told him it got its name because that was where rumrunners landed during Prohibition. The story that Wren had settled on was one I'd also heard here and there—that the name came from the fact that the oyster fleet had always landed there. But that couldn't be right, because in August of 1824, when the oyster fleet still landed at Bivalve, a writer using the pen name "Old Mortality," after Sir Walter Scott's seventeenth-century novel, wrote a story for the Bridgeton newspaper *Washington Whig* whose details disprove the oyster-fleet origin theory. Recounting his travels through Cumberland County, on his way through Newport, Old Mortality had a lot to say about the landscape and its people. "It is said to be a place of considerable trade and the inhabitants are represented to be industrious, hospitable and warm-hearted," he wrote. "A few miles to the westward lays Money Island, and about the same distance to the Southward Fortescue's Island—places famous in traditionary tales as the depositories of the plunder of Blackbeard the pirate. Lord Byron should have visited them before he wrote his 'Corsair.'"

This was the first time the name "Money Island" had ever been used to describe the shoreline on the Downe Township side of the mouth of Nantuxent Creek, and it wouldn't be reused again in print, as far as I could tell, until the 1940s, when Bayview Road and Nantuxent Drive were laid and the land subdivided. Perhaps Old Mortality had gotten the story confused with the many Money Islands of the East Coast, where, the stories go, Blackbeard had also stashed his plunder. I'd been wondering if "Money" was a bastardization of Munyan. But that couldn't have been right, either, since John Munyan hadn't bought the long-since flooded Flax Farm, where the majority of Money Island sits today, until much later than Old Mortality's visit to Newport. There were some things, I guessed, that would never be known. It was fitting that the original Old Mortality of Scott's novel, a Scottish stonemason, had traveled around his country, inscribing the unmarked graves of the martyrs of a forgotten war. The state, the passage of time, the ever-rising sea—they could tear away at the Bayshore land, grain of sand by grain of sand, home by home, person by person, but they could never take its story, even if that story was defined by fleeting fortune.

It was Tony's fifty-eighth birthday. I found him sitting alone on the deck outside the bait shack, staring out at the bay. He'd been having lunch with a friend, he said, who'd just left. There was no one else at the marina now; all the oyster boats were moored at their docks on the creek for the day. There hadn't been much of a spring. It seemed that, one day, the bay was frozen over with ice, and the next the stifling, ninety-degree air was teeming with greenheads. April's back-to-back-to-back nor'easters had left everyone on the Bayshore with only about a month of the kind of weather that they cherished—the kind of weather that, when asked by outsiders why they loved this place so much, they pointed to and said this is why.

In other ways, it hadn't been a good spring. In May, Tony had watched as the mail truck rumbled down Money Island Road and parked at the marina. The mailman got out and handed him a mountainous document. Tony needed only to look at the first page to discern what it was. For the past eight years, the DEP had been building a case against him. Through 567 pages, the "order to show cause," issued by the state's attorney general, outlined, in intricate detail, Tony's purchase of the marina in bankruptcy court in 2012, his own recent bankruptcy filing for his nonprofit, BaySave, and his hundreds of blog and social media posts promoting his grandiose redevelopment plans that had yet to be attained. "Based on Baysave's, and Tony Novak's . . . publicly displayed ambitions of growing his several businesses, as well as his past history of continued development in the absence of any permits . . . I believe it is probable that Mr. Novak will continue to seek new methods of escaping responsibility for his statutory and regulatory violations while simultaneously continuing to develop the marina without any permits," Joseph Traum, one of the DEP investigators assigned to the case, wrote.

A few weeks after the order had arrived in the mail, Tony's steadfast marina manager, Bruce Muenker, succumbed to the cancer he'd been battling for the past year. "He has been the face of the Money Island marina community for the past decade and a very good friend," Tony wrote on the marina's community Facebook page. "We will miss him." Muenker had died in a time and a place that seemed perfectly fitting—after a day of work at the marina, in the trailer at the edge of the bay. "It was probably for the best," Tony said, reminding me that one of the DEP's main targets was Muenker's trailer, his only home. "I don't know where I would've put Bruce."

Despite it all—but not surprisingly—Tony was in a good mood. He was still planning on having his annual Fourth of July barbecue that Saturday, and it seemed like a lot of people were interested in coming. Old Bill Bowen and his wife, Paula, who had recently joined Jim and Carol Giles in reaching out to Blue Acres to arrange a buyout, had bought daisies to hand out to everyone, so they could toss them into the creek, one by one, in honor of Muenker.

Tony was now focusing on Money Island Marina's social media. Like everything he had done in his life, he had dived headlong into this new endeavor. All he knew was that the more he posted—good news and bad—the more it would appear to the outside world that Money Island remained alive and well. He was posting multiple times a day—a dock fisherman's bucket full of perch; the Coast Guard's finally bringing new aids to navigation for the channel; a picture of his Hyundai mini SUV, which he called the "oystermobile"; the first tomato of the season in the marina's "community garden"; the food list for Saturday.

Few of Tony's ventures in life had ever worked out, but this one actually seemed to be working—as we sat together, he received two calls from boat owners who had seen the marina's Facebook page and were interested in renting a slip for the summer. Earlier that day, a "twenty-seven-year-old guy" had put his boat in the water. "I like seeing young people come down," Tony said. "We don't get a lot of them around here."

Tony's main social media target audience might have been potential slip renters, but he was also doing it for the DEP. Because of the state's order, he knew they were watching from their headquarters in Trenton, and he seemed to relish it. He would just flood them with Money Island news day in and day out. It was an old trick, in fact, that he and Campbell shared—buy time by showing proof you're a work in progress. Tony had even gone so far as to publish the state's order on his website, so anyone could read it. "The underlying issue is that the entire Money Island marina, in fact most of the small rural port community of Money Island, was built almost a century ago without building permits, land surveys, tideland leases, etc.," he wrote in the blog post that accompanied the order. "It is, in our opinion, unconscionable for the state to be both the denier of permits and simultaneously bring charges for failure to have permits that should have been addressed decades ago."

I told Tony about Downe Township's receiving money to begin the wastewater project in Fortescue and perhaps even Gandy's Beach. I expected the news to frustrate him, given that Money Island wasn't included in the plans. I should have known better. "It seems to me that once they finish Fortescue and Gandy's, they'll want to do Money Island," he said. "It's just another mile." He stopped, balled in his hands the empty paper bag that he'd packed his lunch in, and looked over the marina. The shedder tanks bubbled quietly on the main dock. A sign for Tony's new marina manager's charter and sight-seeing business wobbled in the satiny breeze. "I know what I have to do now," he said. "I just have to ride it out."

This reminded me of another one of Tony's recent Facebook posts. In the spring, after he'd posted his 2018 business plan for the marina, he added a quote from Ray Bradbury, which Tony wrote summed up his experience living in Money Island and trying to rebuild the marina: "Go to the edge of the cliff and jump off. Build your wings on the way down." Sitting there on the deck and looking out at the bay, however, Tony was thinking of another quote—his favorite line from Janis Joplin. "I think freedom is just another word for nothing left . . ." he said, then went quiet for a moment. "I have nothing left to lose."

Beyond Money Island and Bay Point, beyond the mouth of the bay, and down into the tropics, the 2018 Atlantic hurricane season had already begun. By November, Site Enterprises' claw would again be sinking into another Bayshore home, this time on Bayview Road. By the first days of 2019, there would be nothing left of the Bayview Road side of Money Island but a few purposeless pilings and a line of empty telephone poles. As it happened, the current owner of the old Sileo house had passed away not long after the demolition of Bay Point, and his children had decided to sell the home to Blue Acres. At the last minute, the program obtained the permits to include the home in the Money Island demolition—which would leave, by the spring of 2019, only one structure left on Paris Road: Mike and Kate's honeymoon suite.

After a while, Tony said he thought he'd like to go back to his cabin to take a nap. I left him there still sitting, staring at the water. I got in my car and drove east, back toward the Atlantic coast.

ACKNOWLEDGMENTS

THIS BOOK IS POPULATED WITH REAL PEOPLE who volunteered countless hours of honest, oftentimes difficult, conversation. Without Mike and Kate Nelson and Tony Novak, there would be no story. For that, I am eternally grateful to them.

I would also like to thank some of the other people who appear in, or contributed their knowledge for, this book. Mapping the Bayshore's complicated past and present would not have been possible without the following people:

In Downe Township, Mayor Bob Campbell took time out of his busy schedule to speak with me candidly and passionately about the many needs of his township. At the township office, Nadine Lockley, Nicole Marlette, and April Clifton were enormously helpful and patient, especially with my ambitious public records requests. In Money Island, Jim and Carol Giles and Bill and Paula Bowen allowed me into their homes to talk, and for that I am grateful. Also in Money Island, Meghan Wren and Chuck Bowers shared memories and unique insights that added texture to the hamlet's colorful story.

In Lawrence Township, Carmela Walder opened the doors of the Lawrence Township Historical Society early, allowing me to dig through the society's archives. Bob Thompson and Greg and Susie Bear, formerly of Bay Point, also took the time to speak with me openly and at length about their experiences living on the bay before Sandy.

At the Cumberland County Health Department, Noah Hetzell set aside too many hours to coach me through public health regulations that, he reminded me, took a graduate degree to master. At the Cumberland County Department of Planning, Bob Brewer and Matt Pisarski also sacrificed their time to help me understand open space on the Bayshore, a place they both clearly love.

In Greenwich Township, Larry Niles volunteered poignant insights on the concept of conservation in a state as complicated as New Jersey. Without the early guidance of the entire staff at the Warren and Reba Lummis Genealogical and Historical Research Library, as well as Dan O'Connor, I would not have known how to begin.

In Commercial Township, I am grateful to Steve Fleetwood and Steve Fleetwood Jr. Steve Sr. provided an early, accelerated lesson on the Bayshore's oyster industry. Steve Jr. allowed me to get in his and his crew's way on the *Kelly's Pride* to ask questions and take pictures. Captains Lemmy Robbins and Craig Tomlin were also gracious enough to bring me onboard. Barney Hollinger and Brian Harman, at Cape May Salt Oyster Company, allowed me to observe the inner workings of their aquaculture operations. At the Haskin Shellfish Research Laboratory, Kathy Alcox was brilliant, entertaining, and endlessly helpful, allowing me to dig through the lab's archives and sit in on meetings. And Joe and Mary Linda Lacotte helped me to better understand Port Norris and its rich history.

I would also like to thank Brian Kempf for working on the early versions of the maps found at the start of the book, and Joseph Murgida for his political savvy and help with research.

Purcell Palmer and the Catwalk Institute provided a much-needed residency at the most perfect time, which allowed me to focus on the final stages of the manuscript.

Writing is a tough sport, and those who step in early and support you, even if they don't have much to go on, are the smelling salts a writer needs to endure. Matt Walker is foremost in this category—over the years he has volunteered an incalculable amount of time and wit; without him, I may have never had the confidence to publish a single word. Lis Harris, at Columbia University, supported me from the first day I walked into her classroom, and continues to do so today, as a friend and colleague. Katie Abbondanza, a friend and fellow writer, was an early, keenly observant reader of the manuscript.

My agent, Matt McGowan, took a chance on me and immediately saw the potential of this story, even before the narrative had played out. At Beacon Press, I was lucky to have a wonderful team supporting this project every step of the way. Will Myers believed in the Bayshore's story, and its people, from the outset. Brian Baughan and Susan Lumenello's precise eyes were critical to the book's final touches. And I had the great fortune of having as my editor Amy Caldwell, whose alchemic insights are the reason an unruly manuscript became a polished book.

In Ocean City, I have the Flemings—Conor, Alisabeth, Makenna, Stella, Catherine, and Mimi (also an early reader)—to thank for providing much-needed social diversion and far more free meals, drinks, and laughs than I deserve.

There really is no time off when writing a book, as the narrative and characters within it are constantly conversing in the writer's head, leading them in one unexpected direction after another, often at dinner and in the dead of the night. No one endured these descents into the writerly rabbit hole more than Caitlin Quirk. I cannot thank her enough for her patience and love throughout this project.

I owe my mother and father, Jerry and Betty, an unpayable debt of gratitude, for raising my sister, Renee, brother, Chad, and me to cherish the land upon which we grew up, as well as for sharing their memories and advice for this book. My father's expertise on everything from land use regulations to plant species identifications in Cumberland County was essential. My aunts, Suzan and Donna Lewis, and grandfather, Arthur Lewis, also helped me put together those pieces of our family's history that appear in this book. My uncle, Frank Lewis, who is a true waterman, provided many yarns and crucial information about our home, the Bayshore.

Finally, I thank the many local journalists in the Bayshore area, whose tireless reporting I found to be thorough and indispensable. They, and every other local journalist, are at the beating heart of America, and so they should remain.

SELECTED BIBLIOGRAPHY

THE FOLLOWING WRITINGS were used in the making of this book, but they are by no means a complete record of all the works and sources consulted. Unless noted otherwise in the text, quotations come from interviews—both recorded digitally and by hand—conducted by the author. Additionally, references and quotes attributed to meetings of, and email communications to and from, federal, state, and local officials were obtained through New Jersey's Open Public Records Act.

HISTORY

Bond, Gordon. *Hidden History of South Jersey: From the Capitol to the Shore*. Charleston, SC: The History Press, 2013.

Carlisle, George. *Whiskey, Sun & Fish: The Early Years of Fortescue, a Fishing Village on the Delaware Bay*. Cape May, NJ: Exit Zero Press, 2014.

Cook, George Hammell. *Geology of the County of Cape May, State of New Jersey*. Trenton, NJ: Office of the True American, 1857. https://archive.org/details/geologycountyca02survgoog/page/n9.

Custalow, Dr. Linwood "Little Bear," and Angela L. "Silver Star" Daniel. *The True Story of Pocahontas: The Other Side of History, from the Sacred History of the Mattaponi Reservation People*. Golden, CO: Fulcrum Publishing, 2007.

De Laet, John. *Henry Hudson the Navigator: The Original Documents in Which His Career Is Recorded*. Edited and translated by G. M. Asher. London: Hakluyt Society, 1860. https://archive.org/details/henryhudsonnavig27ashe/page/n10.

Elmer, Lucius Q. C. *History of the Early Settlement and Progress of Cumberland County, New Jersey and of the Currency of This and Adjoining Colonies*. George F. Nixon: Bridgeton, NJ, 1869. Reprint, London: Forgotten Books, 2017.

Fithian, Philip Vickers. *The Beloved Cohansie of Philip Vickers Fithian*. Greenwich, NJ: Cumberland County Historical Society, 2016.

Harrison, Charles. *Cumberland County New Jersey: 265 Years of History*. Charleston, SC: The History Press, 2013.

Hollinger, Thomas F. *Port Norris Pencillings: 1884*. Thomas F. Hollinger, 2016.

Juet, Robert. *Juet's Journal: The Voyage of the* Half Moon *from 4 April to 7 November 1609.* Edited by Robert M. Lunny. Newark: New Jersey Historical Society, 1959. https://hdl.handle.net/2027/mdp.39015010481805.

McMahon, William. *South Jersey Towns: History and Legend.* New Brunswick, NJ: Rutgers University Press, 1973.

Mints, Margaret Louise. *Dallas Ferry on the Wahatquenack: The Story of Historic and Thriving Port Norris, a Village in Cumberland County, New Jersey, Built on a Site Traded for Rum, Guns, and Clothing.* Port Norris, NJ: L. M. Mints, 1964.

Pisarski, Matthew Edward. "One-Room Deep Domestic Architecture of Cumberland and Salem Counties, New Jersey." MS thesis, University of Pennsylvania, 1999.

Reeves, Joseph S., Jr. *Maurice River Memories: Cumberland County, New Jersey, 1937–1947.* Baltimore: Gateway Press, 1993.

Sayreville Historical Society (website). "A Timeline of Sayreville History." https://www.sayrevillehistory.org/timeline.

Smith, Samuel. *The History of the Colony of Nova-Caesaria, or New-Jersey.* Trenton, NJ: Wm. S. Sharp, 1877. Reprint, London: Forgotten Books, 2015.

Weeks, Daniel J. "Quebec and New Amsterdam to 1664: A Comparative Network Analysis." PhD diss., Rutgers, The State University of New Jersey, 2012.

Weslager, C. A. *The Delaware Indians: A History.* New Brunswick, NJ: Rutgers University Press, 1989.

Whitman, Walt. *Specimen Days and Collect: A Winter Day on the Sea-Beach.* Philadelphia: Rees Welsh & Co., 1882–83.

SEA LEVEL RISE

Andrews, Travis M. "Trump Calls Mayor of Shrinking Chesapeake Island and Tells Him Not to Worry about It." *Washington Post*, June 14, 2017. https://wapo.st/2EvfF5M.

Kemp, Andrew C., Benjamin P. Horton, Christopher H. Vane, Christopher E. Bernhardt, D. Reide Corbett, Simon E. Engelhart, Shimon C. Anisfeld, Andrew C. Parnell, and Niamh Cahill. "Sea-Level Change during the Last 2500 Years in New Jersey, USA." *Quaternary Science Reviews* 81 (2013): 90–104. https://doi.org/10.1016/j.quascirev.2013.09.024.

Kummer, Frank. "On the Delaware Bay, N.J. Town Struggles Against Sea Rise." *Philadelphia Inquirer*, June 23, 2017.

Schwartz, Jen. "Surrendering to Rising Seas." *Scientific American*, August 1, 2018. https://www.scientificamerican.com/article/surrendering-to-rising-seas/.

Sweet, William V., Robert E. Kopp, Christopher P. Weaver, Jayantha Obeysekera, Radley M. Horton, E. Robert Thieler, and Chris Zervas. "Global and Regional Sea Level Rise Scenarios for the United States." *NOAA Technical Report NOS CO-OPS 083.*

Swift, Earl. *Chesapeake Requiem: A Year with the Watermen of Vanishing Tangier Island.* New York: Dey Street Books, 2018.

FISHERIES

Anonymous. *Report of a Cause Tried in the District Court of Philadelphia [. . .] John Keen vs. Philip Rice, Involving the Right of New Jersey to the Oyster-Beds in Maurice River Cove.* Bridgeton, NJ: J. Clarke and Co., 1822.

Madrigal, Alexis C. "The Blood Harvest." *Atlantic*, February 26, 2014. https://www
.theatlantic.com/technology/archive/2014/02/the-blood-harvest/284078/.

Mints, Margaret Louise, and Alex Ogden. *Man, the Sea and Industry: A History of Life
on the Delaware Bay from 1492 to 1992*. Port Norris, NJ: L. M. Mints, 1992.

Powell, Eric N., Kathryn A. Ashton-Alcox, John N. Kraeuter, Susan E. Ford, and
David Bushek. "Long-Term Trends in Oyster Population Dynamics in Delaware
Bay: Regime Shifts and Response to Disease." *Journal of Shellfish Research* 27, no.
4 (2008): 729–55.

Radu, Christina, and Penelope S. Watson. "Oystering on the Delaware Bay." In
*Down Jersey: From Bayshore to Seashore, a Guidebook for the Annual Conference of the
Vernacular Architecture Forum*, edited by Robert W. Craig, 39–48. Galloway, NJ:
Richard Stockton College of New Jersey, 2014.

Rolfs, Donald H. *Under Sail: The Dredgeboats of Delaware Bay*. Millville, NJ: The
Wheaton Historical Association, 1971.

Romm, Richard M. "America's First Whaling Industry and the Whaler Yeomen of
Cape May." MA thesis, Rutgers University, 2010.

Sargent, William. *Crab Wars: A Tale of Horseshoe Crabs, Bioterrorism, and Human
Health*. Hanover, NH: University Press of New England, 2002.

Warner, William W. *Beautiful Swimmers: Watermen, Crabs and the Chesapeake Bay*.
New York: Back Bay Books, 1976.

Witty, Anne E. "'Cornshuckers' and 'Sandsnipes': The Oystering Schooners of Delaware Bay." MA thesis, University of Delaware, 1984.

COASTAL ENGINEERING

Dean, Cornelia. *Against the Tide: The Battle for America's Beaches*. New York: Columbia University Press, 1999.

Foster, Janet W. "A Water-Based Landscape: Meadow Banks and Salt Marshes." In
Craig, *Down Jersey*, 26–29.

Godfrey, Matthew C., Joshua Pollarine, and Paul Sadin. *Responsiveness and Reliabil-
ity: A History of the Philadelphia District and the Marine Design Center, U.S. Army
Corps of Engineers, 1972–2008*. Philadelphia: US Army Corps of Engineers,
Philadelphia District, 2012.

Pilkey, Orrin H., and Katharine L. Dixon. *The Corps and the Shore*. Washington,
DC: Island Press, 1996.

Pilkey, Orrin H., Linda Pilkey-Jarvis, and Keith C. Pilkey. *Retreat from a Rising Sea:
Hard Choices in an Age of Climate Change*. New York: Columbia University Press,
2016.

Sebold, Kimberly R. *From Marsh to Farm: The Landscape Transformation of Coastal
New Jersey*. Washington, DC: National Parks Service, 1992. https://hdl.handle
.net/2027/mdp.39015040731740.

Snyder, Frank E., and Brian H. Guss. *The District: A History of the Philadelphia District
U.S. Army Corps of Engineers, 1866–1971*. Philadelphia: U.S. Army Corps of
Engineers, Philadelphia District, 1974.

Teal, John, and Mildred Teal. *Life and Death of the Salt Marsh*. New York: Ballantine,
1969.

US Army Corps of Engineers. *Delaware Bay Shore of New Jersey: Supplemental Information to Accompany Beach Erosion Control and Hurricane Protection Survey Study,*

Contract No. DACW 61-73-C-0678. Philadelphia: US Army Corps of Engineers, Philadelphia District, 1973.

———. *Survey Study Feasibility Report: Beach Erosion Control and Hurricane Protection, Delaware Bay Shore, New Jersey.* Philadelphia: US Army Corps of Engineers, Philadelphia District, 1979.

Wicker, C. F. "History of New Jersey Coastline." *Coastal Engineering Proceedings* 1, no. 1 (January 1950): 33. https://doi.org/10.9753/icce.v1.33.

LAND USE

Berkeley Township Taxpayers Coalition. "Governor Chris Christie Addresses Home Buyout Program." News release, December 20, 2018. bttcnj.org/Governor%20Christie-2013.docx.

Brunetti-Post, Michelle. "Making a New Plan for Conserving Delaware Bay." *Press of Atlantic City,* October 8, 2017. https://bit.ly/2D5veQF.

Cronon, William. *Changes in the Land: Indians, Colonists, and the Ecology of New England.* New York: Hill and Wang, 1983.

Fagin, Dan. *Toms River: A Story of Science and Salvation.* Washington, DC: Island Press, 2013.

Grabas, Joseph A. *Owning New Jersey: Historic Tales of War, Property Disputes & the Pursuit of Happiness.* Charleston, SC: History Press, 2014.

Hurdle, Jon. "A Project Reclaims an Abandoned Stretch of New Jersey Coast." *New York Times,* March 8, 2016. https://nyti.ms/2BRSwZw.

Kov, Daniel J. "Bayshore Residents Unsure of State Buyout Plan." *Daily Journal,* June 26, 2014.

Little, Charles E. *Challenge of the Land: Open Space Preservation at the Local Level.* New York: Pergamon Press, 1968.

Loyer, Susan. "Five Years Later: Sayreville, Woodbridge Works with Rutgers on Floodplain Restoration Plan." *My Central Jersey,* October 28, 2017. http://mycj.co/2lnSzXl.

Mansnerus, Laura. "New Jersey Is Running Out of Open Land It Can Build On." *New York Times,* May 24, 2003. https://nyti.ms/2ULhK3p.

———. "To Sprawl, or Not to Sprawl." *New York Times,* August 13, 2000. https://nyti.ms/2U5aPRf.

McCay, Bonnie J. *Oyster Wars and the Public Trust: Property, Law, and Ecology in New Jersey History.* Tucson: University of Arizona Press, 1998.

"Route 55 Completion Debate Returns, Briefly." Editorial. *South Jersey Times,* October 5, 2018. https://bit.ly/2D0T1Bp.

Salmore, Barbara G., and Stephen A. Salmore. *New Jersey Politics and Government: The Suburbs Come of Age.* New Brunswick, NJ: Rivergate Books, 2008.

Schmidt, Stephan, and Kurt Paulsen. "Is Open Space Preservation a Form of Exclusionary Zoning? The Evolution of Municipal Open-Space Policies in New Jersey," *Urban Affairs Review* 45 (2009): 92–118. https://pdfs.semanticscholar.org/bdb5/18a2f93ee2f9a4314db0fdf79ed8d9b4abc0.pdf.

Shames, Shauna L., and Spencer T. Clayton. "Is South Jersey Getting Its 'Fair Share' of Public Goods?" Camden, NJ: Walter Rand Institute for Public Affairs at Rutgers University. https://rand.camden.rutgers.edu/files/Is-South-Jersey-Getting-its-Fair-Share-of-Public-Goods.pdf.

Solecki, William D., Robert J. Mason, and Shannon Martin. "The Geography of Support for Open-Space Initiatives: A Case Study of New Jersey's 1998 Ballot Measure," *Social Science Quarterly* 85 no. 3 (2004): 624–39. https://doi.org/10.1111 /j.0038-4941.2004.00236.x.

State of New Jersey Department of Environmental Protection. "Christie Administration's Blue Acres Buyout Program Expands into Rahway and Downe Township." News release no. 16/P5, January 29, 2016. http://www.nj.gov/dep/newsrel /2016/16_0005.htm.

———. "Christie Administration Completes Project Restoring Degraded Delaware Bay Wetlands Using Dredge Materials." News release no. 16/P48, May 20, 2016. http://www.nj.gov/dep/newsrel/2016/16_0048.htm.

———. "Christie Administration Marks 500th Blue Acres Demolition with Removal of House Along Delaware Bay." News release no. 17/P118, December 11, 2017. https://www.nj.gov/dep/newsrel/2017/17_0118.htm.

State of New Jersey Department of Environmental Protection (website). "New Jersey Coastal Management Program." Accessed June 20, 2018. https://www.state .nj.us/dep/cmp/fact4.pdf.

SUPERSTORM (HURRICANE) SANDY

Bates, Diane C. *Superstorm Sandy: The Inevitable Destruction and Reconstruction of the Jersey Shore*. New Brunswick, NJ: Rutgers University Press, 2016.

Ellis Nutt, Amy. "One Year After Hurricane Sandy, New Jersey's Forgotten Western Shore Struggles to Rebuild." *Star-Ledger*, October 25, 2013.

———. "Hurricane Sandy Destruction in Bay Point Turned Paradise into Nightmare." *Star-Ledger*, October 25, 2013.

———. "Overlooked After Sandy, Delaware Bayshore Gets Visit from New U.S. Sen. Cory Booker." *Star-Ledger*, December 3, 2013.

———. "18 Months After Sandy, Help Arrives for Homeowners in Cumberland County." *Star-Ledger*, April 20, 2014.

Gurian, Scott, Eve Troeh, and Janet Babin. "Practice Makes Imperfect: Why Do We Keep Getting Disaster Recovery Wrong?" NJ Spotlight, October 30, 2014. https://www.njspotlight.com/stories/14/10/30/why-do-we-keep-getting -disaster-recovery-wrong/.

———. "What New Jersey's Sandy Recovery Experience Has Taught Us for the Future." NJ Spotlight, October 31, 2014. https://www.njspotlight.com/stories /14/10/31/what-new-jersey-s-sandy-recovery-experience-has-taught-us.

O'Dea, Colleen. "Botched Process Denied Thousands of NJ Residents Millions in Sandy Relief." NJ Spotlight, February 6, 2014. https://www.njspotlight.com /stories/14/02/05/botched-process-denied-thousands-in-nj-of-millions-in -sandy-relief.

Office of the Governor. "Governor Christie Announces $300 Million Buyout Plan to Give Homeowners the Option to Sell Sandy-Damaged Residences." News release. May 16, 2013.

Rinde, Meir. "Calls for NJ to Return Millions in Federal Aid for 'Troubled' Sandy Rebuild." NJ Spotlight, October 24, 2016. https://www.njspotlight.com /stories/16/10/23/calls-for-nj-to-return-millions-in-federal-aid-for-troubled -sandy-rebuild.

Star-Ledger. "Gov. Christie's Shameless $2M Self-Promotion." August 6, 2013.

State of New Jersey Department of Environmental Protection. "Christie Adminis-tration Issues Emergency Order Easing Infrastructure Repair Permit Require-ments Following Hurricane Sandy." News release no. 12/P138, November 6, 2012. https://www.nj.gov/dep/newsrel/2012/12_0138.htm.

Sullivan, Sean. "President Obama, Gov. Chris Christie Touring Storm Damage Together in New Jersey." *Washington Post*, October 31, 2012. https://wapo.st /2XjlquX.

INDEX